Why Do You Need This New Edition of *Rhetorical Grammar?*

If you're wondering why you should buy this new edition, here are six good reasons!

❶ A new Chapter 1 on words and phrases provides a solid foundation for the understanding of sentence patterns, now covered in Chapter 2.

❷ A new Chapter 3 on verbs offers expanded explanations about how verbs work, as well as more examples and exercises, to help you understand why successful writers make the choices they do.

❸ A new Chapter 10 on *nominals*— appositives, verb phrases, and clauses used as subjects—offers guidance on using these important parts of speech appropriately and correctly in your own work.

❹ An expanded Chapter 4 extends the important discussion of **coordination and subordination** and provides models and exercises to help you create correct sentences.

❺ New Part Introductions offer summaries of the content of each part for both ease of finding information and quick review.

❻ New examples from written sources and topics for discussion in almost every chapter offer more models that reflect correct usage and help you write with style and accuracy.

Rhetorical Grammar

Grammatical Choices, Rhetorical Effects

SIXTH EDITION

Martha Kolln

The Pennsylvania State University

Loretta Gray

Central Washington University

Longman

Boston   Columbus   Indianapolis   New York   San Francisco   Upper Saddle River
Amsterdam   Cape Town   Dubai   London   Madrid   Milan   Munich   Paris   Montreal   Toronto
Delhi   Mexico City   Sao Paulo   Sydney   Hong Kong   Seoul   Singapore   Taipei   Tokyo

Senior Sponsoring Editor: Virginia L. Blanford
Senior Supplements Editor: Donna Campion
Senior Marketing Manager: Sandra McGuire
Production Manager: Kathy Sleys
Project Coordination, Text Design, and Electronic Page Makeup: Suganya
    Karuppasamy/GGS Higher Education Resources PMG, A division of PreMedia
    Global, Inc.
Design Director: Jayne Conte
Cover Designer: Suzanne Duda
Cover Illustration/Photo: Getty Images
Printer, Binder and Cover Printer: R. R. Donnelley & Sons, Inc.

Library of Congress Cataloging-in-Publication Data
Kolln, Martha.
    Rhetorical grammar : grammatical choices, rhetorical effects / Martha
Kolln, Loretta Gray.—6th ed.
        p. cm.
    Includes index.
    ISBN-13: 978-0-205-70675-4
    ISBN-10: 0-205-70675-4
    1. English language—Rhetoric.   2. English language—Grammar.   I. Gray,
Loretta S.   II. Title.
    PE1408.K696 2010
    808'.042—dc22

                                                                2009034221

Longman
is an imprint of

www.pearsonhighered.com

9 10—DOH—12

ISBN-13: 978-0-205-70675-4
ISBN-10:   0-205-70675-4

Contents

Chapter 3
Our Versatile Verbs   38

Chapter 4
Coordination and Subordination   53

PART II
Controlling the Message   83

Chapter 5
Cohesion   84

Chapter 6
Sentence Rhythm   105

Chapter 7
The Writer's Voice   123

PART III
Making Choices: Form and Function   147

Chapter 8
Choosing Adverbials   149

Chapter 9
Choosing Adjectivals   *167*

Chapter 10
Choosing Nominals   *191*

PART V
Punctuation   259

Chapter 13
Punctuation: Its Purposes, Its Hierarchy, and Its Rhetorical Effects   260

Preface

Grammatical choices. Rhetorical effects. These two phrases tell the story of rhetorical grammar, the marriage of grammar and rhetoric for the composition classroom. Writers who recognize the choices available to them will be well-equipped for controlling the effects of their words. As we explain to students in the Introduction,

> To study grammar in this way—that is, to consider the conscious knowledge of sentence structure as your toolkit—is the essence of rhetorical grammar.

But is there really a place for the study of grammar in the composition class? Is there time for grammar in a syllabus already filled with prewriting, drafting, and revising and with reading what others have written? The answer is "yes." In fact you are already spending time on grammar—when you discuss cohesion and transition; when you explain in a conference why a structure is misplaced or awkward; when you help students understand the effects of certain words on the reader; when you point out redundancy; when you suggest sentence revision; when you praise gems of precision. These are principles of grammar and style and revision that are now part of your writing class. *Rhetorical Grammar: Grammatical Choices, Rhetorical Effects* will help you teach these and many more such principles—and it will do so in a systematic way.

And while the book is addressed to student writers in the composition classroom, we are gratified to know that it is also being used successfully in grammar courses for teacher preparation. In addition to the basics of grammar, those future language arts teachers will gain valuable insight into the teaching of writing.

You'll discover that the lessons in this book are not the definitions and categories and rules of traditional grammar that your students encountered back in middle school. Rather, *Rhetorical Grammar* brings together the insights of composition researchers and linguists; it makes the connection between writing and grammar that has been missing from our classrooms. It also avoids the prescriptive rules and error correction of handbooks, offering instead explanations of the rhetorical choices that are available. And, perhaps what is most important, it gives students confidence in their own language ability by helping them recognize the intuitive grammar expertise that all human beings share.

This difference in the purpose of *Rhetorical Grammar* is especially important. Too often the grammar lessons that manage to find their way into the writing classroom are introduced for remedial purposes: to fix comma splices and misplaced modifiers and agreement errors and such. As a consequence, the study of grammar has come to have strictly negative, remedial associations—a Band-Aid for weak and inexperienced writers, rather than a rhetorical tool that all writers should understand and control.

This book, then, substitutes for that negative association of grammar a positive and functional point of view—a rhetorical view: that an understanding of grammar is an important tool for the writer; that it can be taught and learned successfully if it is presented in the right way and in the right place, in connection with composition. The book can also stimulate class discussion on such issues as sentence focus and rhythm, cohesion, reader expectation, paraphrase, diction, revision—discussions of rhetorical and stylistic issues that will be meaningful throughout the writing process. And the students will learn to apply these grammar concepts to their own writing. This is the kind of knowledge—this toolkit of conscious grammar understanding—that will support not only their academic career but their lifelong literacy as well.

Those of you who are acquainted with past editions will see important changes here in the sixth edition. Perhaps the most important one is the new name on the title page: Loretta Gray has joined Martha Kolln as coauthor, bringing her expertise in linguistics, rhetoric, and composition to this new edition. Other changes include three new chapters:

- A new Chapter 1 that gives an overview of words and phrases, which helps to prepare the reader for the sentence patterns in Chapter 2.
- A new Chapter 3 on verbs, including expanded verbs and time frames that explain the verb choices of successful writers.
- A new Chapter 10 on nominals, along with a discussion of form and function relating to adverbials and adjectivals and nominals.
- An expanded chapter on coordination and subordination.
- A new, comprehensive discussion of structure classes, along with form classes and pronouns in Part IV.
- Introductory descriptions of the book's five major divisions.
- New examples from written sources and topics for discussion.

Retained in this edition are the opening Chapter Preview and the closing sections—Key Terms, Rhetorical Reminders, and Punctuation Reminders—all designed to help students organize and review material. The updated Glossary of Terms provides easy access to definitions of new vocabulary; the Index directs students to other pages where topics are discussed. A self-instructional Answer Key gives students the opportunity to check their work on odd-numbered items in the exercises.

The primary focus throughout the book remains on revision and style, on the importance to students of understanding the writer's tools. For students interested in further study, we have placed at the end of the book a bibliography of sources relevant to the topics discussed.

Depending on the goals of your course, you may find that *Rhetorical Grammar* is the only text your students need; on the other hand, it can certainly work well in conjunction with a reader or rhetoric. In either case, you'll discover that class time can be used much more efficiently when your students come to class with the shared background that the text provides. The Instructor's Manual includes answers to the even-numbered items in the exercises, further explanations of grammatical principles, and suggestions for class activities.

ACKNOWLEDGMENTS

We extend our gratitude to the reviewers whose perceptive comments and valuable suggestions helped us shape this edition of *Rhetorical Grammar*—Rebecca R. Cargile, Freed-Hardeman University; Devan Cook, Boise State University; Don Cunningham, Radford University; Heather M. Hoyt, Arizona State University; Cecil ("Jay") Jordan, University of Utah; Cornelia Paraskevas, Western Oregon University; and Joseph Salvatore, The New School. We'd also like to acknowledge the support received for a Central Washington University research leave.

To our editor and friend, Ginny Blanford, we owe special thanks for making our co-authorship possible and productive.

Martha Kolln
Loretta Gray

Introduction

WHAT IS RHETORICAL GRAMMAR?

To understand the subject matter of a book with the title *Rhetorical Grammar,* you'll obviously have to understand not only the meaning of both *rhetoric* and *grammar* but also their relationship to each other. *Grammar* is undoubtedly familiar to you. You've probably been hearing about, if not actually studying, grammar in your English classes since middle school. *Rhetoric,* on the other hand—as well as *rhetorical*—may not be familiar at all. So, to figure out what rhetorical grammar is all about, we'll begin with the familiar *grammar.*

If you're like many students, you may associate the idea of grammar with rules—various do's and don'ts that apply to sentence structure and punctuation. You may remember studying certain rules to help you correct or prevent errors in your writing. You may remember the grammar handbook as the repository of such rules.

But now consider another possibility: that YOU are the repository of the rules. You—not a book. It might help you to understand this sense of grammar if you think of a grammar rule not as a rule of law created by an authority but rather as a description of language structure. Stored within you, then, in your computer-like brain, is a system of rules, a system that enables you to create the sentences of your native language. The fact that you have such an internalized system means that when you study grammar *you are studying what you already "know."*

Linguistic researchers[1] now tell us that you began internalizing the rules of your language perhaps before you were born, when you began to differentiate the particular rhythms of the language you were hearing. In the first year of life you began to create the rules that would eventually produce sentences.

---

[1]See the section "Language Development" in the Bibliography.

1

You were little more than a year old when you began to demonstrate your grammar ability by naming things around you; a few months later you were putting together two- and three-word strings, and before long your language took on the features of adult sentences. No one taught you. You didn't have language lessons. You learned all by yourself, from hearing the language spoken around you—and you did so unconsciously. When you started to read, your acquisition of language continued. In fact, you are still acquiring language: As you learn new words, you learn (not necessarily through studying) the sentence structures in which those words commonly appear.

This process of language development is universal—that is, it occurs across cultures, and it occurs in every child with normal physical and mental development. No matter what your native language is, you have internalized its basic grammar system. By the time you were five or six years old, you were an expert at narrating events, at asking questions, at describing people and places, probably at arguing. The internalized system of rules that accounts for this language ability of yours is our definition of *grammar*.

When you study grammar in school, then, you are to a great extent studying what you already "know." Note that the verb *know* needs those quotation marks because we're not using it in the usual sense. Your grammar knowledge is largely subconscious: You don't know consciously what you "know." When you study grammar you are learning *about* those grammar rules that you use subconsciously every time you speak or write—as well as every time you make sense of what you hear or read.

But as you know, learning to write involves other rules, the conventions of writing. When you write, you must pay attention to rules about paragraphing and sentence completeness and capital letters and quotation marks and apostrophes and commas and, perhaps the trickiest of all, spelling.

To be effective, however, writing also requires attention to rhetoric—and here is where the term *rhetorical* comes into the picture. *Rhetoric* means that your audience—the reader—and your purpose make a difference in the way you write on any given topic. To a large degree, that rhetorical situation—the audience, purpose, and topic—determines the grammatical choices you make, choices about sentence structure and vocabulary, even punctuation. Rhetorical grammar is about those choices.

This meaning of *rhetoric* is easy to illustrate: Just imagine the difference between texting a friend and writing a letter to the dean of your college, requesting funds for a new film club. Think of the differences there might be in those two different rhetorical situations. One obvious difference, of course, is vocabulary; you wouldn't use the same words with two such different audiences. The grammatical structures are also going to be different, determined in part by the tone or level of formality.

Understanding rhetorical grammar, then, means understanding the grammatical choices available to you when you write and the rhetorical effects those choices will have on your reader. The dean of your college will probably recognize—and approve of—your letter as evidence of a serious-minded, articulate student. She will feel assured that any funding she provides will benefit the students on campus. The good friend who gets your text message will recognize your texting style and understand your abbreviated note.

You can think of the grammatical choices you have as tools in your writer's toolkit. You have a variety of tools for the differences in language that different rhetorical situations call for. To study grammar in this way—that is, to consider the conscious knowledge of sentence structure as your toolkit—is the essence of rhetorical grammar.

We begin this study of the tools by focusing, in Part I, on the words and phrases that constitute basic sentences, the patterns these sentences typically follow, the important role of verbs, and techniques for joining sentences (really *clauses*, but we'll discuss that term later). In Part II you will learn to put these tools to good use in controlling your message to account for reader expectations, while at the same time developing your writer's voice. Part III looks in more detail at expanding sentences and the rhetorical reasons for doing so.

In Part IV, you will find yourself consulting—and appreciating—your subconscious language expertise in the chapter covering word classes. The final chapter, in Part V, describes the purpose and hierarchy of punctuation. The Glossary of Punctuation that follows this chapter pulls together all of the punctuation rules you have studied in context throughout the book.

The Bibliography that follows the Glossary of Punctuation lists the works mentioned in the text, along with other books and articles on rhetoric and grammar. The future teachers among you will find them useful for research purposes and for your teaching preparation.

Throughout the book you will find exercises and issues for group discussion. Answers to the odd-numbered exercise items are included in the back of the book.

Be sure to use the Glossary of Terms and the Index if you are having problems understanding a concept. They are there to provide help.

We'd like to conclude this brief introduction with a piece of advice: Don't be deceived by the bad press the word *grammar* has been given over the years. The study of grammar is not dull, and it's not difficult. If you take the time to read the pages in this book carefully and study the language you hear or read every day, you will easily fill your writer's toolkit to the brim and become confident and skillful at creating sentences appropriate for the rhetorical situations you encounter.

PART I

The Structure of Sentences

Using a language may be compared to riding a horse: much of one's success depends upon an understanding of what it can and will do.

—RICHARD WEAVER

You read in the Introduction that it's useful to think of your grammatical choices as tools in your writer's toolkit. Consider the tools filling the drawers in the mechanic's toolbox and the tools in the carpenter's shop. Each has its name and its place and its particular job to do. The same is true for your writer's tools.

In these first four chapters you will learn about your writing tools: their names, their places, their jobs, what they can and will do:

Chapter 1: An Introduction to Words and Phrases
Chapter 2: Sentence Patterns
Chapter 3: Our Versatile Verbs
Chapter 4: Coordination and Subordination

You will discover that understanding the tools available to you—knowing the terminology of grammar and using it to think about and talk about your writing—will give you confidence as you compose and as you revise.

Some of the terminology will already be familiar. After all, you have spent a dozen years learning to read and write, learning the conventions of spelling and punctuation and paragraphing. In other words, you're not encountering an exotic new subject in these pages. So as you read, don't make the mistake of trying to memorize every new term, every grammatical concept. Instead, filter what you are reading through your own experience; ask yourself how and where that concept fits into your understanding.

An Introduction to Words and Phrases

CHAPTER PREVIEW

The purpose of this chapter is really to *review* words and phrases rather than to introduce them; we assume that most of you have met them before. But even if you haven't, or even if you've forgotten those long-ago lessons, you'll discover that you know more about words and phrases than you suspect—as you read in the Introduction.

For the most part we will be using the terms of traditional grammar, many of which may already be familiar to you. However, instead of the traditional eight parts of speech, we will introduce the word categories of the structural linguists, who classified words in two broad groups: **form classes**[1] and **structure classes.** And we will help you mine your internal grammar expertise to assist you in bringing your subconscious grammar knowledge to a conscious level.

This review will lay the groundwork for the study of the sentence patterns and their expansions in the chapters that follow.

FORM CLASSES

In the middle of the twentieth century, linguists recognized that the traditional classification of words—eight parts of speech based on Latin—did not accurately describe the way words functioned in English. For example, they emphasized that content words—our **nouns, verbs, adjectives, and adverbs**—have special qualities that the other word classes do not

---

[1] Words in bold type are defined in the Glossary of Terms, beginning on page 280.

have. Their numbers alone make them special: These four word classes constitute over 99 percent of our vocabulary. They are also different from other word classes in that they can be identified by their forms. Each of them has, or can have, particular endings, or **suffixes.** And that, of course, is the reason for the label "form classes."

We will begin by looking at nouns and verbs, our two largest word categories, and put them into our simplest kind of sentences: those with a one-word **subject** and a one-word **predicate:**

> Cats fight.
> Mary laughed.

You're probably familiar with the traditional definition of *noun* as the name of a person, place, or thing and *verb* as an action word. These definitions based on meaning are certainly useful (*noun* actually means "name" in Latin) although they're not always accurate. For example, a noun like *kindness* is not exactly a thing, nor is *expect* an action. And many, if not most, so-called "action words," including *fight* and *laugh*, are also nouns: (*The fight lasted only a few minutes; Mary's laugh filled the room.*)

So in the case of our four form classes, we will go beyond meaning and consider a word's form in our definition. Our two sample sentences illustrate one suffix for nouns and one for verbs: the **plural** marker, *-s*, on the noun *cat;* the **past tense** marker, *-ed*, on the verb *laugh.* We will use these "formal" characteristics as criteria in our definitions of *noun* and *verb.*

NOUNS

The plural *-s* is one of two noun endings that we call **inflections;** the other noun inflection is the **possessive case** ending, the apostrophe-plus-*s*— or, in the case of most plural nouns, just the apostrophe. Most nouns will fit into the following framework:[2]

Singular	Plural	Singular Possessive	Plural Possessive
cat	cats	cat's	cats'
horse	horses	horse's	horses'

---

[2] In words where the plural noun has no *-s*, as in the case of irregular plurals such as *men* and *women*, both the singular and the plural possessive forms take the apostrophe-plus-*s*:

man	men	man's	men's
woman	women	woman's	women's

We now have a simple definition of *noun* based on form:

> **A noun is a word that can be made plural and/or possessive.**

We will enhance this simple definition after describing the noun phrase.

THE NOUN PHRASE

The term **noun phrase** may be new to you, although you're probably familiar with the word **phrase,** which traditionally refers to any group of words that functions as a unit within the sentence. A phrase will always have a head, or **headword;** and as you might expect, the headword of the noun phrase is a noun. Most noun phrases also include a noun signaler, or marker, called a **determiner.** Here are three noun phrases you have seen in this chapter, with their headwords underlined and their determiners shown in italics:

> *the* headword
>
> *a* unit
>
> *the* traditional definition

As the third example illustrates, the headword may be preceded by a modifier. The most common modifier in preheadword position is an adjective, such as *traditional.* You will be learning about many structures besides adjectives that function the way adjectives function, as modifiers of nouns.

As you may have noticed in the three examples, the opening determiners are the **articles** *a* and *the.* While they are our most common determiners, other word groups also function as determiners, signaling noun phrases. For example, the function of nouns and **pronouns** in the **possessive case** is almost always that of determiner:

> *Mary's* laugh
>
> *her* new car

Other common words functioning as determiners are the **demonstrative pronouns**—*this, that, these, those:*

> *this* old house
>
> *those* expensive sneakers

Because noun phrases can be single words, as we saw in our earlier examples (*Cats fight, Mary laughed*), it follows that not all noun phrases will have determiners. **Proper nouns,** such as the names of people and places (*Mary*), and plural nouns with a general meaning (*cats*) are among the most common that appear without a noun signaler.

In spite of these exceptions, however, it is accurate to say that most noun phrases do begin with determiners. Likewise, it's accurate to say—and important to recognize—that whenever you encounter a determiner *you can be sure you are at the beginning of a noun phrase*. In other words, articles (*a/an, the*) and certain other words, such as possessive nouns and pronouns, demonstrative pronouns, and numbers, tell you that a noun headword is on the way.

We can now identify three defining characteristics of nouns:

> **A noun is a word that can be made plural and/or possessive; it occupies the headword position in the noun phrase; it is usually signaled by a determiner.**

In the study of syntax, which you are now undertaking, you can't help but notice the prevalence of noun phrases and their signalers, the determiners.

EXERCISE 1

The following six sentences include sixteen noun phrases. Your job is to identify their determiners and headwords.

Note: Answers to the odd-numbered exercises are provided, beginning on page 294.

1. The students rested after their long trip.

2. Our new neighbors across the hall became our best friends.

3. Mickey's roommate studies in the library on rainy weekends.

4. A huge crowd lined the streets for the big parade.

5. This new lasagna recipe feeds an enormous crowd.

6. Jessica made her new boyfriend a batch of chocolate chip cookies.

FOR GROUP DISCUSSION

Turn each list of words into a noun phrase and use it in a sentence. Compare your answers with your classmates'; your sentences will vary, but with one possible exception, your noun phrases should match.

1. table, the, wooden, small,

2. my, sneakers, roommate's, new

3. cotton, white, T-shirts, the, other, all

4. gentle, a, on the head, tap

5. books, those, moldy, in the basement

6. the, with green eyes, girl

Did you discover the item with two possibilities?

VERBS

When the dictionary identifies a word as a verb, it lists three forms: the **base form** (*laugh, eat*) and two inflected forms—the **past tense** (*laughed, ate*) and the **past participle** (*laughed, eaten*). These three forms are traditionally referred to as the verb's "three principal parts." The base form is also known as the **infinitive**, which is often written with *to* (*to laugh, to eat*). All verbs have two other inflected forms as well: the **third-person singular,** which adds an *-s* to the base form, and the **present participle,** which has an *-ing* ending.

Base form	laugh	eat
-s **form**	laughs	eats
Past tense	laughed	ate
Past participle	laughed	eaten
Present participle	laughing	eating

All verbs have these five forms. Notice that the past tense and past participle forms are identical in the case of *laugh,* a **regular verb.** In fact, this characteristic—the addition of *-ed* to the base form to produce a verb's past and past participle—is the essential definition of "regular verb." The verb *eat* is among our 150 or so **irregular verbs,** those in which the past tense and the past participle are *not* produced with the regular inflections. Among the irregular verbs, there's a great variety in these two forms.

The verb *be,* our only verb with more than these five, has eight forms: *am, are, is, was, were, been, being,* and *be*—the infinitive form. *Be* is our only verb that has an infinitive form that is different from the present tense. (You'll read about verbs in more detail in Chapter 3.)

The point to be made here is that in using your knowledge of verb inflections the criterion of form can help you define *verb,* just as it did with *noun.* Note that the following definition mentions only the *-s* form and the *-ing* form (present participle); every verb, both regular and irregular, can occur in these two forms; in other words, any word that has these two forms is, by definition, a verb.

> **A verb is a word that denotes present and past tenses; it has both an *-s* form and an *-ing* form.**

FOR GROUP DISCUSSION

Many words in English can serve as either nouns or verbs.

> I made a *promise* to my boss. (noun)
> I *promised* to be on time for work. (verb)

> He *offered* to help us. (verb)
> We accepted his *offer*. (noun)

Write a pair of short sentences for each of the following words, demonstrating that they can be either nouns or verbs.

> *visit   plant   point   feature   audition*

THE VERB PHRASE

As you would expect, the headword of a verb phrase is the verb; the other components, if any, will depend in part on the subclass of verb, for example, whether it is followed by a noun phrase: A noun phrase follows a **transitive verb** (*The cat chased the mouse*) but not an **intransitive verb** (*Cats fight*). In many, if not most, sentences, the verb phrase will include one or more **adverbials** (*Mary laughed loudly*). In Chapter 2 you will be studying verb phrases in detail because it is the variations in the verb phrases, the sentence **predicates,** that differentiate the sentence patterns.

As we saw with the noun phrase, it is also possible for a verb phrase to be complete with only the headword. Our two earlier examples—*Cats fight; Mary laughed*—illustrate instances of single-word subjects, which are fairly common in most written work, as well as single-word predicates, which are not common at all; in fact, single-word verb phrases as predicates are very rare. So far in this chapter, none of the verb phrases we have used in the discussion come close to the brevity of those two sample sentences.

NP + VP = S

This formula—NP + VP = S—is another way of saying "Subject plus Predicate equals Sentence." Our formula with the labels NP and VP simply emphasizes the form of those two sentence parts, noun phrase and verb phrase. The NP functions as the subject of the sentence; the VP functions as the predicate. The following diagram includes labels of both form and function:

Given what you have learned so far about noun phrases and verb phrases—and with the help of your intuition—you should have no trouble recognizing the two parts of the following sentences. You'll notice right away that the first word of the subject noun phrase in all the sentences is a determiner.

> Our county commissioners passed a new ordinance.
>
> The mayor's husband spoke against the ordinance.
>
> The mayor was upset with her husband.
>
> Some residents of the community spoke passionately for the ordinance.
>
> The merchants in town are unhappy.
>
> This new law prohibits billboards on major highways.

As a quick review of noun phrases, identify the headwords of the subject noun phrases in the six sentences just listed:

_____   _____   _____

_____   _____   _____

Given your understanding of noun phrases, you probably had little difficulty identifying the headwords: *commissioners, husband, mayor, residents, merchants, law.* In the exercise that follows, you are instructed to identify the two parts of those six sentences to determine where the subject noun phrase ends. This time you'll be using your subconscious knowledge of pronouns.

> **EXERCISE 2**

You have at your disposal a wonderful tool for figuring out the boundary between the subject and the predicate: Simply substitute a **personal pronoun** (*I, you, he, she, it, they*) for the subject. In this exercise, find the border between the subject and the predicate of the sentences from the previous discussion; then supply a pronoun for the subject.

Examples: This new lasagna recipe / feeds an enormous crowd. (It)

Our neighbors across the hall / became our best friends. (They)

    1. Our county commissioners passed a new ordinance. (   )

    2. The mayor's husband spoke against the ordinance. (   )

    3. The mayor was upset with her husband. (   )

    4. Some residents of the community spoke for the ordinance. (   )

    5. The merchants in town are unhappy. (   )

    6. This new law prohibits billboards on major highways. (   )

....

As your answers no doubt show, the personal pronoun stands in for the entire noun phrase, not just the noun headword. Making that substitution, which you do automatically in speech, can help you recognize not only the subject/predicate boundary, but the boundaries of noun phrases throughout the sentence.

Recognition of this subject/predicate relationship, the common element in all of our sentences, is the first step in the study of sentence structure. Equally important for the classification of sentences into sentence patterns is the concept of the verb as the central, pivotal position in the sentence. Before moving on to the sentence patterns, however, we will look briefly at two other word classes, adjectives and adverbs, which, like nouns and verbs, can often be identified by their forms. We will then describe the prepositional phrase, perhaps our most common modifier, one that adds information to both the noun phrase and the verb phrase.

ADJECTIVES AND ADVERBS

The other two form classes, **adjectives** and **adverbs,** like nouns and verbs, can usually be recognized by their form and/or by their position in the sentence.

The inflectional endings that identify adjectives and some adverbs are the **comparative** suffix, *-er,* and the **superlative,** *-est:*

Adjective	Adverb
big	near
bigger	nearer
biggest	nearest

When the word has two or more syllables, the comparative and superlative markers are generally *more* and *most,* rather than the *-er* and *-est* suffixes:

beautiful	quickly
more beautiful	more quickly
most beautiful	most quickly

Another test of whether a word is an adjective or adverb, as opposed to a noun or verb, is its ability to pattern with a **qualifier,** such as *very:*

very beautiful	very quickly

You'll notice that these tests (the inflectional endings and *very*) can help you differentiate adjectives and adverbs from the other two form classes, nouns and verbs, but they do not help you distinguish the two word classes from each other.

There is one special clue about word form that we use to help identify adverbs: the *-ly* ending. However, the *-ly* is not an inflectional suffix like *-er* or *-est;* when we add one of these to an adjective—*happier, happiest*—the word remains an adjective (just as a noun with the plural inflection added is still a noun). In contrast, the *-ly* ending that makes adverbs so noticeable is actually added to adjectives to turn them into adverbs:

Adjective				Adverb
quick	+	ly	=	quickly
pleasant	+	ly	=	pleasantly
happy	+	ly	=	happily

Rather than inflectional, the *-ly* is a **derivational suffix:** It enables us to *derive* adverbs from adjectives. Incidentally, the *-ly* means "like": quickly = quick-like; happily = happy-like. And because we have so many adjectives that can morph into adverbs in this way—many thousands, in fact—we are not often mistaken when we assume that an -*ly* word is an adverb. (In Chapter 12 you will read about derivational suffixes for all four form classes.)

In addition to these "adverbs of manner," as the -*ly* adverbs are called, we have an inventory of other adverbs that have no clue of form; among them are *then, now, soon, here, there, everywhere, afterwards, often, sometimes, seldom, always.* Often the best way to identify an adverb is by the kind of information it supplies to the sentence—information of time, place, manner, frequency, and the like; in other words, it answers such questions as where, when, why, how, and how often. Adverbs can also be identified on the basis of their position in the predicate and their movability.

As you read in the discussion of noun phrases, the position between the determiner and the headword is where we find adjectives:

this <u>new</u> recipe   an <u>enormous</u> crowd

Adverbs, on the other hand, modify verbs and, as such, will be part of the predicate:

> Some residents spoke <u>passionately</u> for the ordinance.
>
> Mario <u>suddenly</u> hit the brakes.

However, unlike adjectives, one of the features of adverbs that makes them so versatile for writers and speakers is their movability: They can often be moved to a different place in the predicate—and they can even leave the predicate and open the sentence:

> Mario hit the brakes <u>suddenly</u>.
>
> <u>Suddenly</u> Mario hit the brakes.

Bear in mind, however, that some adverbs are more movable than others. We probably don't want to move *passionately* to the beginning of its sentence. And in making the decision to move the adverb, we also want to consider the context, the relation of the sentence to the others around it.

◀ **FOR GROUP DISCUSSION**

Your job here is to experiment with the underlined adverbs to discover how movable they are. Do you and your classmates agree?

1. I have <u>finally</u> finished my report.
2. Maria has <u>now</u> accumulated sixty credits toward her degree.
3. The hunters moved <u>stealthily</u> through the woods.
4. The kindergartners giggled <u>quietly</u> in the corner.
5. My parents <u>occasionally</u> surprise me with a visit.

6. Our soccer coach will <u>undoubtedly</u> expect us to practice <u>tomorrow</u>.
7. I <u>occasionally</u> jog <u>nowadays</u>.
8. The wind <u>often</u> blows <u>furiously</u> in January.

PREPOSITIONAL PHRASES

Before discussing sentence patterns, we'll take a quick look at the **prepositional phrase,** a two-part structure consisting of a **preposition** followed by an object, which is usually a noun phrase. Prepositions are among the most common words in our language. In fact, the paragraph you are now reading includes eight different prepositions: *before, at, of* (three times), *by, among, in* (twice), *throughout,* and *as* (twice). Prepositional phrases appear throughout our sentences, sometimes as part of a noun phrase and sometimes as a modifier of the verb.

In a noun phrase, the prepositional phrase adds a detail or makes clear the identity of the noun, which it follows in postheadword position. Several of the sentences you saw in Exercise 1 included prepositional phrases:

Our new neighbors <u>across the hall</u> became our best friends.

Here the *across* phrase is part of the subject noun phrase, functioning like an adjective, so we call it an **adjectival** prepositional phrase:

They became our best friends.

This *across* phrase tells "which neighbors." In a different sentence, that same phrase could function adverbially:

Our good friends live <u>across the hall</u>.

Here the purpose of the *across* phrase is to tell "where" the good friends live.
Here's another sentence from Exercise 1:

The students rested <u>after their long trip</u>.

Here the *after* phrase in the predicate functions like an adverb, telling "when"—so we refer to its function as **adverbial.** Another good clue that the phrase is adverbial is its movability; it could open the sentence:

<u>After their long trip</u>, the students rested.

Remember that the nouns *adjective* and *adverb* name word classes; they name forms. When we add that *-al* or *-ial* suffix—*adjectival* and *adverbial*—they become the names of functions—functions that adjectives and adverbs normally perform. In other words, the terms *adjectival* and *adverbial* can apply to structures other than adjectives and adverbs—such as prepositional phrases, as we have just seen.

> **Modifiers of nouns are called *adjectivals*, no matter what their form.**
>
> **Modifiers of verbs are called *adverbials*, no matter what their form.**

EXERCISE 3

In the following sentences, some of which you have seen before, identify the underlined prepositional phrases as either adjectival or adverbial:

1. A huge crowd lined the streets <u>for the big parade</u>.

2. Bill got a new MacBook Air <u>for his birthday</u>.

3. Some residents <u>of the community</u> spoke <u>against the ordinance</u>.

4. The merchants <u>in town</u> are unhappy.

5. I googled Tony's blog <u>on my BlackBerry</u>.

....

Unlike the form classes, a preposition cannot be distinguished by its form; that is, there are no special endings that identify it. Prepositions are one of the word classes called **structure classes.** Other structure classes include determiners, qualifiers (such as *very,* which you saw in the discussion of adjectives and adverbs), **auxiliaries,** also known as helping verbs, and **conjunctions** (connecting words like *and, or,* and *but*).

Because prepositional phrases are such common structures in our language, you might find it helpful to review the lists of **simple** and **phrasal prepositions** in Chapter 12. You'll find them on page 243.

FOR GROUP DISCUSSION

Working either individually or in groups, add modifiers to the noun phrases in the five sentences that follow: an adjective in front of and a prepositional phrase following each noun; you may also add adverbials. You'll want to compare your portrayal of the scene with those of your classmates.

Example: The pipes caused contamination.

The *rusty* pipes *under the sink* caused *serious* contamination *of our water.*

1. The tulips are finally blooming.
2. The children annoyed the neighbors.
3. The carpet matches the furniture.
4. The water glistened in the light.
5. Thunderstorms frightened the residents.

GRAMMATICAL CHOICES

We have begun our discussion of rhetorical grammar with this short outline of sentence components in order to encourage you to think about and appreciate the wide variety of choices you make as a writer. For example, the deliberate selection of the noun headword, the determiner that signals it, and the modifiers that expand the noun phrase are all choices you make in every sentence you write. The same careful selection applies to verbs and adverbials. And while you don't stop to ponder every selection, your conscious understanding of the tools at your disposal—of noun phrases and verb phrases, of adjectivals and adverbials—will give you confidence not only as you write, but also as you revise and polish your prose.

KEY TERMS

In this chapter you've been introduced to many basic terms that describe sentence grammar. This list may look formidable, but some of the terms were probably familiar already; those that are new will become more familiar as you continue the study of sentences.

Adjectival	Headword	Preposition
Adjective	Infinitive	Prepositional phrase
Adverb	Intransitive verb	Pronoun
Adverbial	Inflection	Proper noun
Article	Irregular verb	Qualifier
Auxiliaries	Noun	Regular verb
Base form of verb	Noun phrase	Structure classes
Comparative	Past participle	Subject
Conjunctions	Past tense	Suffix
Derivational suffix	Personal pronoun	Superlative
Demonstrative	Phrase	Transitive verb
pronoun	Plural	Verb
Determiner	Possessive case	Verb phrase
Form classes	Predicate	

Sentence Patterns

CHAPTER PREVIEW

In this chapter we focus on predicates, on verbs and their particular requirements, if any. It's the variation in those requirements that differentiates the
sentence patterns. We also describe the expansion of verbs with auxiliaries
and continue the discussion of adverbials, which all the patterns can include.

The study of sentences may at first seem like a formidable, if not impossible, task when you consider that the potential number of different sentences a speaker or writer can produce is infinite. But of course it's not
impossible. What makes it possible is the systematic nature of sentence
structure and the limited number of elements that make up sentences. So
despite the infinite possibilities, the number of basic sentence forms, or
patterns, is decidedly finite—in fact, the total is quite small: The seven sentence patterns we describe here will account for the underlying skeletal
structure of almost all the possible grammatical sentences in English. And
the sentences in the various patterns share a great many common elements.

The conscious understanding of sentences that you are acquiring will
give you confidence as you write; it will give you the ability to recognize
the choices you have and how those choices can and do affect your reader.
Chapter 1 closed with the first half of the book's subtitle: *Grammatical
Choices.* This chapter opens with the second half: *Rhetorical Effects.*

RHETORICAL EFFECTS

We open our study of sentence patterns by looking at the opening paragraph
of an essay by Annie Dillard, a well-known essayist and observer of nature:

> A weasel is wild. Who knows what he thinks? He sleeps in his
> underground den, his tail draped over his nose. Sometimes he

lives in his den for two days without leaving. Outside, he stalks rabbits, mice, muskrats, and birds, killing more bodies than he can eat warm, and often dragging the carcasses home. Obedient to instinct, he bites his prey at the neck, either splitting the jugular vein at the throat or crunching the brain at the base of the skull, and he does not let go. One naturalist refused to kill a weasel who was socketed into his hand deeply as a rattlesnake. The man could in no way pry the tiny weasel off, and he had to walk half a mile to water, the weasel dangling from his palm, and soak him off like a stubborn label.

> —Annie Dillard, *Teaching a Stone to Talk*

Dillard's opening sentence couldn't be simpler. She has used what may be our most common sentence pattern: "Something is something." You won't have to read far in most modern essays, or in this textbook, to find the use of *be* as a linking verb. (Notice the first sentence following the weasel quotation!)

Dillard could easily have come up with fancier words, certainly more scientific-sounding ones, if she had wanted to:

> Scientists recognize the weasel, genus *Mustela,* as a wild creature. As with other wild animals, one can only speculate about the weasel's thinking process, if, indeed, animals do think in the accepted sense of the word.

Are you tempted to read on? (If you have to, maybe—if there's a weasel test coming up!) It's possible that some people might continue reading even if they didn't have to—weasel specialists, perhaps. But for the average reader, the effect—the rhetorical effect—of this stodgy rewrite is certainly different from the breezy

> A weasel is wild. Who knows what he thinks?

Dillard's reader is likely to think, "Here comes an essay that promises a new glimpse of nature—one that I will understand and enjoy. It's written in my kind of language."

The **linking-*be*** sentence pattern provides a good illustration of both our subconscious grammar ability and the concept of rhetorical awareness, of recognizing the effect our sentences can have on readers. As native speakers, we learn to use *be,* including its irregular past forms—*was* and *were*—and its three present tense forms—*am, are,* and *is*—perhaps without even realizing they are related to the infinitive *to be.* If you are not a native speaker of English, you have probably spent a great deal of time learning the various forms of *be* and how they are used, just as native

English speakers studying a foreign language must do when learning its equivalent of *be.*

The linking-*be* pattern is one of seven basic sentence patterns we describe in this chapter. As you read in the Chapter Preview, these seven represent the underlying skeletal structure of nearly all sentences in English—perhaps 95 percent of them. As you study the patterns, you will find it useful to think of them in terms of their required parts. You've already seen the two basic sentence units: the subject and predicate. The next step is to differentiate among the seven patterns on the basis of the structures in the predicate. Here are the two units in the predicate of the weasel sentence:

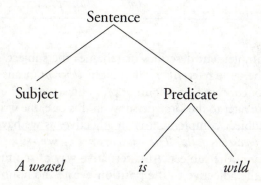

In this pattern the structure following the linking-*be* is called a **subject complement** because it says something about the subject: The adjective *wild* is a modifier of *weasel.* The word *complement* comes from the verb meaning "to complete"; it's useful to think of a complement as a completer of the verb.

There are four categories of verbs that produce our seven patterns: ***be,*** the **linking verbs,** the **intransitive verbs,** and the **transitive verbs.** These categories are differentiated on the basis of their complements. The patterns add up to seven because *be* is subclassified into two groups and the transitive verbs into three.

THE *BE* PATTERNS

Because *be* plays such an important part in sentence structure, not only as a main verb but also as an auxiliary, we put our *be* sentences into patterns separate from the linking verbs. And while most *be* sentences do have a subject complement, like the one we saw in the weasel sentence, some do not. The first pattern describes those sentences in which the second slot of the predicate contains an **adverbial** of time or place rather than a subject complement. Pattern 1 is not generally considered the linking use of *be*.

PATTERN 1	SUBJECT	*BE*	ADVERBIAL
	The weasel	*is*	*in his den.*
	Our final exam	*was*	*yesterday.*

PATTERN 2	SUBJECT	*BE*	SUBJECT COMPLEMENT
	The students	*are*	*clever.* (Adjective)
	I	*am*	*an optimist.* (Noun phrase)

The subject complement describes or renames the subject. If it's a noun phrase, it has the same **referent** as the subject. *Referent* means the person or thing or event or concept that a noun or pronoun stands for; in other words, *I* and *an optimist* refer to the same person—in this case, the writer or speaker.

When the subject complement is an adjective, as we have seen in two examples—*A weasel is wild; The students are clever*—that complement names a quality of the subject. An alternative way of modifying the subject is to shift the adjective to the position before the noun headword: *a wild weasel; the clever students*. That, of course, is precisely what the subject complement means; the difference between the two structures, the prenoun modifier and the subject complement, has to do with emphasis and purpose rather than meaning. The subject complement position puts greater emphasis on the adjective.

THE LINKING VERB PATTERN

The term *linking verb* applies to all verbs other than *be* completed by a subject complement—the adjective or noun phrase that describes or identifies the subject. Among the common linking verbs are the verbs of the senses—*taste, smell, feel, sound,* and *look*—which often link an adjective to the subject. *Become* and *remain* are the two most common ones that connect a noun or noun phrase. Other common linking verbs are *seem, appear,* and *prove*.

PATTERN 3	SUBJECT	LINKING VERB	SUBJECT COMPLEMENT
	The pizza	*looks*	*delicious.*
	My sister	*became*	*a nurse.*

Here again, as with Pattern 2, the subject complement is in line for emphasis.

THE INTRANSITIVE VERB PATTERN

In the intransitive pattern, the predicate has only one requirement: the verb alone.

PATTERN 4	SUBJECT	INTRANSITIVE VERB
	Mary	*laughed.*
	Dogs	*bark.*

As you know, such skeletal sentences are fairly rare in actual writing. The point here is that they are grammatical: No complements are required. In the section "The Optional Adverbial" later in this chapter, we will look again at adverbial modifiers, structures that add information about time and place and manner and reason, which are commonly added to all the sentence patterns, including this one. However, adding a modifier does not change the basic pattern. The following variations of our samples remain Pattern 4 sentences:

> Our dogs always bark at the mail carrier.
>
> Mary laughed at my silly hat.

Other common intransitive verbs are *sit, stand, come, go, walk, run, work, play*—and literally thousands more. They are among the verbs known as *action verbs.* You've probably read or heard advice about using action verbs to enliven your prose. For example, instead of writing

> Henry is a hard worker.

using *be* as your main verb, you could show action with

> Henry works hard.

This is a simple example of what is called *paraphrase,* or finding an alternative way of saying the same thing—or almost the same thing (neither paraphrases nor synonyms are ever identical). One of the reasons for studying sentence structure, as you are doing here, is to develop your ability to paraphrase so as to expand the tools available to you as a writer.

EXERCISE 4

Identify the boundaries of the sentence units in each of the following sentences. Then identify the pattern number. The adverbials are identified with italics. (Remember the trick you learned in Chapter 1 of substituting a pronoun to find the boundaries of a noun phrase.)

Example: The world of computers / remains / a mystery / *to my mother*.
(Pattern ____3____)

1. The bus from Flagstaff arrived *at two o'clock*. (Pattern _____)

2. The public transportation in our area is not reliable.
   (Pattern _____)

3. The breeze from the neighbor's grill smells wonderful.
   (Pattern _____)

4. The weasel sleeps *in his underground den*. (Pattern _____)

5. Annie Dillard is a keen observer of nature. (Pattern _____)

6. Seemingly invisible bits of nature become visible *with her words*.
   (Pattern _____)

7. Our committee meeting is *in the library*. (Pattern _____)

8. The committee meets *there regularly*. (Pattern _____)

THE BASIC TRANSITIVE VERB PATTERN

Transitive verbs are the other action verbs. Unlike intransitive verbs, all transitive sentences have one complement in common: the **direct object**. Pattern 5, which has only that one requirement following the verb, can be thought of as the basic transitive verb pattern.

PATTERN 5	SUBJECT	TRANSITIVE VERB	DIRECT OBJECT
	Weasels	*stalk*	*rabbits.*
	My roommate	*borrowed*	*my laptop.*

Transitive verbs are traditionally defined as those verbs in which the action is directed to, or transmitted to, an object—in contrast to the intransitive verbs, which have no object. The direct objects tells "what" or "whom."

In Pattern 3 we also saw a noun phrase following the verb, and it too answers the question of "what":

My roommate and I became *good friends*.

The distinction between the two patterns lies in the relationship of the complement noun phrase to the subject: In Pattern 3, the two have the same referent; they refer to the same people. We could, in fact, say

My roommate and I *are* good friends,

using the linking *be,* turning the sentence into Pattern 2.

In Pattern 5, on the other hand, the two noun phrases, the subject and the direct object, have different referents. We obviously cannot say, with any degree of seriousness,

Weasels are rabbits.

In the next chapter, you will see another way of testing whether or not a verb is transitive. Can the sentence be turned into the passive voice? If the answer is yes, the verb is transitive.

Incidentally, the pronoun trick you learned for identifying the boundaries of the subject works for all noun phrases in the sentence, including direct objects. For example, in the right context the second sample sentence could be stated,

My roommate borrowed it,

perhaps in answer to the question "Where's your laptop?" However, the use of the pronoun *it* changes the emphasis: When you say the sentence aloud, you'll notice that the main focus is now on the verb rather than on the direct object, as it is in the original sentence, the one with *my laptop.* You'll read about sentence focus again in Chapter 6 in the discussion of sentence rhythm.

TRANSITIVE PATTERNS WITH TWO COMPLEMENTS

The last two patterns have two complements following the verb: In Pattern 6 an **indirect object** precedes the direct object; in Pattern 7 an **object complement** follows the direct object.

PATTERN 6	SUBJECT	TRANSITIVE VERB	INDIRECT OBJECT	DIRECT OBJECT
	Marie	*gave*	*Ramon*	*a birthday gift.*
	Annie Dillard	*gives*	*her readers*	*insights into nature.*

In this pattern, two noun phrases follow the verb, and here all three—the subject, the **indirect object,** and the direct object—have different referents. We traditionally define *indirect object* as the recipient of the direct object or the person to whom or for whom the action is performed. In most cases this definition applies accurately. A Pattern 6 verb—and this is a limited group—usually has a meaning like "give," and the indirect object usually names a person who is the receiver of whatever the subject gives.

Here are some other Pattern 6 sentences with *give*-like verbs:

My father bought my sister a new car.

The judges awarded our debate team the grand prize.

My boyfriend baked me a delicious carrot cake for my birthday.

An important characteristic of the Pattern 6 sentence is the option we have of shifting the indirect object to a position following the direct object, where it becomes the object of a preposition:

Marie gave a birthday gift to Ramon.

You might choose this order if, for example, you want to put the main emphasis, or focus, on Ramon, or if you want to add a modifier. A long modifier often fits the end of the sentence more smoothly than it would in the middle. Compare the two:

Marie gave a birthday gift to Ramon, *a friend from her old neighborhood in Northridge.*

Marie gave Ramon, *a friend from her old neighborhood in Northridge,* a birthday gift.

The original order will be more effective if it's the direct object you wish to emphasize or expand:

Marie gave Ramon a birthday gift, *a necktie she had made herself.*

PATTERN 7	SUBJECT	TRANSITIVE VERB	DIRECT OBJECT	OBJECT COMPLEMENT
	The teacher	*considers*	*the students*	*hard workers.*
	The teacher	*called*	*the students*	*brilliant.*

In this pattern the direct object is followed by a second complement, called an **object complement**—a noun phrase or an adjective that describes the direct object. Note that the relationship between these two complements is the same as the relationship between the subject and the subject complement in Patterns 2 and 3. In fact, we could easily turn these two complement into a Pattern 2 sentence:

> The students are hard workers.
>
> The students are brilliant.

It's obvious that this linking-*be* version of the relationship changes the meaning: To call the students brilliant does not mean that they really are brilliant.

With verbs like *consider,* we also have the alternative of using the infinitive *to be* to introduce the object complement:

> The teacher considers the students *to be* hard workers.

This version has the identical meaning of the original; in fact, the *to be* is really "understood" in the first version. The only differences are in the length of the sentence and in its rhythm. Sometimes you may want the extra beat of rhythm that *to be* provides. If you read both versions aloud, you'll hear a slightly greater emphasis on *students* when the infinitive is included; in other words, both *students* and *hard workers* get emphasis.

Other verbs common to this pattern are *make, prefer, elect,* and *find:*

> I prefer my coffee black.
>
> Some students find grammar challenging.
>
> The teacher made the test too easy.
>
> California voters elected a movie star as their governor.

SENTENCE PATTERN SUMMARY

1. Subject   ***Be***   **Adverbial**
  The weasel   *is*   *in his den.*

2. Subject   ***Be***   **Subject Complement**
  The students   *are*   *clever.* (ADJ)
  I   *am*   *an optimist.* (NP)

3. Subject   **Linking Verb**   **Subject Complement**
  The pizza   *looks*   *delicious.* (ADJ)
  My sister   *became*   *a nurse.* (NP)

4. Subject   **Intransitive Verb**
  Mary   *laughed.*

5. **Subject**	**Transitive Verb**	**Direct Object**	
Weasels	*stalk*	*rabbits.*	

6. **Subject**	**Transitive Verb**	**Indirect Object**	**Direct Object**
Marie	*gave*	*Ramon*	*a birthday gift.*

7. **Subject**	**Transitive Verb**	**Direct Object**	**Object Complement**
The teacher	*called*	*the students*	*brilliant.* (ADJ)
The teacher	*considers*	*the students*	*hard workers.* (NP)

THE OPTIONAL ADVERBIAL

The units that make up the sentence pattern formulas can be thought of as the basic requirements for grammatical sentences. In other words, a linking verb requires a subject complement in order to be complete; a transitive verb requires a direct object. But there's another important unit that can be added to all the formulas, as mentioned in connection with the intransitive pattern: an optional **adverbial,** a structure that adds information about time, place, manner, reason, and the like.

Pattern 4, the intransitive pattern, rarely appears without at least one adverbial. Sentences as short as our two examples (*Dogs bark; Mary laughed*) are fairly rare in prose; and when they do appear, they nearly always call attention to themselves. The adverbials in the following sentences are underlined:

1. <u>During the Vietnam War</u>, Gino's dad was a pilot.
2. <u>Because a weasel is wild</u>, it should be approached <u>with great caution</u>.
3. <u>Yesterday</u> the teacher called the students lazy <u>when they complained about their assignment</u>.
4. <u>This morning</u> I got up <u>early</u> <u>to study for my Spanish test</u>.

As you learned in Chapter 1, the term *adverbial* refers to any grammatical structure that adds what we think of as "adverbial information." It adds the kind of information that **adverbs** add. In the first and second examples, you'll see **prepositional phrases:** *During the Vietnam War* tells "when"; *with great caution* tells "how." The second and third sentences include **dependent clauses:** The *because* clause tells "why"; the *when* clause tells "when." The third and fourth include adverbs of time, *yesterday* and *early.* And sentence four also has a noun phrase, *this morning,* that tells "when," along with an **infinitive phrase,** *to study for my Spanish test,* that tells "why."

It's important to recognize that when we use the word *optional* we are referring only to grammaticality, not to the importance of the adverbial information. If you remove those underlined adverbials from the four sentences, you are left with grammatical, albeit skeletal, sentences. However, even though the sentence is grammatical in its skeletal form, many times the adverbial information is the very reason for the sentence—the main focus. For example, if you tell someone

> I got up early to study for my Spanish test,

you're probably doing so in order to explain when or why about your morning schedule; the adverbials are the important information. The main clause—the fact that you got up—goes without saying!

The variety of structures available for adding information makes the adverbial a remarkably versatile tool for writers. You can add a detail about frequency, for example, by using a single word, a phrase, a whole clause—or a combination—depending on the writing situation:

> My friends and I have pizza <u>regularly</u>.
>
> My friends and I have pizza <u>with persistent regularity</u>.
>
> My friends and I have pizza <u>for breakfast, lunch, and dinner nearly every day of the week</u>.
>
> My friends and I have pizza <u>whenever the mood strikes</u>.

And it's not just their form that makes adverbials so versatile. Perhaps even more important is their movability: They can open the sentence or close it; they can even be inserted between the required units for special effect. Many of the discussions about cohesion and rhythm that you will read in the next few chapters are concerned with the placement of movable structures, including adverbials.

In Chapter 8 the various forms of adverbials are discussed in detail.

EXERCISE 5

A. Draw vertical lines to separate the sentence units, paying special attention to the various adverbials. Identify the verb category: *be*, linking, intransitive, transitive.

Example: The Lincoln penny / first /appeared / in 1909.

> Verb: intransitive

1. Many people now consider the penny a nuisance coin.

    Verb:

2. Early Lincoln pennies are very valuable today.

   Verb:

3. During World War II the government required large amounts of copper for war production.

   Verb:

4. In 1943 zinc-coated steel replaced the copper in the production of pennies.

   Verb:

5. The Philadelphia Mint unwittingly produced twelve copper pennies that year in addition to the new model.

   Verb:

6. The copper blanks for those twelve pennies were already in the press hopper when production of the zinc-coated coins began.

   Verb:

7. Those twelve 1943 copper pennies soon became valuable collectors' items.

   Verb:

8. Even after 100 years, the production of the Lincoln penny continues today.

   Verb:

B. Now revise the sentences in Part A by shifting the adverbials to other locations. You'll find that some are more movable than others.

....

QUESTIONS AND COMMANDS

This two-part structure—subject and predicate—underlies all of our sentences in English, even those in which the two parts may not be apparent at first glance. For example, in questions—also called **interrogative sentences**—the subject is sometimes located in the predicate half of the sentence; to discover the two parts, you have to recast the question in the form of a **declarative sentence,** or statement:

   Question: Which chapters will our test cover?

   Statement: Our test / will cover which chapters.

In the **command,** or **imperative sentence,** the subject—the "understood" *you*—generally doesn't show up at all; the form of the verb is always the base form:

(You)   Hold the onions!

(You)   Be a good sport.

(You)   Come with me to the concert.

Sometimes, for special emphasis, the *you* is included:

You be nice to your sister.

Don't you forget our date.

Questions and commands are certainly not structures to worry about: You've been an expert at asking questions and giving orders for many, many years.

PUNCTUATION AND THE SENTENCE PATTERNS

There's an important punctuation lesson to be learned from the sentence patterns with their two, three, or four required units:

Do not mark boundaries of the required sentence units with punctuation.

That is, never use a single comma to separate

- **the subject from the verb.**
- **the direct object from the object complement.**
- **the indirect object from the direct object.**
- **the verb from the subject complement.**

And, with one exception, never separate

- **the verb from the direct object.**

The one exception to this rule occurs when the direct object is a direct quotation following a verb like *say:*

He said, "I love you."

Here the punctuation convention calls for a comma before the quoted words.

Even though the separate units in the following sentences may be long and may require a pause for breath, there is simply no place for commas:

> The images and information sent back by *Voyager 2* / have given / our space scientists here on Earth / enough information about four of our distant planets to keep them busy for years to come. (Pattern 6)

> All of the discussion groups I took part in during Orientation Week / were / extremely helpful / for the incoming freshmen. (Pattern 2)

> Every sportswriter who saw the preseason contest between the Buckeyes and the Aggies / said / that it was a game that will be remembered for a long time to come. (Pattern 5)

In Chapter 9, in the discussion of adjectivals, we will encounter sentences in which punctuation is called for *within* a unit:

> My roommate, who grew up in New York City, is named Peter Piper.

And sometimes optional adverbial information can be inserted *between* units, where it may call for two commas:

> Weasels, because they are wild, should be approached with great caution.

In both cases, the only reason for the commas is to set off the modifier. Note that the rule, highlighted at the beginning of this section, refers to a *single* comma as a boundary marker.

EXERCISE 6

Draw vertical lines between the separate units of the following sentences, and then identify their sentence patterns. Remember that *be* as the main verb has two possible patterns and the transitive verbs have three. You might want to use pronoun substitution to find all the noun phrases in the sentence: subject, direct object, indirect object, subject complement, object complement, as well as the objects in prepositional phrases.

1. In 1747 a physician in the British navy conducted an experiment to discover a cure for scurvy.

2. Scurvy was a serious problem for men at sea.

3. Dr. James Lind fed six groups of scurvy victims six different remedies.

4. When the men consumed oranges and lemons every day, they recovered miraculously.

5. Although fifty years passed before for the British Admiralty Office recognized Lind's findings, it finally ordered a daily dose of fresh lemon juice for every British seaman.

6. Interestingly, Lind's discovery also affected the English language.

7. In the eighteenth century, the British called lemons "limes."

8. Because of that navy diet, people call British sailors "limeys."

BASIC PATTERNS IN PROSE

You really don't need instruction for writing or punctuating short sentences—as you have seen, most of them need no punctuation—but you may need instruction in using them. Or maybe *encouragement* is a better word: You may need encouragement to use short sentences. It's not unusual for inexperienced writers to believe that writing calls for long sentences rather than short ones, just as they may believe that writing calls for fancy words rather than plain ones. Both notions are wrong. In Chapter 7 we take up the topic of fancy words in the discussion of diction. Here we consider the effectiveness of short sentences, many of which are bare-bones patterns.

The bare sentence pattern as a paragraph opener is a common strategy, especially the Pattern 2, something-is-something, sentence like Annie Dillard's "A weasel is wild." Dillard uses many such sentences in her prose—sometimes with other patterns, sometimes with an added adverbial, but still very short. The following examples are from her book *Pilgrim at Tinker Creek:*

> Today is the winter solstice.
> Bear with me one last time.
> In September the birds were quiet.
> I live in tranquility and trembling.

Richard Ellis opens the first paragraph of his book *The Search for the Giant Squid* with our familiar *be* pattern:

> The giant squid is a real-life enigma.

In his biography of President Harry Truman, David McCullough often introduces a long paragraph with a short *be* sentence:

> He had been a big success as a soldier.
> The store had been a dismal failure.
> His real love, however, was politics.
> Politics was personal contact.

But short sentences like these commonly appear in other positions as well. In the following passage from an Associated Press article by Dina Cappiello about an Audubon Society study on global warming, a simple Pattern 2 sentence closes the first paragraph. It is followed by two one-sentence paragraphs—which, by the way, are common in newspaper articles. In this case, one of the two is another "something is something":

> When it comes to global warming, the canary in the coal mine isn't a canary at all. <u>It's a purple finch.</u>
> As the temperature across the U.S. has gotten warmer, the purple finch has been spending its winters more than 400 miles farther north than it used to.
> <u>And it's not alone.</u>

The story goes on to discuss other species whose wintering grounds are moving northward.

It's also not unusual to find a short sentence in the middle of a paragraph of longer sentences—especially when the writer wants to draw the reader's attention, to focus on a particular point. In the following example, from a *Time* article by J. Madeleine Nash on the movement to demolish dams, the reader can't miss the focus of the short third sentence. The sentence preceding it contains thirty-four words, the one following, thirty-seven. Notice, too, how it changes the focus of the paragraph:

> Shaping up as an important milestone is the demolition of two large dams in Washington State's Elwha River, which flows from the mountains of Olympic National Park into the Juan de Fuca Strait. Their removal, scheduled to begin in 2008, would occur in states, and if it goes as planned, the Pacific Northwest will lose only a tiny amount of hydropower and regain a legendary salmon fishery. <u>But there could be problems.</u> Behind Elwha dams are some 18 million cubic yards of accumulated sediment, enough to fill four

superdomes, and if a lot of that sediment starts to move downstream at once, the ecological consequences could be severe.

Short, focused sentences like this one are bound to draw the attention of the reader.

The linking-*be* pattern is one you may have been warned about using. And such a warning is well taken; you'll certainly want to consider an alternative to *be*, especially if you find yourself using it to the exclusion of other verbs. But bear in mind that, given a particular context, *be* sentences can be just as effective as those of any other verb category. As these examples illustrate, they are commonly used by professional writers to introduce paragraph topics.

◀ FOR GROUP DISCUSSION

The following paragraph opens a chapter of William W. Warner's *Beautiful Swimmers: Watermen, Crabs and the Chesapeake Bay.* The underlining has been added.

Winter

It can come anytime from the last week in October to the first in December. There will be a fickle day, unseasonably warm, during which two or three minor rain squalls blow across the Bay. The sun appears fitfully in between; sometimes there is distant thunder. <u>A front is passing</u>. The first warning that it is more than an ordinary autumnal leaf-chaser comes near the end. The ragged trailing edge of a normal front is nowhere to be seen. Ominously absent is the steady procession of fleecy white puffball clouds that usually presages two or three days of fine weather. Rather, the front picks up speed and passes so rapidly that it is stormy at one moment and unbelievably clear and cloud-free the next. <u>Then it comes</u>. The wind rises in a few minutes from a placid five or ten knots to a sustained thirty or forty, veering quickly first to the west and then to the northwest. <u>The dry gale has begun</u>. Short and steep seas, so characteristic of the Chesapeake, rise up from nowhere to trip small boats. Inattentive yachtsmen will lose sails and have the fright of their lives. Workboat captains not already home will make for any port.

1. Note that the title word *winter*—which is also the topic here—does not appear in the paragraph, represented only by the pronoun *it.*

What effect does that omission have? In what way would *Winter* as the first word, instead of *It,* affect the drama?

2. You saw a three-word, a four-word, and a five-word sentence in this paragraph. What purpose do they serve? How did they affect your reading?

THE SHORT PARAGRAPH

Another attention-getter is the short paragraph that appears on a page of long, well-developed ones. In *Pilgrim at Tinker Creek* Annie Dillard adds drama with an occasional paragraph of one or two sentences, often used for transition from one topic to another, much like the newspaper example we saw earlier. Each of these examples is a complete paragraph:

> The woods were restless as birds.
> The world has locusts, and the world has grasshoppers. I was
> up to my knees in the world.

In his book *Undaunted Courage* , the story of Lewis and Clark's journey to the Pacific, historian Stephen E. Ambrose often uses the short paragraph of transition:

> Thus armed with orders, guns, and goods, Lewis set out to
> meet the Indians of the Great Plains.

Like short sentences in a paragraph of long ones, these short paragraphs call attention to themselves. They, too, say, "Pay attention!" They, too, should be crafted carefully.

KEY TERMS

Adverb	Indirect object	Question
Adverbial	Interrogative sentence	Referent
Be patterns	Intransitive verb	Sentence pattern
Command	Linking-*be*	Subject
Declarative sentence	Linking verb	Subject complement
Dependent clause	Noun phrase	Transitive verb
Direct object	Object complement	Verb phrase
Headword	Predicate	
Imperative sentence	Punctuation	

RHETORICAL REMINDERS

Have I made use of short sentences to focus the reader's attention?

Have I made use of short paragraphs where needed for transition or other special effects?

PUNCTUATION REMINDER

Have I made sure that a comma does not separate the required units of my sentences?

Our Versatile Verbs

CHAPTER PREVIEW

It's probably impossible to count the number of verbs in English. We regularly add new ones when new technology and new ideas require them, and we seem to have no qualms about making verbs out of nouns: We *text* and *fax* and *e-mail* our friends; we *google* to find information. We also have a wide array of affixes we can use to change other word classes into verbs: beaut*ify*, legal*ize*, dark*en*, activ*ate*, *en*courage, *be*friend, *de*rail.

Not only do we have countless verbs, old and new, we have numerous ways of expanding them with auxiliary verbs for expressing subtle variations in time. In the examples and exercises you have seen in the first two chapters, the verbs have been limited to the one-word variety, the simple **present** and **past tenses.** We begin this chapter by examining expansions of those forms, with an outline of the meaning that the auxiliary verbs convey. We also emphasize the importance of choosing effective verbs and of using the passive voice judiciously.

THE EXPANDED VERB

As you are well aware, many of the predicates we use in writing and speech go beyond the simple present and past tenses to include **auxiliary verbs,** also called **helping verbs.** You'll find the auxiliary—sometimes more than one—in the position before the main verb:

Cassie *is* serving vegetable lasagna at her party.

My little brother *has* read all the Harry Potter books three times.

Jamal *has been* volunteering at the food bank on Saturdays.

Sometimes the auxiliaries are separated by an adverb:

I *will* probably *be* <u>taking</u> the bus home this weekend.

Although the way auxiliaries are combined with main verbs may seem chaotic, in fact, it's very systematic. To understand this system, you must be able to distinguish between the two ways verb tenses are labeled. The first is perhaps familiar to you: Verbs are labeled according to time as *present, past,* or *future.* The second is probably less familiar: Verbs are also labeled as *simple, progressive, perfect,* or *perfect progressive.* The following chart shows how these two different ways of labeling combine to create the traditional names for our wide array of tenses. In the chart we use the verb *eat* as our example. (In this chart you will find the five forms of *eat* that you saw in Chapter 1, page 10.) Note that the three columns designate time.

Verb Tenses			
	PRESENT	PAST	FUTURE
Simple	eat, eats (simple present)	ate (simple past)	*will* eat (simple future)
Progressive	*am* (*is, are*) eating (present progressive)	*was* (*were*) eating (past progressive)	*will be* eating (future progressive)
Perfect	*has* (*have*) eaten (present perfect)	*had* eaten (past perfect)	*will have* eaten (future perfect)
Perfect progressive	*has* (*have*) *been* eating (present perfect progressive)	*had been* eating (past perfect progressive)	*will have been* eating (future perfect progressive)

As you can see, in the first row, a verb in the simple present or simple past does not team up with an auxiliary. A verb in the simple future, though, does take an auxiliary, the **modal auxiliary** *will* (which is discussed further on page 43). In the second row, you will find that the **present participle** (the *-ing* form of the verb) appears in all progressive tenses along with *be,* the form of which is determined by the time: *am, is,* and *are* for the present tense, *was* and *were* for the past tense, and *will be* for the future tense. Similarly, in the third row, the **past participle** appears in all the perfect tenses along with a form of the auxiliary *have: Has* and *have* are in the present tense, *had* is in the past tense, and *will have* is in the future tense. The fourth row is a combination of the previous two: In each of the perfect-progressive tenses, you will see *been,* the past participle of *be,* as one auxiliary followed by the main verb, the present participle *eating;* the first auxiliary in the string is a form of *have.*

You may be wondering why there is more than one auxiliary listed in each cell. The form of the auxiliary verb depends on the subject of the sentence. For example, when *I* is the subject, the verb in the present progressive will be *am eating;* the verb will be *are eating* when *you, we,* or *they* is the subject; *he, she,* or *it* as subject calls for *is eating.* (These variations will come up again in connection with point of view in Chapter 7; you'll also read about personal pronouns in Chapter 12.)

Using the Expanded Verbs

In this section, you will be encouraged to pay attention to the verb tenses used in prose. Consider the verb forms in the following paragraph from Scott Turow's essay "An Odyssey That Started with Ulysses":

> At the age of eighteen, after my freshman year in college, I <u>worked</u> as a mailman. This <u>was</u> merely a summer job. My life's calling, I <u>had decided</u>, <u>was</u> to be a novelist, and late at night I <u>was</u> already <u>toiling</u> on my first novel.

This passage includes five main verbs: *work, be, decide, be,* and *toil.* They occur, however, in different tenses:

> *worked*—simple past,
>
> *was*—simple past,
>
> *had decided*—past perfect,
>
> *was*—simple past,
>
> *was toiling*—past progressive.

When you check the chart on page 39, you'll discover they are all in the "Past" column. By using the past tense throughout the paragraph, Turow is able to provide a consistent **time frame** for his narrative. This point may seem obvious. But sometimes, amid the fury of producing that first draft, the writer may inadvertently shift tenses.

> Because the library was open long hours, he spends his free time there.

Something sounds off beat here. You might be asking yourself why the verb *was* is in the past tense, but *spends* is present. Is the library still open long hours? Does the writer still go there? This is the type of confusion that can happen when verb tenses are inconsistent.

You may remember hearing the rule to "avoid shifting tenses" in your writing. What does it mean? Don't writers shift tenses all the time? Yes and no. It's true that Scott Turow has shifted from simple past to past perfect to simple past to past progressive. But as we pointed out, he has stayed in one time frame: All of his verbs fit in the past column. A more accurate statement of the rule is "avoid shifting *time frames* when writing." As long as you use one time frame (present, past, or future), your tenses will be consistent.

There are times, however, when you may want to shift from one time frame to another. You can do this by using a time marker, very likely an adverbial, such as *today, yesterday, soon, in 2002, when I was younger.*

> We <u>take</u> our old magazines to a recycling center. *Soon*, however, we <u>will leave</u> them in curbside recycling bins.

The tense in the first of these two sentences is present; the tense in the second is future. The time marker *soon* signals the shift in time frame.

It is also possible, for writers to shift time frames without using a specific time marker—but only when the reason for shifting is easily understood. The second sentence in the following pair of sentences provides historical information to support the assertion in the first sentence, so the shift from a present time frame to a past time frame is appropriate.

> Our recycling center <u>has moved</u>. The owners of the barn housing the center <u>refused</u> to renew our lease.

Another common shift occurs when a writer wants to add a comment that might aid the reader's understanding. In this example, the opening sentence is in the past tense, but the second sentence, the comment, is in the present.

> We recently <u>established</u> a Web site for reporting local air quality.
>
> Our reports <u>are</u> important to citizens with respiratory diseases.

FOR GROUP DISCUSSION

1. Read the passage below from Robert Grudin's *Time and the Art of Living.*

> In the late November of 1968, I <u>spent</u> a few days in a hotel just off the Piazza San Marco in Venice. At 6 one morning, hearing the loud warning bells, I <u>jumped</u> out of bed, <u>grabbed</u> my camera and <u>rushed</u> out to see the famous Venetian flood. I <u>stood</u> in the empty and as yet dry Piazza and <u>looked</u> out toward the Gulf, for I <u>expected</u> the flood tides to come in from the open water. Many minutes <u>passed</u> before I <u>turned</u> to see that the Piazza <u>was flooding</u>, not directly from the Gulf, but up through its

own sewers. The indented gratings in the pavement <u>had</u> <u>all but</u> <u>disappeared</u> under calm, flat silver puddles, which <u>grew</u> slowly and silently until their peripheries <u>touched</u> and the Piazza <u>had become</u> a lake. That morning I <u>experienced</u> vividly, if almost subliminally, the reality of change itself: how it <u>fools</u> our sentinels and <u>undermines</u> our defenses, how careful we <u>are</u> to look for it in the wrong places, how it <u>does</u> <u>not</u> <u>reveal</u> itself until it <u>is</u> beyond redress, how vainly we <u>search</u> for it around us and <u>find</u> too late that it <u>has occurred</u> within us.

Notice how Grudin begins with one time frame—then shifts to another. Why does he make this shift? Is it effective? Why or why not?

2. Reread Annie Dillard's weasel paragraph at the opening of Chapter 2 with time frames in mind. You'll find that she too has shifted. Did she have a good reason? Does it work? Why or why not?

Special Uses of the Present Tense

Although you might assume that the present tense is used only to refer to present time, this is not the case. In some rhetorical situations writers use the present tense to refer to past events. For example, fiction writers sometimes use the simple present tense to make action more immediate or suspenseful. The following passage is from the first chapter of William Trevor's novel *Felicia's Journey*. In this scene Felicia is riding on a train:

The train <u>judders</u> on, rattling on the rails, slowing almost to a halt, gathering speed again. Felicia <u>opens</u> her eyes. A hazy dawn <u>is distributing</u> farmhouses and silos and humped barns in shadowy fields. Later, there <u>are</u> long lines of motor cars creeping slowly on nearby roads, and blank early-morning faces at railway stations.

The present tense is also used in the analysis of literature. In this passage, John Elder discusses Robert Frost's poem "Directive":

Frost's opening lines not only <u>point</u> up to the ridge above Bristol, they also <u>identify</u> a tension fundamental to America's environmental movement. We <u>long</u> to save wild beauty from heedless development, to guarantee a modicum of biodiversity in the world of internal combustion engines and electronic monoculture.

We also use the simple present form of the verb to refer to habitual actions:

> The news comes on at six o'clock.
>
> I always vote a straight party ticket.

And we use the present in reference to propensities of nature:

> Beavers build dams.
>
> Bears hibernate in winter.
>
> Thunder follows lightning.

Other Auxiliaries

Do-Support. So far we have looked at three auxiliary verbs: *be, have,* and *will.* Another common auxiliary is *do.* We call on *do,* or one of its other two forms, *does* and *did,* when we need an auxiliary for converting a positive sentence into a negative or turning a statement into a question or for carrying the emphasis—but only when the sentence has no other auxiliary:

> I *don't like* horseradish.
>
> *Do* you *like* horseradish?
>
> Jose *does like* horseradish.
>
> *Do* sit down.

This auxiliary use of *do* is called **do-support.** In other words, *do* comes to the rescue when an auxiliary is needed. Like *be* and *have, do* can also serve as a main verb; in fact, all three are among our most common verbs.

Modal Auxiliaries. You're already familiar with one of the **modal auxiliaries:** *will,* sometimes called "the sign of the future." Unlike *be, have,* and *do,* the job of the modals is to add nuances to the meaning of the main verb. The other modal auxiliaries are equally familiar: *can, could, may, might, must, shall, should, would, ought to.* These verbs signal a variety of meanings:

> This weekend I <u>*can*</u> go to the library. (ability)
>
> This weekend I <u>*might*</u> go to the library. (possibility)
>
> This weekend I <u>*should*</u> go to the library. (advisability)
>
> This weekend I <u>*must*</u> go to the library. (obligation)

THE PASSIVE VOICE

You're probably familiar with the definition of a verb as an "action word," a description commonly applied to both intransitive and transitive verbs:

> The baby cried. (Pattern 4)
>
> My roommate wrote the play. (Pattern 5)

In these sentences the subjects are performing the action; they are making something happen. Linguists use the term **agent** for this "doer" of the verbal action. Another term that describes this relationship of the subject to the verb is **active voice.**

What happens when we turn the Pattern 5 sentence around, when we remove the agent from the subject position and give that role to the original direct object, *the play?*

> The play was written by my roommate.

This reversal has changed the sentence from active to **passive voice.** However, while *my roommate* is no longer the sentence subject, it is still the agent; and while *the play* is no longer the direct object, it is still the so-called receiver of the action. What has changed are their functions, their roles, in the sentence, not their relationship to each other.

The transformation from active to passive involves three steps:

1. The direct object becomes the subject.
2. A form of *be* is added as an auxiliary (in this case the past form *was*, because *wrote* is past); it joins the past participle of the main verb.
3. The original agent, if mentioned, becomes the object of the preposition *by* (or, in some cases, *for*).

If you think about the first step in the list, you'll understand why the other example of an action verb, *The baby cried,* is not being used to illustrate the passive voice: Intransitive verbs, such as *cry,* cannot be made passive because they have no direct object.

The passive voice has an important purpose: to shift the focus of the sentence, changing the topic under discussion. This shift is an important tool for sentence cohesion, a feature of writing you will explore in Chapter 5.

Using the Passive Voice

The core of the passive verb is the auxiliary *be* and the past participle. Here is an abbreviated form of the tense chart you studied earlier; this time, though, it is filled with verbs in the passive voice.

Verb Tenses (Passive Voice)			
	PRESENT	PAST	FUTURE
Simple	*am, is, are* assigned	*was, were* assigned	*will be* assigned
Progressive	*am, is, are being* assigned	*was, were being* assigned	*will be, being* assigned
Perfect	*has, have been* assigned	*had been* assigned	*will have been* assigned

We can cite good reasons for using the passive voice, as you will see in Chapter 5, where we discuss the role of the passive in cohesion. The passive voice may also be called for when the agent is unknown or has no bearing on the discussion:

> So far as we know, from Einstein's Special Theory of Relativity, the universe <u>is constructed</u> in such a way (at least around here) that no material object and no information <u>can be transmitted</u> faster than the velocity of light.
>
> —Carl Sagan (*Broca's Brain*)

> The Vikings have had a bad press. Their activities <u>are equated</u> with rape and pillage and their reputation for brutality is second only to that of the Huns and the Goths. Curiously, they also <u>have been invested</u> with a strange glamour which contradicts in many ways their fearsome image.
>
> —James Graham-Campbell and Dafydd Kidd
> (*The Vikings*)

The authors' purpose in the last passage is not to explain who equates the Vikings with rape and pillage or who invests them with glamour. The use of the passive puts these statements in the category of accepted beliefs. In some cases the passive voice is simply more straightforward:

> Joe <u>was wounded</u> in Iraq.

And sometimes, in order to add modifiers to the agent, we put it where we can do so more conveniently, at the end of the sentence:

> Early this morning a campus van <u>was hit</u> by a delivery truck traveling at high speed through the intersection of James Avenue and Water Street.

Note that if we switched the agent to the subject position, the result would be a fairly wide separation of the subject headword and the verb:

> Early this morning a delivery truck traveling at high speed through the intersection of James Avenue and Water Street hit a campus van.

The choice, of course, also depends on where the main focus should be.

The passive voice is especially common—and deliberate—in technical and scientific writing, in legal documents, and in lab reports, where the researcher is the agent, but to say so would be inappropriate:

> *Active:* I increased the heat to 450° and allowed it to remain at that temperature for twenty minutes.
>
> *Passive:* The heat was increased to 450° and allowed to remain at that temperature for twenty minutes.

EXERCISE 7

It's important to recognize the passive voice when you see it—so that you'll know when you've used it and thus will use it deliberately and effectively. In the first section of this exercise, you'll transform active sentences into the passive voice; in the second part you'll do the opposite—change the passive into the active. And in the third part, the voice of the sentence is not identified: You'll have to figure it out.

A. Transform the following active sentences into the passive voice; remember that the direct object of the active functions as the subject in the passive.

1. My roommate wrote the lead article in today's *Collegian*.

2. Bach composed some of our most intricate fugues.

3. Our homecoming committee has organized an elaborate celebration.

4. I should have washed the car before our trip.

5. The county commissioners are proposing a new tax-collection system this year.

6. Your positive attitude pleases me.

B. Transform the following passive sentences into the active voice; remember that the subject of the passive is the direct object in the active. (Note: If the agent is missing, you will have to supply one to act as the subject for the active.)

1. This year's cheerleading squad was chosen by a committee last spring.
2. Bill's apartment was burglarized last weekend.
3. The election of the class officers will be held on Tuesday.
4. Your car's oil should be changed on a regular basis.
5. The suspect is being kept in solitary confinement.
6. The kidnap victim has been found unharmed.

C. First decide if the following sentences are active or passive; then transform them.

1. Barack Obama was elected president in 2008.
2. You should read the next six chapters before Monday.
3. The cities in the Northeast have been affected by migration in recent years.
4. After the dot-com bubble burst, many employees of financial institutions were cheated out of their retirement savings.
5. Our company is trying out a new vacation schedule this year.
6. The streetlights on campus are finally being repaired.

FOR GROUP DISCUSSION

Surely the most famous words in our country's history are those written by Thomas Jefferson in the Declaration of Independence. Here is the opening of the Declaration's second paragraph:

> We hold these truths to be self-evident, that all men are created equal, that they are endowed by their Creator with certain unalienable Rights, that among these are Life, Liberty and the pursuit of Happiness. That to secure these rights, Governments are instituted among Men, deriving their just powers from the consent of the governed. That whenever any Form of Government becomes destructive of these ends, it is the Right of the People to alter or to abolish it, and to institute a new government, laying its foundation on such principles and organizing its powers in such form, as to them shall seem most likely to effect their Safety and Happiness. Prudence, indeed, will dictate that Governments long established should not be changed for light and transient causes; and accordingly all experience hath shown, that mankind are more disposed to suffer, while evils are sufferable, than to right themselves by abolishing the forms to which they are accustomed.

Underline the passive sentences. Rewrite all or some of them in the active voice and compare the two versions.

The Obscure Agent

Certainly the passive voice has a place in every kind of writing; it is a legitimate tool—but like any tool it must be right for the job. Too often the purpose of the passive voice is simply to obscure the agent. For example, one of the most common responses that governmental investigative committees hear from individuals accused of mismanagement is

> "Yes, Senator, mistakes were made."

And the passive is common in the "official" style used by bureaucrats:

> It was reported today that the federal funds to be allocated for
> the power plant would not be forthcoming as early as had been
> anticipated. Some contracts on the preliminary work have been
> canceled and others renegotiated.

Such "officialese" or "bureaucratese" takes on a nonhuman quality because the agent role has completely disappeared from the sentences. In the foregoing example we do not know who is reporting, allocating, anticipating, canceling, or renegotiating.

This kind of agentless passive is especially common in official news conferences, where press secretaries and other government officials explain what is happening without revealing who is responsible for making it happen:

> Recommendations <u>are being made</u> to the Mexican government
> concerning drug enforcement.
> A tax hike <u>has been proposed</u>, but several other solutions to the
> federal deficit <u>are</u> also <u>being considered</u>.
> The president <u>has been advised</u> that certain highly placed officials
> <u>are being investigated</u>.

The faceless passive does an efficient job of obscuring responsibility, but it is neither efficient nor graceful for the writing that most of us do in school and on the job.

Sometimes writers use the passive to avoid the first-person *I*, perhaps because the paper has too many *I*'s already or because the teacher has ruled out the first-person point of view:

> The incessant sound of foghorns <u>could be heard</u> along the waterfront.

But remember that English is a versatile language; first person is not the only alternative to the passive. You don't have to write, "I [or we] heard the sound of foghorns. . . ." Here's a version of the sentence using *sound* as the verb:

> The foghorns <u>sounded</u> along the waterfront.

And here's one that describes the movement of the sound:

> The incessant sound of foghorns <u>floated</u> across the water.

Many times, of course, the writer simply doesn't realize that the passive voice may be the culprit producing the vagueness or wordiness of that first draft. For example, a student writer ended his family Christmas story with an impersonal, inappropriate passive:

> That visit from Santa was an occurrence that <u>would never be forgotten by the family</u>.

Clearly, he needed to ask himself, "Who was doing what?"

> <u>The family would never forget</u> that visit from Santa.

And if for purposes of transition or rhythm he had wanted to retain *visit* as the subject, he could easily have done so in an active way:

> That <u>visit</u> from Santa <u>became</u> part of our family legend.

EXERCISE 8

1. The writer of the following passage has managed to avoid using the first-person point of view but in doing so has obliterated any resemblance to a personal voice. Revise the passage, avoiding both the passive and the first person. Remember to think about the agent as subject.

   > The woods in the morning seemed both peaceful and lively. Birds could be heard in the pines and oaks, staking out their territory. Squirrels could be seen scampering across the leaves that covered the forest floor, while in the branches above, the new leaves of the birches and maples were outlined by the sun's rays. The leaves, too, could be heard, rustling to the rhythm of the wind.

2. Identify the passive verbs in the following passage from *Stalking the Wild Asparagus* by Euell Gibbons. Why do you think he chose the passive instead of the active voice? Can you improve the passage by revising some or all of the sentences?

> Wild food is used at our house in a unique method of entertaining. Our "wild parties," which are dinners where the chief component of every dish is some foraged food, have achieved a local fame. Many different meals can be prepared almost wholly from wild food without serving anything that will be refused by the most finicky guest. Such dinners are remembered and talked about long after the most delicious of conventional dinners have been forgotten.

WELL-CHOSEN VERBS: SHOWING, NOT TELLING

When writing teachers promote the virtues of "showing" rather than "telling," what do they mean? They mean that you don't have to tell us that the old woman on the park bench is sad; you can show us:

> The old woman on the park bench wept quietly.

You don't even have to tell us that she's old:

> Wearing a shawl around her shoulders, the woman on the park bench wept quietly, wisps of gray hair escaping the woolen cap, frail bony fingers clutching her handkerchief.

Annie Dillard doesn't tell us that building a road through the Everglades between Miami and Tampa was an arduous job; she shows us:

> To build the road, men stood sunk in muck to their armpits. They fought off cottonmouth moccasins and six-foot alligators. They slept in boats, wet. They blasted muck with dynamite, cut jungle with machetes; they laid logs, dragged drilling machines, hauled dredges, heaped limestone. The road took fourteen years to build up by the shovelful.
>
> —*An American Childhood*

And Barbara Ehrenreich doesn't tell us that she was glad her day of hard work as a housecleaner was over; she shows us:

> I rush home to the Blue Haven [Motel] at the end of the day, pull down the blinds for privacy, strip off my uniform in the

kitchen—the bathroom being too small for both a person and her discarded clothes—and stand in the shower for a good ten minutes, thinking all this water is *mine*. I have paid for it. In fact, I have earned it.

—*Nickel and Dimed*

A well-chosen verb not only heightens the drama of a sentence and makes its meaning clear, it also sends a message to the reader that the writer has crafted the sentence carefully, that the idea matters. We certainly get that message from the examples of prose we have just seen.

The overuse of the linking-*be* is a common signal that a writer is telling rather than showing: "The old woman *is* sad." "The old woman *is* old." "Building a road through the Everglades between Miami and Tampa *was* an arduous job." "She *was* glad her day of hard work as a housecleaner *was* over."

You saw in Chapter 2 that the *be* patterns commonly serve not only as topic sentences but also as supporting sentences throughout the paragraph. You may be surprised, in checking a paragraph or two of your own prose, at how often you've used a form of *be* as the main verb. An abundance of such examples—say, more than two or three in a paragraph—constitutes a clear "revise" message.

Certainly, the potential drama and meaning of your prose are weakened or missing altogether when the verbs don't pull their weight. Sometimes the culprit is one of our other common, garden-variety verbs, such as *have, make, go, do, say, get, take*. Because these verbs have so many nuances of meaning, you can often find a more precise one. For example, where you have selected the verb *make*, you could probably express yourself more exactly with *constitute, render, produce, form, complete, compel,* or *create*, all of which are indexed under *make* in *Roget's Thesaurus*, along with *make believe, make good* (demonstrate), *make out* (discover, know, interpret), and *make up* (complete).

It's important to note, too, that these alternatives to *make* are not uncommon or esoteric words; they're certainly a part of your active vocabulary. Unfortunately, however, the precise verb doesn't always come to mind when you need it—especially when you're composing the first draft. Rather than stop right there in midsentence or midparagraph to find it, just circle the word you've used—or highlight it with boldface type if you're using a word processor. Then, during the revision stage you can take time to think about it again. At that point, in fact, you may want to consult your dictionary or thesaurus just to remind yourself of some of these more specific verbs.

(*A word of warning:* Every word in the thesaurus is not for you. If it's not your word, if you're not sure of it, if it doesn't sound natural in your voice, then don't use it. Sometimes the dictionary is a better reminder: It often provides synonyms in context, along with the distinctive meanings of each.)

EXERCISE 9

Find time today to watch someone doing something for five or ten minutes. Then write a paragraph-long description of the person in action. Try to use as few *be* patterns as possible. The next time you're in class, compare your paragraphs with those of your friends, paying special attention to the verbs.

··

KEY TERMS

Active voice	Intransitive verb	Present participle
Agent	Linking-*be*	Present tense
Auxiliary verb	Modal auxiliary	Showing
Be patterns	Passive voice	Telling
Do-support	Past participle	Time frame
Helping verb	Past tense	Transitive verb

RHETORICAL REMINDERS

Have I remembered to show, not tell?

Have I kept my use of the linking-*be* to a minimum?

Have I put the agent in subject position whenever possible?

Have I used the passive voice effectively?

Have I used time frames consistently?

Are the shifts I make in time frames signaled by a time marker? If they aren't, will my readers understand why I have made the shifts?

CHAPTER
4

Coordination and Subordination

In Chapter 2 we introduced basic sentence patterns, emphasizing the separate units of each; here we examine the ways in which we expand units and even sentences themselves, using **coordination, subordination,** or both. The technique of coordination, of putting together like structures in sentences, is old hat; you've been using it all your life. Coordination is a natural part of language, one that develops early in speech. If you pay attention to sentence structure the next time you're within hearing distance of a small child, you'll hear the **coordinating conjunction** *and* used frequently to link parts of sentences:

> We built a new snow fort <u>and</u> threw snowballs.
>
> Robbie is mean, <u>and</u> I'm not going to play with him anymore.

Coordination shows up early and often in writing as well. Certainly in this book you can't read very far without coming to a coordinating conjunction—an *and* or a *but* or an *or.* Your own writing is probably filled with these conjunctions, too.

Subordination is another technique you use or encounter frequently without even realizing that it has a special name. When you come across the following types of newspaper announcements, you're reading sentences that contain **subordinating conjunctions** such as *because* and *after:*

> School was canceled <u>because</u> many roads were closed.
>
> All games will be rescheduled <u>after the strike is over</u>.

So why do we need to study coordination and subordination? Because they're so essential to communication! Any technique that we use as often as we do coordination or subordination needs to be under our control. Remember, a written sentence is there to be looked at and pondered, to be read over and over again. We want to be sure that every one of our sentences containing coordinate or subordinate structures is grammatical and logical. And, equally important, we want to use the most efficient and accurate conjunctions possible.

This chapter is also about punctuation. Make no mistake, it is important to follow the conventions of punctuation; the effectiveness of your prose diminishes with every error the reader notices. As we're sure you know, punctuation rules can seem complicated in sentences with coordinate or subordinate structures. You already know how to use these structures in your sentences; it's also important to know when they require a special punctuation mark, usually a comma. Having punctuation under control will give you the confidence to construct long sentences. And, just as important, such control will send a message to your reader that you are a writer with authority.

COORDINATION WITHIN THE SENTENCE

In this chapter you'll find it useful to think again about the sentence parts you studied in Chapters 1 and 2. Most of the coordination that takes place within the sentence results from compounding one or more of those parts. *Compounding* means simply "joining" or "linking." Here we've compounded the subject:

> <u>Gino's father *and* my uncle</u> flew helicopters in Vietnam.

In the following sentence the complete predicate is compounded:

> The kids <u>played outdoors all morning *but* stayed inside all afternoon</u>.

In the following sentence, only the direct object is compounded

> He usually drinks <u>a cappuccino *or* a latte</u> before class.

Now is a good time to review the important punctuation rule you learned in Chapter 2:

> **Do not mark boundaries of the required sentence units with punctuation.**

Here's another, a non-comma rule of sorts, that describes the sample sentences you have just seen:

> **Use *no* comma with a coordinating conjunction when it joins a two-part compound *within* a sentence.**

The connectors in the preceding examples—*and, but, or*—are the three primary coordinating conjunctions we use for connecting both full sentences and their parts; you can think of them as "the big three."

You may have had a teacher in elementary or middle school who taught you a list of seven conjunctions—and perhaps helped you remember them with an acronym: *fanboys.* (The *a, b,* and *o* of *fanboys,* of course, stand for *and, but,* and *or.*) That list includes *for,* which has features of both a coordinating conjunction and a subordinating conjunction; it also includes *yet* and *so,* which share features of **conjunctive adverbs** (words like *however,* defined later in this chapter). The *n* of *fanboys* is even further removed from the big three in that it has a built-in negative meaning and is generally used only with its partner, *neither,* or, sometimes, *not.* (You'll read more about the **correlative conjunction** *neither–nor* later in the chapter.) All of these lesser conjunctions are certainly words you use in writing from time to time, but their in-between status means they do not have the wide range of use that the big three have.

Although the non-comma rule will apply to most of your sentences containing coordinate pairs, you may at times want to give special emphasis to the second part of the pair, in which case, a comma can be used to signal a slight pause:

> I didn't believe her, and said so.
>
> The running back charged ahead, but missed the goal line by an inch.

The emphasis is even stronger with a dash instead of a comma:

> I didn't believe her—and said so.
>
> The running back charged ahead—but missed the goal line by an inch.

The dash also sends the message that the punctuation was deliberate—not a comma error, a judgment some readers might make. Because an emphatic comma can be misjudged, be sure to use it with care.

Parallel Structure

One of your most important writer's tools is the concept of **parallel structure,** or **parallelism.** A coordinate structure is parallel only when the parts are of the same form. The parallel structure is an effective one—and this feature is just as important—only when the two ideas are equal, when they belong together. Annie Dillard clearly understood the effectiveness of parallel forms when she wrote this sentence:

> We could live under the wild rose as weasels, <u>mute</u> and <u>uncomprehending</u>.

For contrast, examine this compound structure that is unparallel in form:

> *<u>My new exercise program</u> and <u>going on a strict diet</u> will make me stronger and healthier.

Here the conjunction *and* connects the parts of a compound subject. The first part (*My new exercise program*) is a noun phrase in form; the second (*going on a strict diet*) is a special type of verb phrase, a **gerund.** (*Gerund* is the label we give an *-ing* verb when it is used as a noun. Gerunds are discussed further in Chapter 10.) In this case the ideas are equal, so in that sense they belong together. But for the sentence to be grammatical, the two parts of the compound must be the same form:

> <u>My new exercise program</u> **and** <u>a strict diet</u> (NP + NP)
> <u>Sticking to my exercise program</u> **and** <u>going on a diet</u> (VP + VP)

You may be thinking that these unparallel structures sound perfectly normal—like sentences you hear every day. And you're right: They do sound normal. We use sentences like these in our conversation all the time—and no one accuses us of being ungrammatical. But writing is different. We want to be as precise and effective as possible. And as writers we have a second (and third and fourth!) chance to improve our sentences. We don't have to show that first draft to anyone. Sentences with unparallel features can always be improved.

Coordination of the Series

In the **series**—a coordinate structure with three or more components—we use commas to separate the parallel coordinate elements:

> Among the lands on the frozen fringes of the Arctic Ocean are Alaska, Canada, and Greenland.

These commas represent the pauses and slight changes of pitch that occur in the production of the series. You can hear the commas in your voice

---

*An asterisk marks the sentence as ungrammatical or of questionable usage.

when you compare the series of three with a two-part structure, which of course has no comma:

> Among the lands on the frozen fringes of the Arctic Ocean are
> Alaska and Canada.

You probably noticed a leveling of your voice in reading the pair, a certain smoothness that the series does not have.

Some writers—and some publications as a matter of policy—leave out the **serial comma,** the one immediately before the coordinating conjunction. One such publication is *The New York Times.* Here is the sentence from which the previous example was taken, as published in the *Times:*

> Unlike Antarctica, a continent surrounded by ocean, the Arctic
> is mostly ocean ringed by land—the frozen, inhospitable fringes
> of Alaska, Canada, Greenland, Iceland, Scandinavia and Russia.
> —Darcy Frey

The open, or light, punctuation style leaves out the comma where a boundary is otherwise marked. Here, of course, the conjunction *and* marks the final boundary of the series.

This punctuation style, however, does have a drawback: It may imply a closer connection than actually exists between the last two elements of the series, such as the connection in the following sentence:

> Throughout college Herbie survived on pizza, ramen, and
> <u>macaroni and cheese</u>.

Climax.   In addition to parallelism, a second structural principle should be emphasized in connection with the series: **climax,** the arrangement of words or phrases or clauses in the order of increasing scope, length, or importance. Consider the three-part series in this sentence:

> With <u>his bright sunflowers, searing wheat fields and blazing
> yellow skies,</u> Vincent van Gogh was fanatic about light.
> —Paul Trachtman

This parallel series consists of three noun phrases functioning as the object of the preposition *with.* Notice also the climactic ordering of these phrases, starting with *sunflowers,* moving to *wheat fields,* and ending with *skies.* When you use climactic ordering, you might think of yourself as a photographer, shifting a camera's focus from close-up to wide angle. To get a sense of the effect when a sentence follows neither of these principles, compare Trachtman's sentence with the following version:

> With his searing wheat fields, bright sunflowers, and skies that are
> blazing yellow, Vincent van Gogh was fanatic about light.

In this example, the first two elements in the series begin with adjectives (*searing* and *bright*), but the third begins with a noun (*skies*). The third element makes the series unparallel; the climactic ordering has also been lost, the series now beginning with wheat fields instead of sunflowers.

Let's return now to coordination that *is* effective. The next two sentences, with coordination in a series, exemplify both principles, parallelism and climax:

> Thus political language has to consist largely of euphemism,
> question-begging and sheer cloudy vagueness.
> > —George Orwell

Note that Orwell, like Trachtman, omits the serial comma, but his ordering is impeccable: first one, then two, then three words. The parallel items in the following sentence are also ordered according to length:

> Those of us who manage the public's dollar will be held to
> account—to spend wisely, reform bad habits, and do our busi
> ness in the light of day—because only then can we restore the
> vital trust between a people and their government.
> > —Barack Obama

You can probably hear the special rhythm in these examples with **triplets,** the three-item series. Clearly, there must be something special about triplets, a natural inclination of some kind that encourages writers to write them and satisfies the readers who read them.

◀ FOR GROUP DISCUSSION

If you read extensively, you're bound to note many sentences that include parallel forms; sometimes, however, you'll find a sentence such as the following. Find the form that is not parallel with its partners.

> But it is her [Francine du Plessix Gray's] voice that says the
> most about her: deep, earthy and so in love with words that

her syllables roll up against one another like Vouvray on a vintner's tongue.

Did you choose the long phrase *so in love with words that her syllables roll up against one another like Vouvray on a vintner's tongue?* The principle of climax is certainly at work here. The last element in a series is often longer and more important than the other elements. Why do you suppose the writer, Marie Arana, used this form in her sentence? Would you agree that she broke the parallelism rule to good effect?

Coordination with Correlative Conjunctions

In Chapter 6 you will learn about "power words," words that command special attention; among them are the correlative conjunctions:

both–and	*either–or*
not only–but also	*neither–nor*

The power of the correlatives lies in their ability to change the rhythm and focus of the sentence and so set up different expectations in the reader. Read these two sentences aloud and listen to the change in your voice when you add *both:*

Individuals <u>and</u> nations must learn to think about the environment.

<u>Both</u> individuals <u>and</u> nations must learn to think about the environment.

The change may seem like a small one. But notice what the added *both* does: It shifts the emphasis from the predicate to the subject, which normally gets little, if any. Now the reader expects to read on about the response of individuals and nations. Here's another example of the difference that *both–and* can make in contrast to *and* alone. This is a revised version of a sentence you just read:

The power of the correlatives lies in their ability to change <u>both</u> the rhythm <u>and</u> the focus of the sentence and so set up different expectations in the reader.

If you listen carefully, you'll notice that the addition of *both* adds stress, or loudness, to *and.* The same kind of change in emphasis occurs with *not only–but also* (or *not only–but . . . as well*):

> As citizens of this global village, we must be concerned <u>not only</u> with our own health and safety <u>but</u> with the needs of others <u>as well</u>.
>
> As citizens of this global village, we must be concerned <u>not only</u> with our own health and safety <u>but also</u> with the needs of others.

In reading these two sentences aloud, you'll notice that in the second there is less emphasis on *others;* the main focus falls on *also.*

Probably the least common correlative is *neither–nor;* and it's probably accurate to say that inexperienced writers avoid it. But because it is rare, it sends a strong message, one that says the writer has constructed the sentence carefully:

> <u>Neither</u> individuals <u>nor</u> nations can afford to ignore what is happening to the environment.

The use of *both–and* carries a restriction the other correlatives do not have: It cannot connect full sentences. The other correlatives are more versatile in that they can connect both sentences and the units within the sentence.

> I should *either* spend more time studying *or* get a part-time job.
>
> *Either* I should spend more time studying, *or* I should get a part-time job.

As with other compound structures, the two parts connected by the correlatives will be parallel in structure: two noun phrases, two prepositional phrases, two verb phrases, and so on. In the case of correlative conjunctions, the problem of unparallel structure is usually easy to spot and easy to fix: It's a matter of paying attention to the conjunctions. *Either* signals that *or* is on the way—and your reader knows it! Just be sure that the same form follows both parts of the correlative, because that's what the reader is expecting. The writer of the following sentence suffered a lapse in attention:

> *I will **either** <u>take the train</u> **or** <u>the bus</u>.

Here we have a verb phrase (*take the train*) connected to a noun phrase (*the bus*). To correct this unparallel structure, simply move *either:*

> I will take **either** <u>the train</u> **or** <u>the bus</u>.

Now the same form, a noun phrase, follows both *either* and *or.*

EXERCISE 10

Revise the following sentences by substituting correlatives for the coordinating conjunctions. In your revisions, use all four of the correlatives at least once: (*both–and, either–or, neither–nor, not only–but also*).

1. Tea and coffee contain caffeine.

2. Caffeine quickens metabolism and increases the heart rate.

3. Some people drink coffee or tea, but not both.

4. Coffee and tea cannot make you intelligent, but a little caffeine can help you concentrate for a short period of time.

5. Japanese blue-collar workers work more hours per day than American workers do and typically do so with more dedication and energy.

6. Workers and schoolchildren in Japan put in more time than their American counterparts.

7. Blue-collar workers and students in the United States do not spend as much time at their respective jobs as their Japanese counterparts.

SUBJECT-VERB AGREEMENT

The topic of **subject–verb agreement** is often at issue in sentences that have compound subjects. The concept can perhaps best be illustrated by looking at examples where the subject and verb "disagree":

> We was at the movies last night.
> He don't work here anymore.

The subject-verb pairings in these sentences, though acceptable in some dialects, differ from what is expected in standard English—*We were; He doesn't.*

	Singular	**Plural**	**Singular**	**Plural**
1st	I was	we were	I do	we do
2nd	you were	you were	you do	you do
3rd	she was	they were	he does	they do

A comparison of these differences highlights the importance of understanding when to use the -*s* form of the verb, the third-person singular. The first comparison—*we was* versus *we were*—shows that in the nonstandard dialect, *was* is the only form of the verb *be* used to indicate past tense. In standard English, however, *be* has two forms for the past tense, both *was* and *were*. The second comparison—*don't* versus *doesn't*—reveals a similar pattern. The nonstandard dialect has just one form of negative *do* in the present tense (*don't*), whereas standard English has two (*don't* and *doesn't*). When your writing situation calls for standard English (not all writing situations do), be sure to use the two past-tense forms of *be* and the two present-tense forms of *do*.

In writing, too, the issue of subject–verb agreement is concerned with the -*s* form of the verb and the number (whether singular or plural) of the subject. In standard English, we use the -*s* form only when the subject is singular *and* third person (a subject that can be replaced by *he, she,* or *it*). But when subjects are compound, agreement can get a bit tricky.

When nouns or noun phrases in the subject position are joined by *and* or by the correlative *both–and,* the subject is plural:

> <u>My friends and relatives</u> **are** coming to the wedding.

However, the coordinating conjunction *or* and the correlatives *either–or* and *neither–nor* do not have the additive meaning of *and*. In compound subjects with these conjunctions, the verb is determined by the closer member of the pair:

> Neither the speaker nor <u>the listeners</u> **were** intimidated by the protestors.
> Either the class officers or <u>the faculty adviser</u> **makes** the final decision.

If the correct sentence sounds awkward because of the verb form, you can simply reverse the compound pair:

> Either the faculty adviser or <u>the class officers</u> **make** the final decision.

When both members of the pair are alike, of course, there is no question:

> Either <u>the president or the vice president</u> **is** going to introduce the speaker.
> Neither <u>the union members nor the management representatives</u> **were** willing to compromise.

For most verb forms, there is no decision to be made about subject–verb agreement; the issue arises only when the present tense -*s* form of the verb or auxiliary is involved. In the following sentences with the past tense, there is no choice:

> Either the class officers or the faculty adviser <u>made</u> the final decision.

> Either the faculty adviser or the class officers <u>made</u> the final decision.

Another situation that sometimes causes confusion about number—that is, whether the subject is singular or plural—occurs with subjects that include a phrase introduced by *in addition to* or *along with:*

> *The sidewalk, in addition to the driveway, need to be repaired.

> *Mike, along with his friend Emilio, often help out at the bakery on weekends.

These additions to the subject are parenthetical; they are not treated as part of the subject. In both sentences, the subjects are singular; the verb should be the *-s* form—*needs* and *helps*. To make the subject compound—to include the additions—the writer could use a coordinating conjunction, such as *and:*

> The sidewalk <u>and</u> the driveway <u>need</u> to be repaired.

> Mike <u>and</u> his friend Emilio often <u>help</u> out at the bakery on weekends.

EXERCISE 11

Choose the verb that agrees in number and in person with the subject. If a compound subject is joined by *either . . . or* or *neither . . . nor*, the verb should agree with the closer member.

1. The students in Biology 101 (goes/go) on a field trip each spring for a full day.

2. Either the students or the instructor (chooses/choose) a site in the region to explore.

3. Neither the instructor nor the students (goes/go) to any other classes that day.

4. A lunch, along with plenty of water, (is/are) essential for the trip.

5. A field guide, as well as a writer's notebook, (finds/find) a place in most students' backpacks.

COMPOUND SENTENCES

The sentence patterns you learned in Chapter 2 can also be called *clause patterns:* The two words **clause** and **sentence** are close in meaning. First, we'll define *clause* as a structure that contains a subject and a predicate. That definition, of course, conforms precisely to the illustration of *sentence* shown in Chapter 1. When a clause functions independently, we call it an **independent clause.** When it begins with a capital letter and ends with a period (or other terminal mark of punctuation), we call it a **simple sentence:**

> A weasel is wild.

As you well know, however, not all sentences in the English language are simple. Often we want to show that the ideas expressed in two independent clauses are related, so we join them together into a **compound sentence:**

> Acupuncture has been effective in healing muscular disorders, **and**
>   it has no side effects.
> Acupuncture is cheaper than conventional medicine, **but** most
>   Americans do not understand how it works.

The punctuation convention for compound sentences calls for a comma at the end of the first clause, signaling that another independent clause is on the way. Here, then, is the second punctuation rule in connection with coordination:

> **Use a comma before the coordinating conjunction joining the two independent clauses of a compound sentence.**

As you can see, it's important to understand exactly what it is you're compounding: If it's only two words or phrases within the sentence, then no comma is called for; if it's two independent clauses, then the conjunction needs a comma to send a signal to the reader that a second independent clause is on the way. It's not unusual to see in published works compound sentences without the comma, especially when both independent clauses are short. However, most professional writers follow the rule consistently.

FOR GROUP DISCUSSION

You may remember hearing a rule for writers that warns, "Never begin a sentence with *and* or *but*." Is it true? Does it accurately describe how writers write? Frankly, no. According to the fifteenth edition of *The Chicago*

Manual of Style, "a substantial percentage (often as many as 10 percent) of the sentences in first-rate writing begin with conjunctions" (193).

The reason for this common usage is that starting a sentence with a coordinating conjunction can provide a rhetorical punch, as in this example from the Introduction to *Earth: The Sequel* by Fred Krupp and Miriam Horn:

> A revolution is on the horizon: a wholesale transformation of the world economy and the way people live. This revolution will depend on industrial technology—capital-intensive, shovel-in-the-ground industries—and will almost certainly create the great fortunes of the twenty-first century. But this new industrial revolution holds a more important promise: securing the world against the dangers of global warming.

A. Rewrite their last sentence, following the so-called rule. Has your revision changed the impact of the sentence?

B. To see if the estimate of sentence-opening conjunctions given in *The Chicago Manual of Style* is accurate, check the textbooks or other readings you have done for your classes. Also check daily newspapers and/or weekly newsmagazines.

Conjunctive Adverbs and Transitional Phrases

In Chapter 5, on the topic of cohesion, you will read about *metadiscourse,* a term that refers to certain signals that help the reader understand the writer's message. Among the most useful of such signals are the conjunctive adverbs, also known as adverbial conjunctions. As their name suggests, conjunctive adverbs join sentences to form coordinate structures as other conjunctions do, but they do so in a different way. The following list includes some of the most common adverbs that function as sentence connectors:

> *Addition:* moreover, furthermore, further, also
> *Time:* meanwhile, then, afterwards, previously
> *Contrast:* however, instead, rather
> *Result:* therefore, consequently, thus
> *Concession:* though
> *Reinforcement:* indeed, nevertheless, still

Conjunctive adverbs differ from other conjunctions in that, like ordinary adverbs, most of them are movable; they need not only introduce their clause. It is that movability that makes them such an important tool for writers:

> We worked hard for the Consumer Party candidates; <u>however,</u> we knew they didn't stand a chance.
>
> We worked hard for the Consumer Party candidates; we knew, <u>however,</u> that they didn't stand a chance.
>
> We worked hard for the Consumer Party candidates; we knew they didn't stand a chance, <u>however</u>.

Bear in mind, though, that the farther along in the sentence the conjunctive adverb appears, the less value it has as a connector. If the reader needs the signal that the connector carries—such as the message of *however,* indicating that a contrast is coming—you will probably want the reader to get it in a timely fashion, not wait until the end, especially when the second clause is fairly long.

A different emphasis occurs when the conjunctive adverb is used with no punctuation. Read these pairs of sentences aloud and note where you put the main stress in the second clause of each:

> Our main speaker canceled at the last minute; the rally was <u>therefore</u> postponed until the following weekend.
>
> Our main speaker canceled at the last minute; the rally, <u>therefore,</u> was postponed until the following weekend.

In the versions *without* commas, it is the word *following* the conjunctive adverb that gets main stress; *with* commas, it's the word *preceding.*

This punctuation choice occurs with only a limited number of the conjunctive adverbs; most of them require the commas to send their message. And it's also important to recognize that without punctuation they lose some of their connective power, functioning more like adverbials, less like conjunctions. In the example without commas, *therefore* seems more like a modifier of the word *postponed* rather than a comment relating to the clause as a whole.

You'll also want to consider the tone that conjunctive adverbs tend to convey. Some of them—such as *moreover, nevertheless, therefore,* and even the fairly common *however*—may strike the reader as formal, perhaps even stiff. You can often diminish that formality by using coordinating conjunctions: Instead of *however,* use *but;* instead of *moreover,* use *and;* for *nevertheless,* use *yet.*

Many prepositional phrases are also used as sentence connectors. They are called **transitional phrases.** Note that they serve the same purposes as conjunctive adverbs:

> *Addition:* in addition to
> *Time:* in the meantime
> *Contrast:* in contrast, on the contrary
> *Result:* as a result, in the end
> *Concession:* of course, at any rate, at least
> *Reinforcement:* in fact, above all, in particular

And like conjunctive adverbs, many of these prepositional phrases can appear at various points in a sentence.

> The campaign contributions we had been counting on didn't materialize; <u>in fact,</u> the campaign was broke.
> The campaign contributions we had been counting on didn't materialize; the campaign, <u>in fact,</u> was broke.
> The campaign contributions we had been counting on didn't materialize; the campaign was broke, <u>in fact</u>.

Unless you want to stress the word following the connector, the rule to remember when using either conjunctive adverbs or transitional phrases is as follows:

> **Use commas to set off conjunctive adverbs and transitional phrases.**

Compound Sentences with Semicolons

You've seen a great many semicolons used in the discussions throughout these chapters. And in the previous section you saw them in sentences illustrating the use of conjunctive adverbs. However, you can't assume from these examples that you'll find them in great numbers everywhere. Some people manage to go through life without ever making their acquaintance. If you belong to that group of non-users, you can be sure of one thing: Your punctuation is not as effective as it could and should be. But take heart! The semicolon is easy to use.

In her book *Woe Is I,* Patricia T. O'Conner calls the semicolon the flash-ing red of punctuation traffic signals:

> If a comma is a yellow light and a period is a red light, the semicolon is a flashing red—one of those lights you drive through after a brief pause. (139)

Think of the semicolon as the equivalent of the comma-plus-conjunction that connects compound sentences. You could even put this relationship into a formula:

$$(, + and) = (;)$$

In the last section you saw semicolons in compound sentences with conjunctive adverbs, but don't get the idea that the conjunctive adverb is required. Semicolons can be used with no conjunction at all:

> There was silence; I stood awkwardly, then moved to the door.
> There was silence; white faces were looking strangely at me.
> —Richard Wright

In compound sentences like these, the semicolon sends a message to the reader: "Notice the connection." To understand the importance of the semicolon, imagine these sentences without the semicolons, with periods instead. The connection of the silence to what follows in each case would be lost.

These two uses of the semicolon to connect clauses—by itself and with a conjunctive adverb—are perhaps the most common; but there are times when you will want to use a coordinating conjunction along with the semicolon, as in this compound sentence you are reading. As you can see, the second clause includes a comma, so we use a semicolon before the conjunction *but* to signal clearly the boundary between the two inde-pendent clauses. In Chapter 10 you will read about the one other place we use the semicolon: to separate the parts of a series when the individual parts include punctuation of their own. Here's an example:

> The study of language includes three main areas: phonology, the study of sounds; morphology, the study of meaningful combinations of sounds; and syntax, the study of sentences.

Because each of the three items in the series includes an explanatory phrase set off by commas, the use of semicolons between them helps keep the reader on track.

Compound Sentences with Colons

Inexperienced writers often avoid using semicolons simply because they don't understand them; even less understood is the colon as a sentence connector. In Chapter 10 you will read about the colon in its more familiar role—as a signal of a list of items:

> Three committees were set up to plan the convention: program, finance, and local arrangements.

In this sentence the message of the colon is "Here it comes, the list of committees I promised."

In connecting two complete sentences, the message of the colon is similar. As with the list in the preceding example, the independent clause following a colon also completes or explains or illustrates the idea in the first clause:

> Rats and rabbits, to those who injected, weighed and dissected them, were little different from cultures in a petri dish: they were just things to manipulate and observe.
>
> —Steven Zak

> It's not that Japanese consumers are eager to throw their money away: to judge by the way shoppers prowl through the neighborhood supermarket and electronics store, they are extremely cost conscious.
>
> —James Fallows

> I came to a conclusion that I want to pass on to you, and I hope nobody gets too mad: Medical science does everything it can.
>
> —Carolyn See

The preceding examples are all taken from essays in popular magazines. The following sentence is from fiction:

> Jem and I found our father satisfactory: he played with us, read to us, and treated us with courteous detachment.
> —Harper Lee (*To Kill a Mockingbird*)

Notice how the first clause sets up an expectation in the reader. The colon says, "Here comes the information you're expecting," or "Here's what

I promised." In the second passage, the *not* in the first clause sets the reader up for a contrast in the second. In general, if you can mentally insert *namely* or *that is* or *in fact,* as you can in the preceding examples, you should consider using a colon to connect the sentences.

It's important to recognize that this way of connecting two clauses is quite different from the connection with semicolons. The two clauses connected with the semicolon have parallel ideas. And unless you include a signal to the contrary, your reader will expect the relationship to be an additive one, an *and* connection. If you try to replace the colon with *and,* you'll see that it won't work.

Two other common structures that the colon signals are questions and direct quotations:

> Everyone at the news conference wondered what was coming next: Would the senator actually admit her part in the cover-up?

> A Northwestern University psychiatrist explained the purpose of brain chemicals rather poetically: "A person's mood is like a symphony, and serotonin is like the conductor's baton."
> —*Time*

Another situation that calls for the colon as a signal, which you are probably familiar with, is the block quotation—the long indented quotation.

There is one detail of punctuation in these compound sentences that varies. Except in the case of the direct quotation, you have the choice of using either a capital or a lowercase letter following the colon. (The first word of a direct quotation following a colon is generally capitalized.) Some publications capitalize all independent clauses following colons (the style of this book); others capitalize only questions; some use lowercase for all independent clauses except direct quotations. Whichever style of punctuation you choose, be consistent.

Punctuation Pitfalls

If you've ever encountered a teacher's "CS" or "FS" or "RO" notation in the margin of an essay, you're in good company. The **comma splice** and the **fused sentence,** sometimes called a **run-on sentence,** are among the most common—and probably the most perplexing to teachers—of all the punctuation errors that writers make. They are perplexing because they are based on such a straightforward and common situation: a sentence with two independent clauses.

Consider again the sentence patterns you saw in Chapter 2—those simple *subject–verb–complement* sentences. When you write one of those—when you begin it with a capital letter and end it with a period—you've created an independent clause, actually a sentence that can stand on its own. It's true, of course, that most of the sentences we write aren't as simple as the bare sentence patterns—and often not as easy to identify. Every subject and every complement can be expanded with all sorts of structures; further, there are all shapes and sizes of adverbials that can be added to the beginning and the end of the sentence. So the key is first to recognize a sentence pattern when you see it—to recognize the boundaries of its various units—bearing in mind that certain units can themselves be clauses (which we'll discuss in more detail later). Let's examine again a sentence we discussed earlier in this chapter.

> Acupuncture has been effective in healing muscular disorders, **and** it has no side effects.

The punctuation in this sentence follows the highlighted rule you saw in the last section:

> **Use a comma before the coordinating conjunction joining the two independent clauses of a compound sentence.**

What happens if we leave out the conjunction?

> *Acupuncture has been effective in healing muscular disorders, it has no side effects.

We've produced a *comma splice.* In other words, we've spliced, or joined, two independent clauses together with a comma. But a comma alone is not strong enough: It needs the support of a conjunction. *Remember, we want the reader to know that another independent clause is coming.*

If you have ever committed a comma splice—left out the *and* (well, maybe *committed* is too strong a word!)—you may have done so for what you thought was a good reason: to create a tighter connection. The sentence may have sounded or looked better. It's true that sometimes the conjunction adds a certain flabbiness, and maybe the sentence would be better off without it. There is a solution, though, and it's often a good one—the semicolon. Notice how slim and trim the following sentence is with a semicolon instead of *and:*

> It's true that sometimes the conjunction adds a certain flabbiness; maybe the sentence would be better off without it.

In the version with the semicolon, the reader will give more emphasis to the second clause.

However, if we were feeling miserly and decided to leave out the semi-colon as well, we would be creating a fused sentence—two sentences run together without any punctuation—another error best to avoid.

At this point you may be asking yourself, "How about the conjunction by itself? Is that ever allowed in a compound sentence?"

> *It's true that sometimes the conjunction adds a certain flabbiness and maybe the sentence would be better off without it.

Again, the wrong message—another fused sentence of sorts, although not as serious as the one with neither conjunction nor comma. The use of *and* without the comma tells the reader that a coordinate structure *within the sentence* is coming—not that a new independent clause is coming.

In an earlier section, you saw examples of the semicolon used to join sentences beginning with a conjunctive adverb or transitional phrase:

> We worked hard for the Consumer Party candidates; <u>however,</u> we knew that they didn't stand a chance.
>
> The campaign contributions we had been counting on didn't materialize; <u>in fact,</u> the campaign was broke.

Inexperienced writers sometimes use a comma in these sentences where the semicolon should be, thus creating a sentence with a comma splice. When you use a conjunctive adverb to begin a clause, be sure that it follows a semicolon (as shown previously) or a period (as in the following):

> We worked hard for the Consumer Party candidates. However, we knew that they didn't stand a chance.
>
> The campaign contributions we had been counting on didn't materialize. In fact, the campaign was broke.

It's certainly possible to find examples in both contemporary and older prose of two sentences, usually short ones, put together with the conjunction alone or with the comma alone—deliberate deviations from conventional punctuation practices. However, most academic and business writing assignments call for the compound sentence to follow the rules stated earlier—*comma-plus-conjunction* or *semicolon-plus-conjunctive adverb/transitional phrase*—so that the punctuation provides the reader with information about the kinds of structures that will come after it. These are the rules followed in this book.

The importance of accurate punctuation cannot be overemphasized. Not only will readers be guided efficiently through your ideas, they will also gain confidence in you as a writer—and as an authority on your topic. It's easy for a reader to conclude—perhaps subconsciously and, yes, perhaps unfairly—that slipshod punctuation equals slipshod thinking.

Your image, your credibility as a writer, can only be enhanced when you make accurate, effective, and helpful punctuation choices.

THE COMPOUND SENTENCE: PUNCTUATION REVIEW

We have seen five styles of punctuation for joining the clauses in compound sentences. Every writer should understand all five and be able to use them effectively.

1. COMMA-PLUS-CONJUNCTION

    Every ride at an amusement park has a history, and the history of the roller coaster begins with the Russian Ice Slides of the seventeenth century.

Remember that the comma by itself is not strong enough to make that connection; without the conjunction, the result is a comma splice. Without either the conjunction or the comma, the sentence becomes a fused sentence.

2. SEMICOLON

    Every ride at an amusement park has a history; the history of the roller coaster begins with the Russian Ice Slides of the seventeenth century.

You can think of this connection as a tighter version of the comma with *and.*

3. SEMICOLON-PLUS-CONJUNCTION

    Every ride at an amusement park has a history; and the history of the roller coaster begins with the Russian Ice Slides of the seventeenth century, located primarily in the area around present-day St. Petersburg.

A semicolon, instead of a comma, is used between two independent clauses, especially when one of the clauses already includes a comma.

4. SEMICOLON-PLUS-CONJUNCTIVE ADVERB/TRANSITIONAL PHRASE

The inclusion of a conjunctive adverb has the advantage of being movable, so you can manipulate the rhythm pattern to focus the emphasis on different words. You can decide how the reader reads the sentence:

    Every ride at an amusement park has a history; <u>however,</u> the roller coaster has one of the most unusual stories to tell.

> Every ride at an amusement park has a history; the roller
> coaster, <u>however,</u> has one of the most unusual stories
> to tell.

Strong stress falls on the word preceding the comma.

5. COLON

> Many of the ice slides built in Russia were quite elabo-
> rate: Some rose to eighty feet and accommodated sev-
> eral large sleds at once.

Here the colon is saying, "Here it comes, the elaboration you're
expecting." Note that the full sentence following the colon does
not always begin with a capital letter, as it does here. Some publications prefer lowercase in this position.

These, then, are the five ways we connect the two clauses of a compound
sentence. Be sure to take time to understand all of them. Using them correctly also means understanding the structure of clauses, their parameters.
These two concepts—the structure of clauses and the conventions for connecting them—are basic tools that every writer needs for every writing task.

EXERCISE 12

Add punctuation to the following passages, if necessary. In some cases
there may be more than one possibility.

1. The Smithsonian Institution comprises nineteen museums nine
   research centers and the National Zoo.

2. Most of the museums are located on the National Mall in
   Washington, DC but the National Air and Space Museum has
   two locations.

3. You can find one of the museums on the National Mall and the
   other near Dulles International Airport.

4. The National Air and Space Museum on the National Mall contains in its collection the Wright Flyer Sputnik 1 and the Apollo 11
   lunar module.

5. The museum on the National Mall opened in 1976 however, its
   collection was so large that an additional museum was built near
   Dulles International Airport.

6. Visitors to the Steven F. Udvar-Hazy Center can view the Boeing
   B-29 Superfortress *Enola Gay* the MacCready *Gossamer Albatross*
   and the space shuttle *Enterprise*.

7. Together, these two museums maintain a vast collection of air- and spacecraft they also sponsor vital research into aviation and related technologies.

8. These museums share the same mission they are dedicated to the commemoration of the nation's aeronautic history.

9. Approximately 260 employees work at the museums but the museums could not open their doors without the help of their 500 volunteers, whose tasks range from staffing the information desk to serving as docents.

10. Admission to both these spectacular museums is free but donations are accepted.

SUBORDINATION: THE DEPENDENT CLAUSES

So far we've discussed sentences in terms of independent clauses: The simple sentence consists of one independent clause; the compound sentence consists of two, sometimes three or more, independent clauses. But a clause need not be independent. It can also function within a sentence as a **dependent clause,** also called a *subordinate clause.*

In Chapter 2 we saw examples of dependent clauses functioning as adverbials:

<u>Because a weasel is wild</u>, it should be approached with great caution.

Yesterday the teacher called the students lazy <u>when they complained about their assignment.</u>

Remember that movability is a good clue that a structure is functioning as an adverbial. And as you can see in the first example, when an adverbial clause opens the sentence, it is followed by a comma. We'll discuss this comma rule in more depth in Chapter 8.

Another type of dependent clause functions adjectivally, as the modifier of a noun. In the following sentence a *who*-clause is a modifier of the subject *the man:*

The man <u>who lives upstairs</u> bothers the neighbors.

Again you can recognize the three units of the sentence when you substitute pronouns for the noun phrases:

He	bothers	them.
(subject)	(verb)	(object)

Recall that a pronoun stands in for the entire noun phrase, including all the modifiers. Because this type of dependent clause functions as an adjective to modify a noun, it is called an **adjectival clause.** Like the prepositional phrases you saw in Chapter 1, the adjectival clause follows the headword of the noun phrase:

the man	who lives upstairs
our new neighbors	across the hall

Dependent clauses can also function as **nominals,** filling noun phrase positions. For example, we could use our original weasel clause as a direct object following a transitive verb like *say,* creating a Pattern 5 sentence:

Annie Dillard says *that a weasel is wild.*

This sentence has the same three units as this sample Pattern 5 sentence from Chapter 2:

My roommate	borrowed	my laptop.
Annie Dillard	says	something.

But in the Annie Dillard sentence, the "something" in the direct object position is a clause, not a noun phrase. This type of dependent clause is called a **nominal clause** because it functions as a noun. Note that the term *nominal,* the *–al* form of *noun,* is the name of a function, not a form, just as *adverbial* and *adjectival* are. (In Chapter 1 you learned that the terms *adverbial* and *adjectival* apply to all forms that function the way adverbs and adjectives do.)

These then are the three roles that dependent clauses fill in sentences, their three functions: adverbial, adjectival, and nominal. You will learn more about the functional categories in Chapters 8, 9, and 10.

EXERCISE 13

In his textbook *Classical Rhetoric for the Modern Student,* Professor Edward P. J. Corbett reports on a study of style he conducted in his Honors Freshman English class. His students compared the length of their own sentences and paragraphs with those of a professional writer, F. L. Lucas. They selected eight paragraphs from an essay by Lucas, avoiding short transitional paragraphs and any that contained two or more sentences of quoted material. Then they calculated the average number of words per sentence (20.8) and the average number of sentences per paragraph (7.6). In addition, they calculated the percentage of sentences that were ten words longer than the average (17 percent) and the percentage that were five words shorter than average (40 percent). Then they did the same with an expository theme of their own.

We cannot, of course, judge the effectiveness of a paragraph on the basis of statistics. However, data gathered can sometimes show us our strengths (or perhaps bad habits); they can also point out structures we might consider using.

Do a contrastive study of your own writing style and that of a professional, following Professor Corbett's model. For the analysis, choose eight paragraphs from an article published in a magazine (e.g., *Harper's, Atlantic Monthly, The New Yorker, Smithsonian, Nature*) or from an article published in a professional journal in your major field. For purposes of this analysis, a sentence is defined as "a group of words beginning with a capital letter and ending with some mark of end punctuation." In some cases these sentences will be fragments; even so, you should include them in your analysis. However, among the eight do not include short transitional paragraphs or any paragraph that contains two or more sentences of quoted material. Do the same analysis with eight paragraphs from an expository essay of your own.

	PROFESSIONAL	STUDENT
1. Total number of words	_____	_____
2. Total number of sentences	_____	_____
3. Longest sentence (in # of words)	_____	_____
4. Shortest sentence (in # of words)	_____	_____
5. Average sentence length	_____	_____
6. Number of sentences with more than ten words *over* the average length	_____	_____
7. Percentage of sentences with more than ten words *over* the average	_____	_____
8. Number of sentences with more than five words *below* the average	_____	_____
9. Percentage of sentences with more than five words *below* the average	_____	_____
10. Paragraph length	_____	_____
longest paragraph (in # of sentences)	_____	_____
shortest paragraph (in # of sentences)	_____	_____
average paragraph (in # of sentences)	_____	_____

REVISING COMPOUND STRUCTURES

In compound sentences, as well as sentences with compound predicates, verb forms that are unparallel can sometimes produce a kind of fuzziness. Notice in the following sentence that only one of the two verbs includes an auxiliary:

> Experts in sports medicine <u>emphasize</u> the importance of water intake and <u>are recommending</u> a half-ounce per day for every pound of body weight.

A related source of fuzziness can occur in the compound sentence. Our example could easily be turned into a compound sentence with the simple addition of a second subject:

> Experts in sports medicine emphasize the importance of water intake
>
> , and
>
> <u>they</u> are recommending a half-ounce per day for every pound of body weight.

The sentence is now parallel in *form.* But a question remains: Are the two *ideas* parallel? Do they belong together as equal partners? (And remember, that's what the message of *and* is: "These two structures are equal partners.")

If the two ideas were fuzzy partners as predicates—a judgment suggested by the form of the verbs—then they are just as likely to be fuzzy partners as sentences. The problem is not just that one verb has an auxiliary and the other doesn't (*are recommending* and *emphasize*); it's the underlying reason for that difference. We generally use the simple present tense (*emphasize*) to describe an accepted truth or timeless quality; we use the present progressive tense (*are recommending*) for an ongoing action. It's not that the two ideas don't belong together: They do—but not as equal partners. *And* is simply the wrong connection.

Because the sentence is out of context, we don't know which of the two ideas should be emphasized, but a good guess would be the recommendation:

> Experts in sports medicine, who emphasize the importance of water intake, are recommending a half-ounce per day for every pound of body weight.

Here we've used a dependent clause for one of the two ideas. Another possibility is the **participial phrase** to open the sentence. (An *-ing* verb used as an adjective is called a **participle** or, as in this case, a participial phrase.)

Emphasizing the importance of water intake, experts in sports
medicine recommend a half-ounce per day for every pound of
body weight.

We will look at both of these noun modifiers—the adjectival clause and
the participial phrase—in Chapter 9.

You may find it helpful to think in terms of **foregrounding** and
backgrounding when you have two ideas to combine. Which idea should
get the foreground, the prominence of the main clause? Which should be
thought of as background and given the supporting role of the dependent
clause? This concept is related to the concept of known and new information, which you will study in the next chapter.

The following sentence illustrates another common coordination
problem: a fact and a conclusion based on that fact put together as parallel ideas.

The African killer bees are less predictable than European bees and
tend to attack in vast swarms.

One clue that the two predicates don't belong together is a difference in
verb classes: linking and transitive. Again, we need context to know which
idea should get the main focus, which idea should be foreground, and
which should be treated as the background:

The African killer bees, which are less predictable than European
bees, tend to attack in vast swarms.

The African killer bees, which tend to attack in vast swarms, are
less predictable than European bees.

A mismatch in verb forms certainly doesn't guarantee a problem, but it's
the kind of sentence you'll want to notice when you're revising.

EXERCISE 14

Revise the following sentences, paying particular attention to the unparallel structures.

1. At the new recreation center, students have the privilege of deciding whether to lift weights or swimming in an Olympic-size pool.

2. The Baltimore Orioles' stadium at Camden Yards has all the
   virtues of the beloved ballparks of another era and is in the great
   tradition of classic baseball architecture.

3. I neither enjoy flying across the country nor particularly want to take the train.

4. The movie's starting time and whether we could afford the tickets were both more important to us than were the opinions of the reviewers.

5. The academic adviser introduced a number of programs and said that we could make individual appointments to see her.

6. Lance Armstrong won the Tour de France seven times but is also known for his philanthropy.

7. I almost never watch television: There is either nothing on that appeals to me, or the picture disappears at a crucial moment.

8. Blue whales are the largest of all animals and up to 80 percent of them congregate seasonally in Antarctic waters.

....

FOR GROUP DISCUSSION

The following excerpt is from Malcolm Gladwell's *Outliers: The Story of Success*. Comment on the uses of coordination, subordination, and parallelism. Be sure to go beyond finding examples to discuss the effects the author's choices have on his message and on you, the reader.

> You can't buy your way into Major Junior A hockey. It doesn't matter who your father or mother is, or who your grandfather was, or what business your family is in. Nor does it matter if you live in the most remote corner of the most northerly province in Canada. If you have ability, the vast network of hockey scouts and talent spotters will find you, and if you are willing to work to develop that ability, the system will reward you. Success in hockey is based on *individual merit*—and both of these words are important. Players are judged on their own performance, not on anyone else's, and on the basis of their ability, not on some other arbitrary fact.
> Or are they?

KEY TERMS

Adjectival clause
Backgrounding
Clause
Climax
Colon
Comma
Comma splice
Compound sentence
Conjunction
Conjunctive adverb
Coordinating
   conjunction
Coordination

Correlative
   conjunction
Dependent clause
Foregrounding
Fused sentence
Gerund
Independent clause
Nominal
Nominal clause
Parallelism
Parallel structure
Participial phrase
Participle

Run-on sentence
Semicolon
Sentence
Serial comma
Series
Simple sentence
Subject–verb
   agreement
Subordinating
   conjunction
Subordination
Transitional phrase
Triplet

RHETORICAL REMINDERS

Parallelism

Do the coordinate structures within the sentence belong together? (Are the ideas equal? Are the forms the same?)

Climax

When writing a series, have I ordered phrases or clauses in the order of increasing importance, scope, or length?

Coordinating Conjunctions

Have I used coordinating conjunctions to begin sentences when I would like to stress addition or contrast?

Correlatives

Have I taken advantage of the strong focus that the correlatives provide: *either–or, neither–nor, both–and, not only–but also?*

Conjunctive Adverbs

Have I used the versatile conjunctive adverbs to good advantage?

Have I placed them where I want the reader to focus?

Colons

Have I used the colon to connect those sentences that set up an expectation in the reader?

PUNCTUATION REMINDERS

Have I remembered that in the case of a two-part compound within the sentence no comma is required?

Have I used commas between elements in a series?

Have I used a comma with the conjunction joining the two independent clauses of a compound sentence?

Have I used commas to set off conjunctive adverbs and transitional phrases, especially when they begin a clause?

Have I used a comma after a dependent clause at the beginning of a sentence?

Have I made good use of a semicolon to connect clauses when it would effectively signal a close connection?

Have I used a colon effectively to signal the expected information that follows in a second independent clause?

Have I used a dash (or dashes) to lighten the comma load?

PART II

Controlling the Message

Good prose is a kind of speech, more deliberate and shapely than the words we utter aloud, yet still akin to the living voice.
—SCOTT RUSSELL SANDERS

The writer's toolkit that you brought to this course already had a good many tools in it. As you studied the previous four chapters, you learned the names of many of those tools, along with some new ones. You can think of the next three chapters as the training manual for their use:

Chapter 5: Cohesion
Chapter 6: Sentence Rhythm
Chapter 7: The Writer's Voice

These three chapters all focus on helping you gain control of your prose and its effects on your reader: controlling your message. They will help you feel confident in making choices as you draft and revise. And having that control, that confidence, means more than simply avoiding error: It means creating sentences that flow, that work together to send your readers the message you want them to hear.

In these chapters, you will learn the *whats* and the *whys*—what options are available to you and why they have the effects they do. By the end of Chapter 7, you'll be able to use your tools to develop your own repertoire of writer's voices, one to suit each of the writing situations you encounter.

CHAPTER
5

Cohesion

CHAPTER PREVIEW

Cohesion refers to the connection of sentences to one another, to the flow of a text, to the ways in which a paragraph of separate sentences becomes a unified whole. In Chapter 4 we discussed the role coordinating conjunctions, subordinating conjunctions, conjunctive adverbs, and transitional phrases play in connecting clauses. They may signal that the content in the second of two adjoining clauses contrasts with the content in the first. *But, while, however,* and *on the contrary* all indicate contrast. Other connections commonly signaled by conjunctions, conjunctive adverbs, and transitional phrases include addition, result, time, concession, and reinforcement.

In our examination of cohesion in this chapter, we first look at **reader expectation,** which means, simply, imagining yourself—you, as writer— in your reader's shoes. Then we examine three important features of cohesive writing:

- **Repetition:** key words and phrases that keep the reader on course.
- The **known-new contract:** a simple but powerful concept that reflects one aspect of reader expectation—that a sentence will have both known, or old, information as well as new and that the known information will precede the new.
- **Parallelism:** the repetition of structures of the same form for purposes of clarity and emphasis. In the previous chapter you looked for parallel forms within a sentence; in this chapter you will study parallel forms across sentences.

By studying these topics, you are essentially learning to put labels on features of the language that often make the difference between merely adequate prose and genuinely effective prose. When you recognize them and learn to manipulate them, they become writing tools at your disposal.

In every aspect of rhetoric—especially in the matter of connections—the writer must keep the reader and the reader's expectations in mind. So before taking up the separate features of cohesion, we will look at this important concept affecting all the connections: reader expectation.

READER EXPECTATION

Have you ever come across a teacher's "awk" noted in the margin of a written assignment, or have you yourself ever judged a piece of writing as awkward? Perhaps in reading a composition of your own or one written by a classmate, you have felt that something was amiss—but you couldn't quite put your finger on the something. Such problems can often be traced to thwarted expectations. Something may have struck you as awkward simply because you weren't expecting it.

Both in reading and in conversation our language is loaded with expectations; we have a sense of direction about language. Although we may not know exactly what's coming next, when we hear it—or read it—we recognize if it's appropriate. It's when the ideas take an unexpected turn that the "awk" response can set in, when a passage fails to fit that expectation, that sense of appropriateness: "I didn't know exactly what was coming next—but I certainly didn't expect *that!*"

In conversation, we can call a halt to the speaker: "Wait! What was that you just said?" But as readers, we don't have that option. Instead, we find ourselves thinking, "Why am I reading this now?" Even though it's only a fleeting thought, it doesn't take many such interruptions—the pause, the second thought, the backtracking—to obstruct the cohesive flow of a piece of writing.

Where do a reader's expectations come from? Obviously, from what has gone before, from the prior text, or, in the case of an opening paragraph, from the title or, possibly, from the author's reputation. Within a paragraph, reader expectation begins with the opening sentence. The writer, of course, has all manner of possibilities for setting up that expectation. The first sentence of this paragraph, because it is a question, sets up the expectation of an answer—or perhaps a second question.

Following is the opening sentence from a paragraph in an article about the "most glamorous sweepstakes in sports"—the Triple Crown of thoroughbred racing. This paragraph follows the article's opening section discussing the eleven horses that have successfully swept the three races of the Triple Crown since its inception in 1914, the most recent being

Affirmed in 1978. The paragraph is preceded by a subheading: "Three races become the ultimate test."

> The sweep is so rare and difficult because each race has unique demands and the series as a whole requires unusual ruggedness.

This opening sentence has no doubt set up an expectation in you about what is coming next, something about the difficulties, demands, and/or ruggedness of the Triple Crown sweep. Now read the complete paragraph:

> The sweep is so rare and difficult because each race has unique demands and the series as a whole requires unusual ruggedness. Racehorses usually do best with about a month between races. In the Triple Crown they must race three times in 36 days, over three different tracks, and at three different distances, all longer than most have ever tried before.
> —Steven Crist (*USAir Magazine*)

That second sentence is surely a letdown: We were expecting something else. The topic has shifted. Not that this new topic is unimportant. But the writer did not prepare us to expect this shift from the ruggedness of the race to the ideal interval between races.

The effective topic sentence nearly always suggests the direction the paragraph will take, calling up a response in the reader: "Prove it" or "Tell me more." The following sentence opens a paragraph in *Time* about the friendship between Abraham Lincoln and Frederick Douglass, the third paragraph in an article by John Stauffer entitled "Across the Great Divide":

> Despite the immense racial gulf separating them, Lincoln and Douglass had a lot in common.

After reading that statement, we expect to read facts that prove the point. The writer meets our expectations, first with what we might call a subtopic sentence and then the supporting details:

> They were the two preeminent self-made men of their era. Lincoln was born dirt poor, had less than a year of formal schooling and became one of the nation's greatest Presidents. Douglass spent the first 20 years of his life as a slave, had no formal schooling—in fact, his masters forbade him to read or write—and became one of the nation's greatest writers and activists.

The paragraph ends with two additional sentences about Douglass as writer and activist. As you can see, the promise of the topic sentence has been kept. It led us to believe we would be given proof of its proposition—and the rest of the paragraph does just that.

While you're in the early drafting stage of your essay, you have lots of details to think about: deciding which ideas should be emphasized, which main ideas require support, and which words convey meaning most effectively. At this early stage the response of your reader may not even occur to you. But certainly at the various revision stages along the way—and, by the way, revision does go on all the time—you'll want to think about the reader's expectations.

Remember that, as with many other facets of language, a reader's expectations are not necessarily conscious thoughts. A thwarted expectation may constitute only a fleeting break in concentration, a momentary blip in the flow. But remember, too, it's that blip that produces the "awk."

Active readers do more than simply process the words and meanings of a particular sentence as they are reading it. They also fit the ideas of the current sentence into what they already know: knowledge garnered both from previous sentences and from their own experience. At the same time, they are developing further expectations.

To become aware of the reader's expectations means to put yourself in the reader's shoes—or head. It requires the ability to read your own ideas objectively, to see and hear your own words as someone else might read them. All the sections that follow in this chapter, covering various features of cohesion, emphasize this relationship between writer and reader.

FOR GROUP DISCUSSION

1. Look again at the weasel paragraph at the opening of Chapter 2. Delete the second sentence, the question. Discuss how that deletion alters reader expectation. In what way does the presence of the question change the expectation set up by the opening sentence? Compose an alternative second sentence in the form of a statement, rather than a question. Compare your version to Dillard's in terms of its effect on a reader's expectation.

2. Revise the second sentence of the Triple Crown paragraph to eliminate that blip of awkwardness. In other words, prepare the reader for the information about the time between races; prepare the reader to expect it.

3. The following excerpt comes from a paragraph in *The Life and Wars of General Phil Sheridan* by Roy Morris, Jr. For this exercise, the excerpt is divided into four separate sentences. Take a slip of paper and cover all the sentences but the first. Then, read the first and discuss what you expect to follow. Do the same with the second and third sentences. Are the sentences in this excerpt cohesive? Is there anything that could be done to make them more cohesive?

Before 1870, large buffalo herds still roamed the Southern plains, and many thousands of Native people still lived as they preferred, with the buffalo at the base of their economies.

The slaughter of the vast buffalo herd that roamed the plains and prairies until the 1840s reached a million animals a year during the 1870s.

Along the newly opened tracks, the railroads ran special excursions from which self-styled sportsmen shot buffalo from the comfort of their seats.

General Phil Sheridan remarked that the buffalo hunters had done more in two years to defeat the Indians than the entire regular Army had been able to do in the previous thirty years.

REPETITION

Instead of "Repetition," this discussion could be headed **"Lexical Cohesion,"** a term that refers to the contribution of particular words to the cohesion, or continuity, of text. (*Lexicon,* the noun form of *lexical,* means the words of the language; you can think of your lexicon as the dictionary in your head.) The repetition of words from one sentence to another is an obvious cohesive link, one that logically occurs in a paragraph on a particular topic.

In *Constructing Texts,* George Dillon characterizes the conflicting advice about repetition that student writers often encounter as a "no-man's land":

> [A] no-man's-land where they are caught in the crossfire of Never Use the Same Word Twice on a Page and Repeat Key Terms, Use Your Thesaurus to Find Synonyms and Avoid Needless ('Elegant') Variation. (p. 96)

Dillon notes that the journalism class is more often the source of "Never Use the Same Word Twice" and the English class the source of "Repeat Key Terms." He points out that sportswriters are especially good at avoiding repetition, at finding synonyms. In the following paragraph from a *New York Times* description of the 2009 Super Bowl, notice the variety of verbs:

> On the Steelers' first drive, on the offense's second play, Roethlisberger <u>faked</u> a handoff to Willie Parker, <u>rolled</u> right and <u>fired</u> a strike to receiver Hines Ward that <u>gained</u> 38 yards. Two plays later, he <u>found</u> tight end Heath Miller for 21 yards up a seam on the left side of the field.
>
> —Greg Bishop

Here is another example from the *Times*, a paragraph from the Associated Press's "National League Roundup" column about a Cubs-Cardinals game:

> [Derrek Lee's] two-run shot off Matt Morris (11–3) with two outs in the fifth sailed over the visitors' bullpen in left before clanging off a guardrail, a drive estimated at 421 feet that put the Cubs ahead, 5–3. Morris gave up all three homers and has allowed 10 this season after surrendering 35 last year.

In the first sentence, the batter's successful hit is referred to as both a *shot,* and a *drive;* and the three verbs in the last sentence—*gave up, has allowed, surrendering*—are all synonyms for delivering a home-run pitch. In fact, among the major word classes in the paragraph—nouns, verbs, adjective, and adverbs—there's not a single repeated word!

It's not only the sports reporters who avoid repetition. News writers in other departments also rely on synonyms. During the 2008 election campaign, for example, we often read news reports that started off with "John McCain," then changed to "the Republican candidate," then "the nominee," then "the senator from Arizona" in successive sentences or paragraphs. And political writers often use "the White House," "the administration," and "the executive branch" as alternatives to "the president."

On the other hand, you'll find that the paragraphs you've been reading in this textbook reflect the English-class advice that Dillon identifies: "Repeat Key Terms." For example, the second paragraph in Chapter 2, headed "Chapter Preview," includes the word *sentence* eight times in its five sentences and the word *pattern* three times, with no synonyms for either word—simply because there are no synonyms that would do the job as well. And, of course, it makes sense to repeat key concepts in a book designed to teach those concepts. But you'll also find from time to time alternative phrasing for the sake of variety or for the purpose of adding a new dimension to the discussion. In the writing you do for your English class, the best advice is probably the middle ground. It would certainly be a mistake to conclude that repetition should be avoided. In fact, the opposite is true: Repetition strengthens cohesion.

But what happens when your teacher writes "rep" in the margin of your essay, a comment usually aimed at unnecessary repetition? How can you tell the difference between the good kind, the repetition that enhances cohesion, and the kind that calls negative attention to itself? Unnecessary repetition goes by the name of **redundancy.** It's possible that the redundant word the teacher noticed is part of a redundant sentence, one that adds nothing new to the discussion. As you'll read in the next section, most sentences contain both known (old) and new information. The lack of new information may be the source of that "rep" comment.

Lexical cohesion also refers to synonyms and other related words, not just actual repetition: *birds/robins, rodents/mice, meal/supper, friend/companion, vacation/trip/holiday.* And of course our grammar itself calls for the use of pronouns in lieu of repeating a noun or noun phrase. Such substitutes constitute strong cohesive ties.

THE KNOWN-NEW CONTRACT

Seeing the sentence as a series of units, as you did in Chapter 2, will help you understand the feature of cohesion called the **known–new contract.** It relates to both what the reader knows and what the reader expects.

The first sentence in a paragraph, like the first paragraph of a chapter or an essay, sets up expectations in the reader about what is coming. Certainly one of those expectations is that the following sentences will stick to the topic. Another is that the sentence will have new information, not just a repeat of what the reader already knows.

The term *known-new* also describes the most common order for that information, with the known information coming first, generally in the subject position, and the new information—the reason for the sentence—in the predicate, where the main emphasis of the sentence naturally occurs. This pattern is obvious in the Lincoln/Douglass paragraph you read earlier in this chapter, with *Lincoln and Douglass* as the subject of the topic sentence, *they* as the subject of the second, and their separate names as subjects in the sentences that follow. In the Triple Crown paragraph, that blip of awkwardness we encountered occurred in the subject position of the second sentence. We expected a known subject, old information, such as *each race;* instead we encountered *racehorses.*

The repeated known information is not always repeated in the exact words, as it is in the Lincoln/Douglass example—as the sports reports in the preceding section clearly demonstrate. We saw another example in the paragraph about dams in Chapter 2, where the known information in the second sentence is a paraphrase of the topic in the first:

> Shaping up as an important milestone is <u>the demolition of two large dams</u> in Washington State's Elwha River, which flows from the mountains of Olympic National Park into the Juan de Fuca Strait. <u>Their removal</u>, scheduled to begin in 2008, would occur in stages, and if it goes as planned, the Pacific Northwest will lose only a tiny amount of hydropower and regain a legendary salmon fishery.

In other words, *removal* is another way of saying *demolition.*

The Lincoln/Douglass example illustrates a common pattern wherein the repeated topic, information that the reader knows, remains fairly constant throughout the paragraph, in subject position. In some paragraphs, however, the new information that appears in the predicate of one sentence becomes the known information in the next, functioning as the subject. Here, for example, is a newspaper paragraph written by a meteorologist in response to a reader's question about thunderstorms; it begins with a one-sentence paragraph:

Thunderstorms can be categorized as single cell or multicell.

Basically, *a single-cell thunderstorm* is the lone thunderstorm that forms on a hot humid day. The *heat and humidity of the day* is the only trigger for the storm. This type of storm forms in an environment with little difference in the wind speed and direction—or wind shear—between the surface and cloud level.

—Joe Murgo (*Centre Daily Times*)

Here's another paragraph in which you can find known-new links:

This desire to deepen my alternate language [Ojibwe] puts me in an odd relationship to my first love, English. *It* is, after all, the language stuffed into my mother's ancestors' mouths. English is the reason she didn't speak her native language and the reason I can barely limp along in mine. English is an all-devouring language that has moved across North America like the fabulous plagues of locusts that darkened the sky and devoured even the handles of rakes and hoes. Yet *the omnivorous nature of a colonial language* is a writer's gift. Raised in the English language, I partake of a mongrel feast.

—Louise Erdrich ("Two Languages in Mind,
but Just One in the Heart")

The ⟶ in these examples highlight this pattern: The new information in the predicate of one sentence (underlined) becomes the known information (italicized) in the next one.

In another paragraph pattern, or information pattern, the proposition in the topic sentence is followed by supporting details suggested by the topic and expected by the reader. This pattern of development is fairly standard for writing various kinds of description, where the topic sentence sets up the expectation of the details that will prove its point, specific examples to support the generalization in the topic sentence:

Our trip to Florida for spring break turned out to be a disaster. The hotel room we rented was miserable—shabby and stuffy and downright depressing. The food we could afford made our dining hall remembrances from campus seem positively gourmet. The daily transportation to the beach we had been promised showed up only once and even then was an hour late. . . .

Here the subjects of the supporting sentences are what we can think of as subtopics of the main subject, "our trip to Florida for spring break." Paragraphs like this one generally cry out for more details, and the place to add them is under those subtopic sentences, with specifics of the room and the food and other events that make the trip come alive for the reader—in other words, another layer of detail. If, after finishing the disaster details, you decide to add some happy events of the trip, either in the same paragraph or in the next one (assuming there were indeed some happy events), you'll have to signal that change to your reader with "on the other hand" or "however" or "but" or some other indication that you're shifting gears.

If you are writing a descriptive essay about your apartment, perhaps to let a future roommate know what to expect, chances are you'd use this same pattern. You might begin with an overall assessment of the apartment's adequacy or inadequacy, its efficiency or lack thereof, in your topic sentence. The subjects of the sentences that follow would support that assessment with details about cost, location, furnishings, neighbors, and so on.

It might appear that the sentences of such a paragraph, like those in the description of spring break, contain no known information, when each brings up a new topic, or subtopic. But in both cases the subtopics really are known information; they are all part of the domain, the sphere, of apartment living—or of spring breaks in Florida. We can think of them as essentially given information, information that a reader can be expected to recognize as relevant.

◀ FOR GROUP DISCUSSION

The following paragraphs are from Chapter 15 of *Undaunted Courage* by Stephen E. Ambrose, the story of the Lewis and Clark expedition. The passage here describes an event in October 1804, a year into the trip. As you read the sentences, note the information patterns and cohesive ties that Ambrose has used. You might begin by marking the known information in each sentence and noting its connection to the preceding text:

> Beginning in October, as the expedition made its way through present northern South Dakota, it passed numerous abandoned villages, composed of earth-lodge dwellings and cultivated fields. Some of the fields, although unattended, still had squash and corn growing in them. These had once been home to the mighty Arikara tribe. About thirty thousand persons strong in the year the United States won its independence, the tribe had been reduced by smallpox epidemics in the 1780s to not much more than one-fifth that size. Another epidemic

swept through in 1803–4, devastating the tribe. What had been eighteen villages the previous year had been reduced to three by the time Lewis arrived.

EXERCISE 15

Revise the following passages to improve their cohesion. Think especially about reader expectation and the known-new contract.

1. The Gateway Arch at the edge of the Mississippi River in St. Louis is the world's tallest monument. Eero Saarinen designed the stainless steel structure that commemorates the Westward Movement.

2. Psychologists believe that color conveys emotional messages. Advertisers routinely manipulate consumers using color psychology. The pure white backgrounds and bold primary colors of detergent boxes are thought to influence buyers. Cleanliness and strength are associated with those colors.

3. The relentless heat of California's great Central Valley makes the summer almost unbearable at times. Over 110° is not an unusual temperature reading from June through September. Bakersfield often records the hottest temperature in the valley.

4. Getting chilled or getting your feet wet won't cause a cold. Weather is not the culprit that causes the common cold. Viruses are to blame.

5. The federal witness-protection service began in 1968. The U.S. Marshal Service directs the program. Over four thousand people have been relocated under the program. New identities are created for people in the program. The people are in extreme danger because they have testified against criminals.

The Role of Pronouns

Personal Pronouns. Perhaps our most common known element, equally as strong as the repeated noun phrase, is the pronoun. In Chapter 1, you'll recall, we used personal pronouns—*he, she, it, they, we*—to identify the boundaries of noun phrase units. When we use those pronouns in writing (and we often do use a pronoun instead of repeating a noun phrase), we call that noun phrase the pronoun's **antecedent.** You can think of the antecedent as the pronoun's back-up system. And because it has that back-up noun phrase, the pronoun is, by definition, known information.

But the pronoun will work only when its antecedent is clear to the reader, in the foreground of the reader's consciousness.

Let's look at a portion of the weasel paragraph we saw in Chapter 2:

> (1) A weasel is wild. (2) Who knows what **he** thinks? (3) **He** sleeps in **his** underground den, **his** tail draped over **his** nose. (4) Sometimes **he** lives in **his** den for two days without leaving. (5) Outside, **he** stalks rabbits, mice, muskrats, and birds, killing more bodies than **he** can eat warm, and often dragging the carcasses home.

The pronoun *he* connects the second sentence to the first—only that one word, but clearly a strong grammatical tie. The third sentence repeats *he*. The fourth and fifth sentences both begin with *he*.

As you learned in Chapter 1, personal pronouns in the **possessive case,** such as *his* in the third and fourth sentences of the weasel passage, function as **determiners,** or noun signalers. These **possessive pronouns** also signal a link between new and known information. In the following passage, the possessive pronoun *its* provides strong cohesive ties:

> Portland, sixty miles from the Pacific Ocean, is by no means immune to the suburbanization that has sapped the vitality from many cities. **Its** suburbs now contain about two thirds of the area's 1.4 million residents and about half of the area's jobs. Yet as the suburbs have grown, the downtown has become more attractive and popular than ever.
>
> Downtown Portland has distinct edges. **Its** eastern border is the deep, navigable Willamette River, lined for more than a mile by Tom McCall Waterfront Park, a grassy, mostly level expanse suited to events that draw thousands such as the Rose Festival (Portland calls itself the "City of Roses"), a blues festival, and a summer symphony series. **Its** western border is the steep West Hills, which contain Washington Park, home of the International Rose Test Gardens, where more than 400 varieties of roses are cultivated, and Forest Park, whose 4,800 acres of Douglas fir, alder, and maple constitute one of the largest nature preserves and hiking areas in any American city.
> —Philip Langdon (*The Atlantic Monthly*)

In the weasel paragraph, *he* constitutes the entire subject; in the Portland paragraph, in all three cases, *its* stands for the possessive noun *Portland's* and acts as a signal for the headwords: *suburbs, eastern border,* and *western border.* But no matter how it functions—whether it occurs by itself or acts as a determiner—the pronoun represents known information.

It is this known information that helps provide the cohesive tie between sentences. The three *its* sentences here are typical, with the known information in the subject, the new information in the predicate.

Demonstrative Pronouns. Like the personal pronouns, the **demonstrative pronouns**—*this, that, these,* and *those*—take the place of a noun phrase; in doing so, they provide a strong cohesive tie. And, like the possessive pronouns, they also serve as determiners:

> <u>That</u> sounds like a good plan. (noun phrase replacement)
> <u>That</u> plan sounds good to me. (determiner for *plan*)

When you read the second sentence aloud, you can hear the special focusing quality that the demonstrative adds to the noun *plan,* a focus that the determiner *the* would not have:

> The plan sounds good to me.

The demonstratives include the feature of proximity, in reference to both space and time, with *this* and *these* indicating closeness, *that* and *those* more distance. You'll find many sentences in these chapters (note the use of *these*) that demonstrate the close proximity indicated by *these* and *this* in their roles as determiners.

In the following example from Chapter 2, the demonstrative pronoun *these* occurs without a noun headword:

> <u>These</u> seven [sentence patterns] represent the underlying skeletal structure of nearly all our sentences.

When a writer uses a pronoun, the reader has the right to assume that the antecedent is not just known information but that, in fact, the information is located in the foreground of his or her consciousness. The demonstratives, especially *this* and *these,* represent extra emphasis for foregrounding. We saw an example of this emphasis in the Ambrose passage about Lewis and Clark:

> Some of the fields, although unattended, still had squash and corn growing in them. <u>These</u> had once been home to the mighty Arikara tribe.

And in the sentence introducing the quote you just read, there's another example: *this emphasis.*

Writers can easily introduce weak spots when a pronoun has no clear antecedent. For example, in the following sentence there is no specific noun phrase to back up either the demonstrative pronoun *this* or the personal pronoun *it:*

> My roommate told me she has decided to drop out of school and look for a job. <u>This</u> has taken me completely by surprise, and I know <u>it</u> will shock her parents.

The problem here is not one of communication; we can easily figure out what the sentence means. But notice the absence of a specific noun in the first sentence to which the demonstrative *this* refers; rather, the pronoun refers to the idea in the sentence as a whole. This use of the pronoun is called **broad reference.** And while this example may not cause the reader to stumble, sometimes the understood antecedent is a bit troublesome to figure out. The point is that we, as readers, shouldn't have to do the figuring: That job belongs to the writer. Often the best way to fix a vague *this* or *that* is to turn the pronoun into a determiner and supply the missing headword:

> <u>This decision of hers</u> took me completely by surprise.

By turning *this* into a complete noun phrase, we also provide the vague *it* with a backup antecedent.

When you're revising the first draft of your essay—or perhaps rereading a sentence you just wrote—always pay attention to those sentences with a lone pronoun as subject, especially the demonstratives. Make sure that the antecedent of *this* or *that* or *these* or *those* is clear to the reader. If the noun phrase the pronoun stands for is not obvious, consider using the pronoun as a determiner and adding a headword. Pay special attention to *it* and *they* as well. It's important to recognize that pronouns without clear antecedents are in violation of the known–new contract.

◄ FOR GROUP DISCUSSION

You could make the argument that a bare *this, that, these,* or *those* is perfectly capable of communicating without a noun headword, as the example in the Lewis and Clark passage by Steven Ambrose demonstrates. In fact, the original draft of the sentence that introduces the quotation also had a bare determiner: "We saw an example of *this* in the Lewis and Clark passage."

Do you think the revised version with the word *emphasis* added is an improvement? Would the addition of *fields* improve the Ambrose passage? And how about the roommate example? Did it really need the headword added? Check some of your reading material from this or another class to find out how common it is for demonstratives to appear without headwords. Are the missing headwords obvious, easy to retrieve?

EXERCISE 16

Revise the following passages to eliminate the vague pronouns. In some cases the most effective revision will be to turn *this* or *that* into a determiner. Another possibility is to combine the sentences.

1. Many women in the nineteenth century joined the fight for equal legal and political status. This eventually led to the establishment in 1890 of the National American Woman Suffrage Association.

2. Women in the labor force protested against long hours and poor working conditions. The National Consumers' League, founded in 1899, tried to improve that.

3. Some married women in the 1830s were able to have their own property, but it didn't mean they could vote.

4. Elizabeth Cady Stanton and Susan B. Anthony insisted that the fourteenth amendment gave women the rights of citizenship; because of this, they also argued that the fifteenth amendment should be expanded to guarantee a woman's right to vote.

5. In 1920 the Constitution was finally amended to give women the right to vote. That did not, however, provide *all* women with the right to vote: In some states, many African American women (and men) had to pass tests in order to vote.

6. Today equal rights are still denied to women in many countries either because of their sex, their ethnic identity, or their economic status. This will not change without pressure from international organizations dedicated to promoting and protecting human rights.

The Role of the Passive Voice

It's possible that everything you've heard about the **passive voice** up to now has been negative; English teachers often declare it out of bounds. Such edicts come about—those "pass" comments appear in the margins—because writers so often use passives when they shouldn't. And it's true that ineffective passives do stand out. But there's a great deal of misunderstanding about the passive. All good prose includes both active and passive voice.

In Chapter 3 you practiced changing active sentences to passive by making the direct object of the active sentence the subject of the passive. That shift of focus is one of the main strengths of the passive voice, one of its purposes: It allows known information to be in the subject position. Here, for example, is the beginning of a paragraph from a *Time* article by

Michael D. Lemonick about the destruction of the Brazilian rain forests. Note how the subject of the passive second sentence provides a cohesive tie:

> If Americans are truly interested in saving the rain forests, they should move beyond rhetoric and suggest *policies* that are practical—and acceptable—to the understandably wary Brazilians. *Such policies* cannot be presented as take-them-or-leave-them propositions. If the U.S. expects better performance from Brazil, Brazil has a right to make demands in return. In fact, the U.S. and Brazil need to engage in face-to-face negotiations as part of a formal dialogue on the environment between the industrial nations and the developing countries. [Emphasis added.]

In the first sentence, *policies* is new information; in the second it is known. You'll note that the agent is missing from the passive sentence; however, "by the Americans" is clearly understood. Note also how the information patterns work in the two sentences following the passive, with the known information, *U.S.* and *Brazil*—the agents—in subject position and the new information in the predicates.

   The following example of the passive voice appears in a sentence you read earlier in this chapter in the discussion of the known–new contract. It opens a paragraph:

> In another paragraph pattern, or information pattern, the proposition in the topic sentence is followed by supporting details suggested by the topic and expected by the reader.

Here the term *supporting details* is the new information, so it belongs in the predicate, where it gets the main emphasis. You'll be reading more about this important feature—the connection of information and sentence rhythm—in the next chapter.

Other Sentence Inversions

As you have seen, the *passive transformation,* as the passive voice is called, inverts the active word order, with the original direct object shifted to subject position. Another, much more common, method of rearranging information is to open the sentence with an adverbial modifier, as you saw in Chapter 2 under the heading "The Optional Adverbials" (page 28). Adverbials are called optional because, with few exceptions, sentences are grammatical without them. However, when we do add them—and adverbials are very common indeed—they are considered modifiers of the verb; that is, they are part of the predicate. But they don't have to stay in the predicate position. Here are two opening adverbials from the discussion in Chapter 2, the first a prepositional phrase and the second a dependent clause:

> <u>During the Vietnam War</u>, Gino's dad was a pilot.
>
> <u>Because a weasel is wild</u>, it should be approached with great caution.

In that discussion of adverbials, these examples were presented without context. But let's assume that the second one is the opening of a paragraph following our old standby weasel passage. You probably remember its opening sentence: *A weasel is wild.* Clearly, if our *because* clause opened a second paragraph on weasels, the clause itself would be adding no new information, so we don't want it at the end of the sentence. We want to save the sentence end for the new idea—in this case, the idea of great caution. The *because* clause, with its known information, provides the transition from the previous sentence; it is the glue that connects them. One of the main points of the adverbial discussion in Chapter 2 is the movability—and thus the versatility—of the optional adverbial. When you put that feature together with the concept of the known–new contract, you can appreciate how important a tool movable adverbials can be for you as a writer.

Still another inversion of information involves switching the position of the subject and the predicate. Here's the topic sentence of a paragraph you've seen before:

> Shaping up as an important milestone is the demolition of two large dams in Washington State's Elwha River, which flows from the mountains of Olympic National Park into the Juan de Fuca Strait.

Here's the underlying subject-predicate structure:

> The demolition of two large dams . . . is shaping up as an important milestone.

The writer's purpose for making that subject-predicate switch is connected to the previous paragraphs in the article, which relate the history and consequences of dam removal. The word *milestone* refers to that history, so it becomes the transition to the new information about these two particular dams. It's an unusual grammatical situation, for the old information to occur in the verb phrase, the predicate. Using her inversion tool, the writer has set aside the subject-predicate order so that the new information is in line for emphasis. The position at the end of the sentence also makes it easier to add those two long modifiers, a prepositional phrase and a *which*-clause.

We look more closely at word-order variations in Chapter 11.

FOR GROUP DISCUSSION

The following paragraph is the beginning of a short description of Thomas Jefferson by Lee A. Jacobus:

> Thomas Jefferson, an exceptionally accomplished and well-educated man, is probably best known for writing the Declaration of Independence, a work composed under the eyes of Benjamin Franklin, John Adams, and the Continental Congress, which spent two and a half days going over every word. The substance of the document was developed in committee, but Jefferson, because of the grace of his style, was chosen to do the actual writing. The result is one of the most memorable statements in American history.

Explain why the author used the passive voice where he did. Try writing a version of the paragraph using only the active voice. Is it equally effective?

PARALLELISM

Early in this chapter you read that it's okay to repeat words, that repetition can have a positive effect on the reader. In this section we look at a specific kind of repetition called **parallelism,** the repetition of whole structures, such as phrases and clauses. Parallelism is usually thought of as a device for enhancing a writer's style—and indeed it is that—as you learned in Chapter 4. It can certainly add polish and flavor to prose that otherwise might be the plain vanilla variety. But it can also provide cohesion, especially when the repeated elements extend through a paragraph or from one paragraph to the next.

Parallelism refers to repeated grammatical elements, often combined with repeated words. The quality of being parallel means that the repeated elements have the same structure, such as noun phrases with noun phrases, prepositional phrases with prepositional phrases. One of the most famous sentences in President Kennedy's inaugural address includes parallel verb phrases: "pay any price, bear any burden, meet any hardship, support any friend, oppose any foe." And we're all familiar with Lincoln's "of the people, by the people, and for the people."

Parallelism becomes an especially strong cohesive device when a structure echoes a structure from a previous sentence or paragraph. In the second paragraph of the Portland passage on page 94, the subject "Its eastern border" names one of the "distinct edges" referred to in the opening sentence. The next sentence not only fulfills the reader's expectation with the word *western,* it does so using parallel structure:

> Its eastern border is the deep, navigable Willamette River . . . .
> Its western border is the steep West Hills . . . .

In the following passage the author's use of repetition adds intensity and drama to his argument:

> That knowledge has become the key resource means that there is a world economy, and that the world economy, rather than the national economy, is in control. Every country, every industry, and every business will be in an increasingly competitive environment. Every country, every industry, and every business will, in its decisions, have to consider its competitive standing in the world economy and the competitiveness of its knowledge competencies.
> —Peter F. Drucker (*The Atlantic Monthly*)

The two repeated series as subjects are the most obvious repetitions, but note also in the first sentence two instances of *world economy* contrasted with *national economy* and a third repetition of *world economy* in the last sentence. And in the second and third sentences we read *competitive standing, competitive environment,* and *competitiveness.*

The repeated series in this paragraph by Stephen Jay Gould from *Ever Since Darwin* illustrates another fairly common feature of parallelism, that of **antithesis,** the introduction of contrasting, or dissimilar, ideas:

> Why imagine that specific genes for aggression, dominance, or spite have any importance when we know that the brain's enormous flexibility permits us to be aggressive or peaceful, dominant or submissive, spiteful or generous? Violence, sexism, and general nastiness are biological since they represent one subset of a possible range of behaviors. But peacefulness, equality, and kindness are just as biological—and we may see their influence increase if we can create social structures that permit them to flourish.
> —Stephen Jay Gould (*Ever Since Darwin*)

Note in the following passage how the point of view changes in the middle of the paragraph where the parallel *it* clauses begin. Each of them introduces a clause in the second person, one with *you* as the subject.

> A thin broken strand of islands curves out into the Atlantic Ocean and then back again in a sheltering embrace of North Carolina's mainland coast and its offshore sounds. These are the Outer Banks of North Carolina. For thousands of years these barrier islands have survived the onslaught of wind and sea. Today their long stretches of beach, sand dunes, marshes, and woodlands are set aside as Cape Hatteras National Seashore. <u>It can be a lonely place</u>; you may walk along the beach unseen except by shore birds searching for a meal. <u>It can be a place of discovery</u>; you may visit the 1870 Cape Hatteras Lighthouse, one of many monuments to man's encounter with the sea. <u>It can be a wild place</u>; you may be buffeted by an approaching gale or surprised by the honking of large flocks of migrating geese. <u>And it can be an exciting place</u>, where you may explore many opportunities for recreation: surf fishing, sunbathing, swimming, beach combing, canoeing, sailing, surfing, snorkeling. Part land, part sea, Cape Hatteras offers rewards from each.
>
> —National Park Service Brochure

From all of these examples it should be clear that parallelism is more than mere stylistic décor: The parallel structures are, in fact, among the strongest cohesive ties that the writer has available. They highlight those ideas that should be in the foreground of the reader's consciousness, sending the message that the parallel structures are not only connected but also significant.

Repetition Versus Redundancy

Rather than commending these authors for effective parallelism, you may be tempted to accuse them of unnecessary repetition, a problem that goes by the label **redundancy.** How do we distinguish between them? How do we tell the difference between good repetition and bad?

Parallelism of the kind we see here—parallelism as a stylistic device—invariably calls attention to itself. Did these authors intend to do that, to call attention to these structures? Clearly, the answer is "Yes—and for good reason." In all of these passages, the use of repetition has added a dramatic dimension to the prose.

The repetition in these passages might also tempt you to accuse the authors of wordiness; their sentences certainly don't pass the test of brevity or conciseness, features of writing so often touted in composition textbooks. Clarity, of course, is always a goal. And, yes, sometimes clarity calls for brevity, for a lean version of a sentence. But there are many occasions that call for a celebration of words. We certainly don't expect the president to be brief in an inaugural address; neither should we expect a writer to be brief in describing Cape Hatteras or in explaining the concept of a world economy or in arguing for the biological basis of kindness.

In Chapter 8 redundancy is addressed in a section called "The Proliferating Prepositional Phrase." And the use of repetition as a stylistic device is discussed further in Chapter 11, "Making Stylistic Choices."

FOR GROUP DISCUSSION

Find the parallel structures in the following paragraph from Jay Wink's *The Great Upheaval* and explain how they provide cohesion:

> Soldiers marched that day in Manhattan. For almost as long as anyone could remember, the sight of soldiers had invariably meant the same thing, whether they were French or Russian, Austrian or English, whether they belonged to kings or were battle-hardened mercenaries, whether they moved in great formations or galloped along on horseback. Too often their presence was ominous, signaling that the campaign was beginning and the war was deepening, that the dead would increase and the bloodshed would continue, and the suffering would go on. But today their footsteps were unique, booming out the rites of nationhood. They called out a celebration of victory and the raising of the flag—the American flag. It was November 25, 1783. Evacuation Day in New York City.

KEY TERMS

Antecedent	Determiner	Possessive case
Antithesis	Known–new contract	Possessive pronouns
Broad reference	Lexical cohesion	Pronouns
Cohesion	Parallelism	Reader expectation
Demonstrative	Passive voice	Redundancy
pronouns	Personal pronouns	Repetition

RHETORICAL REMINDERS

Have I anticipated my reader's expectations?

Do my paragraphs profit from lexical cohesion, the repetition of words?

Is the known information in the beginning of the sentence, where it can provide a cohesive tie to the previous sentence, with the new information in end-focus position?

Have I taken advantage of parallelism as a cohesive device?

CHAPTER 6

Sentence Rhythm

CHAPTER PREVIEW

In this chapter we look at a feature of language you might not have thought about before: its **rhythm.** Yes, our language has a rhythm, just as music does—a regular beat. When you learn to listen to that beat and think about it when you write, you gain control of an important writing tool.

We begin by examining the valleys and peaks of **intonation** and the connection of those patterns with **end focus,** which is tied up with the known–new contract you learned about in Chapter 5. You will learn how to control sentence rhythm using **cleft sentences,** the *there*-**transformation, power words,** and punctuation.

Even though these terms may be new to your vocabulary, the concepts they name are part of your everyday language, in both speech and writing. This chapter is really about consciousness raising; it's about awareness. That awareness will help you control the message that your reader gets.

INTONATION: THE PEAKS AND VALLEYS

One of the most important aspects of your expertise with sentences is your sense of rhythm. For example, if you read the opening sentence in this paragraph out loud, you'll hear yourself saying "one of the most" in almost a monotone; you probably don't hear a stressed syllable, a beat, until you get to *important:*

one of the most imPORTant

And you probably rush through those first four words so fast that you pronounce "of" without articulating the *f,* making "one of" sound like the first two words in "won a prize."

The rhythm of sentences, what we call the **intonation pattern,** can be described as peaks and valleys, where the loudest syllables, those with **stress,** are represented by peaks:

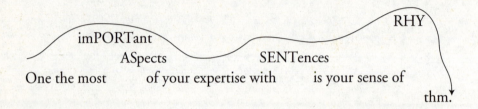

Not all the peaks are of the same height—we have different degrees of stress—but they do tend to come at fairly regular intervals. As listeners we pay attention to the peaks; that's where we'll hear the information that the speaker is focusing on. And as speakers we manipulate those peaks and valleys to coincide with our message, reserving the loudest stress, the highest peak, for our main point of focus.

Such sentence manipulation is not something we ordinarily think about, nor is it a skill we were taught; for native speakers it's automatic, part of our native language ability. On the other hand, if you're not a native speaker of English, mastering the rhythm of sentences may be difficult, especially if the sentence rhythm of your native language does not have a regular beat like English does. Certainly, a dominant feature of some accents is the absence of that rhythm, with peaks and valleys in unexpected places or missing altogether.

But even for you who are not native speakers, recognizing the relationship between the rhythm of sentences and the message, which we examine in this chapter, will be helpful to you as writers. You will also find it helpful in practicing your own listening skills to focus on sentence rhythm, with its peaks and valleys.

END FOCUS

The rhythm of sentences is closely tied to their two-part structure (subject and predicate) and to the known–new contract. In Chapter 5 you learned that known information often occurs in the subject position. When it does, you'll note a valley or a low peak in the intonation contour. The prominent peak of stress occurs in the predicate, on the new information, generally on the last or next-to-the-last unit in the sentence. Linguists describe this common rhythm pattern as **end focus.**

The contrast between the peaks and valleys of rhythm is easy to demonstrate in short sentences. As you read the following, listen for the syllable that gets main stress:

> The common cold is caused by a virus.
>
> My chemistry book cost almost a hundred dollars.
>
> Barbara wrecked her motorcycle.
>
> Sentence rhythm is characterized by end focus.

We normally don't read sentences in lists, of course; we read them in context. And as readers we count on the context, on the meaning, to guide the reading, to help us put the emphasis where it belongs. Our job as writers, then, is clear: If we want readers to understand our intentions and to focus on the important information, we must help them by taking sentence rhythm into account.

The following passages provide a simple lesson on the way in which end focus and sentence rhythm work together:

> Dennis told me that Barbara had an accident this morning on her way to work. But I think he got his facts wrong. She wrecked her motorcycle yesterday.
>
> Dennis told me that Barbara had an accident this morning on her way to work. But I think he got his facts wrong. Yesterday she wrecked her motorcycle.

As you probably noticed, the one difference in the wording of the two passages is the placement in the last sentence of the adverb *yesterday*. And, when you read the two, that difference probably produced a difference in the rhythm pattern. In both passages the words *but* and *wrong* in the second sentence led you to expect information refuting something in the first sentence: perhaps the fact of the accident itself; if not that, its time or place. And recognizing that *yesterday* fulfilled your expectation, that's the sentence unit that got the main stress. However, by putting *yesterday* in the opening position, the writer disregarded your expectation as the reader that the new, important information would be in end-focus position.

As you have read before in these chapters—in Chapter 2 under the heading "The Optional Adverbials," in your study of the sentence patterns, and in Chapter 5 in connection with the known–new contract—the movability of adverbials is an extremely important and versatile tool in your writer's toolbox. The term *optional* refers only to the fact that most sentences do not need adverbials to be grammatical; however, when we do add them, we usually do so for good reason: to add information about time and place and manner and reason and so on. Often that information provides transition from the prior text, so the opening position is the right place for it. And time adverbials, like *yesterday,* often belong there at the opening. But not always. Not in the sentence we've just looked at, where *yesterday* is the new information.

So in case you're tempted to make that kind of switch—to move an adverbial to the beginning of a sentence, perhaps for the sake of variety, to relieve the monotony of starting every sentence with the subject— think again! Remember the principle of end focus. If the adverbial is the new information, save it for the end of the sentence, the point of main stress. Otherwise, when the reader happens to be your composition teacher, you're likely to find "awk" noted in the margin of your essay.

In Chapter 5 we discussed the use of the passive voice to facilitate cohesion. But it has another job: to ensure that new information is in the predicate. Compare the following passages. Does the end of the second sentence in each pair focus on known or new information?

> Each year since 1901, scientists, artists, and peacemakers from around the world have received the Nobel Prize for helping humanity. The creator of dynamite and other explosives, Alfred Nobel, founded this award.

> Each year since 1901, scientists, artists, and peacemakers from around the world have received the Nobel Prize for helping humanity. This award was founded by Alfred Nobel, the creator of dynamite and other explosives.

Clearly, the second passage takes advantage of end focus. And this grammatical choice does have a rhetorical effect. In fact, choosing a passive sentence here has the dual effect of placing new information where it will be stressed and making the second passage more cohesive. The message is thus clear; and the reader satisfied.

FOR GROUP DISCUSSION

The following paragraph opened a *Sports Illustrated* article called "The Dominance Theory." As you read it, locate the main peaks of stress, keeping in mind both end focus and the known–new contract. Do you have any revision suggestions for the author?

> We watch sports to see great plays and great games, great athletes and, of course, great teams. Dynasties form the foundation upon which sports history is built. The Yankees, the Canadiens, the Celtics, the 49ers: They're the standard against which all other teams are judged.

Notice also the author's use of parallel noun phrases, with the repetition of *great* in the first sentence and the team names in the last. Describe the effect these series have on the stress pattern.

EXERCISE 17

Read the following passages, listening carefully to the intonation contour of each sentence. Indicate the words (or syllables) that get main stress. Compare your reading with that of your classmates.

1. Never invest in something you don't understand or in the dream of an artful salesperson. Be a buyer, not a sellee. Figure out what you want (be it life insurance, mutual funds or a vacuum cleaner) and then shop for a good buy. Don't let someone else tell you what you need—at least not if he happens to be selling it.

   —Andrew Tobias (*Parade*)

2. Plaque has almost become a household word. It is certainly a household problem. But even though everyone is affected by it, few people really understand the seriousness of plaque or the importance of controlling it. Plaque is an almost invisible sticky film of bacteria that continuously forms on the teeth. Plaque germs are constantly multiplying and building up. Any dentist will tell you that controlling plaque is the single most important step to better oral health.

   —advertisement of the American Dental Association

3. Frank evaluation of its [caffeine's] hazards is not easy. There is a vast literature on the effects of caffeine on the body, and for every study reaching one conclusion, seemingly there is another that contradicts it. Although most major health risks have been ruled out, research continues at a steady clip.

   —Corby Kummer (*The Atlantic Monthly*)

CONTROLLING RHYTHM

Because end focus is such a common rhythm pattern, we can think of it as part of the contract between writer and reader. The reader expects the main sentence focus to be in the predicate, unless given a signal to the contrary. But of course not all sentences are alike; not every sentence has end focus. In speech, especially, the focus is often shifted elsewhere. The speaker can easily stress the new information, no matter where in the sentence it appears. Consider, for example, these alternative ways of saying the motorcycle sentence, the variety of messages that are possible for the speaker:

> BARBARA wrecked her motorcycle yesterday morning. [Not someone else.]
>
> Barbara wrecked HER motorcycle yesterday morning. [Her own, not someone else's.]
>
> Barbara wrecked her motorcycle yesterday MORNING. [Not in the afternoon.]

And we can add extra stress to *motorcycle:*

> Barbara wrecked her MOTORCYCLE yesterday morning. [Not her car.]

Or we can give the whole sentence added emphasis:

> Barbara DID wreck her motorcycle yesterday morning. [Believe me, I'm not making this up.]

The speaker is in control of the message that the listener is meant to hear. The spoken language is powerful, much more powerful than writing, far more capable of expressing feelings and nuances of meaning.

The It-*Cleft*

It's true that the speaker has a much easier job than does the writer in getting the message across and preventing misinterpretation. But the writer is certainly not powerless—far from it. As we saw earlier, the careful writer can take control simply by understanding the reader's expectations about the sentence and by making sure that the important information coincides with the prominent stress. You'll recall the first version of the motorcycle passage, where the sensitive reader would almost certainly delay the stress until the word *yesterday.* But in the following revision, the writer has left nothing to chance:

> Dennis told me that Barbara had an accident on the way to work this morning. But he apparently got his facts wrong. <u>It was yesterday that she wrecked her motorcycle.</u>

In this version it's impossible for the reader to misinterpret the emphasis on *yesterday* with the *it* construction, known as a **cleft sentence.** This use of *it* is called an **expletive.** (The term *cleft* comes from the verb *cleave,* which means to divide or split.) The **it-cleft** enables the writer to shift the emphasis to any unit in the sentence, forcing the reader to focus on the structure following "it was" (or "it is," "it has been," etc.):

> It was Barbara who wrecked her motorcycle.
>
> It was her own motorcycle that Barbara wrecked.

Instead of the usual end focus, the reader will recognize that the emphasis belongs on the word or phrase following that opening unstressed valley of "it was" and will automatically make that the highest peak in the intonation contour of the sentence. The following *it*-cleft is from a *Time* article on killer microbes by Michael D. Lemonick:

> It is by killing individual cells in the body's all-important immune system that the AIDS virus wreaks its terrible havoc. The virus itself isn't deadly, but it leaves the body defenseless against all sorts of diseases that are.

The *it* construction enables the writer to control the reader's valleys and peaks of stress, to determine precisely what the rhythm of the sentence will be.

The What-*Cleft*

Another kind of cleft sentence uses a *what* clause in subject position; here a form of *be* separates the original sentence into two parts:

> Barbara wrecked her motorcycle.
>
> <u>What Barbara wrecked was her motorcycle.</u>

The **what-cleft** can also shift the original verb phrase into subject position; that shift will put the original subject in line for end focus:

> What is always needed in the appreciation of art, or life, is the larger perspective.
>
> —Alice Walker

See how the emphasis changes in this sentence without the *what*-cleft:

> The larger perspective is always needed in the appreciation of art, or life.

Here is another example of a sentence in which the verb phrase appears in subject position:

> Thick fog reduced the visibility to zero.
>
> <u>What reduced the visibility to zero was the thick fog.</u>

This example could also be revised as an *it*-cleft:

> It was thick fog that reduced the visibility.

The There-*Transformation*

Another method of changing word order to shift the stress is known as the **there-transformation:**

> A stranger is standing on the porch.
> <u>There's a stranger standing on the porch.</u>
> No concert tickets were available this morning.
> <u>There were no concert tickets available this morning.</u>

Again, this reordering puts the main stress on the subject by shifting its position. Remember that the normal subject position, the opening position, is usually an unstressed valley in terms of the intonation pattern. This addition of *there,* like *it* in the *it*-cleft, is known as an expletive; it delays the subject, thereby putting it in line for stress.

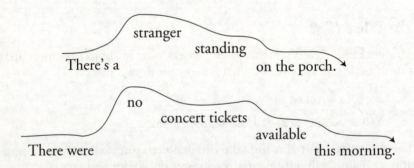

In addition to its focusing ability, the *there*-transformation gives the writer a way of introducing a new topic, both within the paragraph and at the opening, as the topic sentence. You'll find many such introductory sentences in the books you read. These two come from two different chapters of Tom Vanderbilt's book *Traffic:*

> There is an iron law in traffic engineering: The longer pedestrians have to wait for a signal to cross, the more likely they are to cross against the signal.

> There are times when we do not want to signal our intentions.

This use of *there is* or *there are* is sometimes referred to as "the **existential there**"; in other words, the use of "there is something" affirms that the something is, or exists. You can hear that same affirmation of existence in the *there* example we looked at in Exercise 17:

> There is a vast literature on the effects of caffeine on the body, and for every study reaching one conclusion, seemingly there is another that contradicts it.

In all of these *there*-transformations you can hear the main stress focus on the structure following *there is* or *there are*.

Why, if these are important structures, do handbooks frequently warn writers against starting sentences with the *it* and *there* constructions? You'll find that these warnings generally appear in discussions of wordiness and brevity, with advice about deleting extra words. This is also the reason sometimes given for avoiding the passive voice. And while it's true that "it is" and "there are" do add words, when they are used in the right place and for the right reason, they are not redundant, unnecessary words; they are, in fact, doing an important job.

It's certainly possible to overuse these structures (and the passive voice as well)—and perhaps it's that overuse that teachers and handbook writers worry about. So as you reread that first (or second or third) draft, do pay special attention to sentence focus, to the way the reader will read your sentences: Think about end focus, about known and new information, about sentence rhythm. Make sure you have used these focusing tools for the right reason.

EXERCISE 18

Rewrite the following sentences, shifting the focus by using sentence transformations: the *it*-cleft, the *what*-cleft, and the *there*-transformation. For example, you could use a cleft structure in the first sentence to focus either on the date or the place or the ship.

1. The *Titanic* hit an iceberg and sank in the North Atlantic in 1912.

2. Our defense won the Stanford game in the final three minutes with a crucial interception.

3. Hundreds of angry parents were protesting the senator's position on day care at yesterday's political rally in the student union.

4. Lightning causes many of the forest fires in the Western states.

5. Countless travelers have lost their lives in the Bermuda Triangle.

6. Herbert Spencer used the phrase "survival of the fittest" to label the competition among human beings.

> ## FOR GROUP DISCUSSION

The following short article by Dale Conour accompanies a dramatic two-page photograph in *Sunset* (October 2004) of an enormous black cloud of starlings nearly covering the sky. Notice especially the author's methods of controlling rhythm. Part of that control comes with the use of *it*—seven times, in fact: as an expletive *it* and as the personal pronoun. Can you justify all those *its*? Consider cohesion as well as the rhythm and focus that they produce. Could the essay get by with fewer *its*? Is it possible to eliminate all or most of them? Would the revision be an improvement? Try your hand at revising the article.

> It's an eerie sight to anyone—a massive swarm of European starlings, some million strong, sweeping over a fallow field off State 46 north of Bakersfield, California. But to birders, it's even more disturbing: They know it's an invasion.
>
> It began in 1890 when New Yorker Eugene Schiffelin made it his quest to introduce to the New World every Old World bird mentioned in Shakespeare's works. Compelled by a single mention of the starling in *Henry IV,* Schiffelin loosed 60 birds in Central Park.
>
> The result today: Millions of starlings—voracious, aggressive, and smart (they're members of the myna family)—have blanketed the U.S., while the number of cavity-nesting songbirds has plummeted.
>
> It may have been *Henry IV* in which the Bard mentions the starling directly, but it's *Henry VI* in which he's prophetic: "Hung be the heavens with black, yield day to night!"

RHYTHM AND THE COMMA

The sentence transformations with *it* and *what* and *there* are not the only ways we have to control the focus and rhythm of sentences. Other ways, in fact, are much more common and, in most cases, more subtle. The phrase *in fact* in the preceding sentence illustrates one such method—a set phrase that interrupts the rhythm pattern. The inserted phrase not only adds a new intonation contour; it also adds emphasis to the subject. We can illustrate the difference with a picture of the contours:

Other ways are much more common.

Other ways, in fact, are much more common.

The visual signal of the comma causes the reader to give added length and stress to the preceding word. And, as the contour lines illustrate, the sentence has gone from having one intonation contour to having three. The main focus is still on the new information at the end, but the sentence rhythm has changed, with part of the reader's attention shifted to the subject. Notice in the second version how much more length and stress you give to the subject headword, *ways,* when it is followed by a comma.

This role for the comma, to shift the peak of stress, is probably one you hadn't thought about before. You've probably considered the comma in the more traditional way, as a signaler of the pause in speech. But, as you learned in Chapter 2 regarding the sentence units, not every pause translates to a comma in writing. And when we do include a comma, the pause goes beyond simple hesitation. It includes the rising intonation illustrated by the arrows, along with stress and added length given to the preceding word. Even the common *and* gets that extra attention in the second sentence of the previous paragraph. The inserted *as* clause lengthens the opening *and;* because of the comma, that one word has its own intonation contour:

And, as the contour lines illustrate, the sentence . . .

Among the most versatile tools for manipulating sentence rhythm are the **conjunctive adverbs** and **transitional phrases,** which we examined in Chapter 4. The conjunctive adverbs create cohesion with an adverbial emphasis between sentences. Their versatility lies in their movability. That earlier sentence could have been written like this:

Other ways are much more common, in fact.

In this version, the word *common* gets all the attention.

Here are some other examples of sentences with movable phrases— examples from previous passages:

1. One obvious difference, <u>of course,</u> is vocabulary.

2. Consider, <u>for example,</u> these alternative ways of saying the motorcycle sentence . . . .

3. You might choose this order if, <u>for example</u>, you want to put the main emphasis . . . .

4. When you study grammar at school, <u>then,</u> you are studying what you already "know."

5. To be effective, <u>however</u>, writing also requires attention to rhetoric . . . .

Notice especially how many different places in these sentences a conjunctive adverb or a transitional phrase occurs: in (1) between the subject and the predicate; in (2) between the verb and the direct object; in (3) between a subordinating conjunction and the rest of the dependent clause; in (4) and (5) between the introductory adverbial and the main clause.

An important point to understand is that there are other places in all five of these sentences where that word or phrase could have been placed. Writers position these structures to help their readers: How do I want the reader to read this sentence? What is important here for the reader to stress? Will the reader understand how this sentence fits in with what follows?

Other familiar words and phrases are listed on pages 65 and 67.

FOR GROUP DISCUSSION

1. Several of the sentences in the following passage, from *The Birds* by Roger Tory Peterson, illustrate another method of putting the subject in line for main stress. Read the passage aloud and mark the peaks of stress. Using your understanding of the sentence units, identify the subject and predicate of each clause. What technique has the author used to control the rhythm? In thinking about the subject-predicate order of the sentences, you might want to review the discussion of inversion on pages 98–99. (The sentences are numbered so that the discussion of them will be easier.)

   > [1] A bird's feathers have to do many things. [2] Not only must they provide lift surfaces for wings and tail, but they must protect the bird against the weather and insulate it against loss of heat. [3] Feathers come in almost infinite variety, but they fall into four main categories. [4] Most numerous are the contour feathers which coat the body, giving it a streamlined shape. [5] A house sparrow wears about 3,500 of these in winter, and they are so efficient at sealing in heat that it can maintain a normal temperature of 106.7°F without difficulty in below-freezing cold. [6] Lying beneath them are the soft down feathers, also used for insulation. [7] Scattered among both types are the hairlike filoplumes, which sometimes protrude from the coat and may serve as a kind of decoration, or possibly as sensory organs.

2. Read a draft of your own essay (or a classmate's) with sentence rhythm in mind. (Don't hesitate to read it aloud and listen for your own peaks and valleys.) Think especially about end focus and the difference in rhythm that commas make.

POWER WORDS

We have just seen how conjunctive adverbs set off by commas can override the principle of end focus, the expected rhythm pattern. We've also seen how the use of *it* and *there* can change the emphasis. But some words are powerful enough to interrupt the usual rhythm pattern on their own—even without commas or sentence shifts.

Read the following pairs of sentences aloud and listen for the words that get main stress:

> In the first gallery we admired a display of Tiffany glass.
>
> In the first gallery we admired a magnificent display of Tiffany glass.
>
> The senator spoke about the problems of the homeless.
>
> The senator spoke eloquently about the problems of the homeless.

Both its meaning and its length may contribute to a word's inherent attention-getting power, as in the case of the adjective *magnificent* and the adverb *eloquently.* Words that convey strong emotions and words that have a superlative or absolute quality are hard to compete with for attention in most sentences.

Adjectives and adverbs are especially powerful when they are preceded by another modifier (*secretly jealous, cautiously hopeful, quite gracefully*) and when they are in the superlative degree, ending in *-est* (*loudest, fastest*) or marked by *most* (*most aggressively, most incredible*). Noun phrases too have the power to take control of the sentence, especially when they include one of those powerful modifiers (*complete chaos, dangerous undertaking, overwhelming courage, bewildering array*).

A word of warning is called for here. To label these words as power words is not necessarily to recommend that you use them. The point to remember is that when you do use them they will command attention. Like movie stars who inevitably create a stir wherever they go, these words change the atmosphere of the sentences they inhabit. Here is what happened to the sentence about the senator's speech:

The senator spoke about the problems of the homeless.

The senator spoke eloquently about the problems of the homeless.

The word *eloquently* shifts the limelight from the topic of the speech to the senator's style of speaking; and, in doing so, it sets up a different expectation in the reader. We would not be surprised if the subject of the next sentence turned out to be *he* or *she* (the senator) rather than *they* (the homeless).

It's important to recognize that in each example the added word—*magnificent, eloquently*—changes a statement of fact into an arguable proposition. The reader has every right to expect supporting evidence for these opinions. What was there about the speech that was eloquent? In what way is the display magnificent? In other words, those power words that change the rhythm also change the reader's expectations.

Correlative Conjunctions

The correlative conjunctions that you read about in Chapter 4—*either–or, neither–nor, both–and, not only–but also*—are among the power words that change the focus and rhythm pattern of the sentence and change the expectation of readers. When you read the following sentence, you probably give the loudest stress to *environment:*

Individuals and nations must learn to think about the environment.

Now add one word. Instead of the simple conjunction *and,* use the correlative *both–and* and listen to your rhythm pattern.

Both individuals *and* nations must learn to think about the environment.

It's important to recognize that these two possibilities—the two different kinds of conjunctions—cannot be used interchangeably. After reading the version with *both–and,* the reader's expectations will be different from those of the version with *and.* The main stress shifted to the subject, especially to *nations,* so the reader is probably expecting to read further about the role of nations.

Now try it with *not only–but also* (or . . . *as well*):

Not only individuals *but also* nations must learn to think about the environment.

Not only individuals *but* nations *as well* must learn to think about the environment.

Now the subject, especially the second half of it, has acquired even more emphasis.

Adverbials of Emphasis

As you read in Chapter 2, adverbials provide their information of time, place, manner, and the like in a variety of shapes; they also give the writer special flexibility because they are movable. And in the previous section on "Rhythm and the Comma," you saw how the conjunctive adverbs can change the focus by shifting position. But there's another group of adverbials, mainly single-word adverbs, whose purpose is to emphasize a particular structure and thus control the pace and rhythm of the sentence.

Read the following sentences and note where you apply the main stress:

> I could hardly sleep last night.
>
> I slept hardly at all last night.
>
> My roommate also had trouble sleeping.
>
> Some people are always looking for trouble.
>
> Joe tells me that he rarely stays awake past midnight.
>
> The country has never before faced the kind of crisis it faces now with terrorism.

You probably put the emphasis on *hardly, all, also, always, rarely,* and *never before.*

Given these examples, you can think of other words that you use for emphasis: other negatives, such as *seldom, barely, scarcely;* other time and frequency words, such as *afterwards, finally, sometimes;* and others expressing duration, such as *already, no longer, still.*

Negative adverbials produce an even stronger emphasis when they open the sentence, the result of switching the position of the subject and the auxiliary:

> Never before <u>has the country encountered</u> the kind of crisis it now faces with terrorism.

This shift, in fact, requires an auxiliary unless the main verb is a form of *be:*

> I seldom <u>get</u> a good night's sleep on weekends.
>
> Seldom <u>do I get</u> a good night's sleep on weekends.

This is another instance where we call on *do*-support when we need an auxiliary. (This use of *do*-support is discussed briefly on page 43.) And, as you can hear, the auxiliary–subject combination shares the main stress with the adverbial. It's possible, of course, to write sentences in which these words would not have main stress, where the principle of end focus, for example, would still be in effect. But certainly these are words that you, as a writer, need to recognize; they often wield the power in a sentence, controlling its intonation contour and making a difference in the message.

The Common *Only.* One of our most versatile—but also most frequently misused—adverbials of emphasis is the common *only.* Like other emphasizers, *only* can change the focus of the sentence by directing the reader's attention to a particular word:

> I'm taking <u>only twelve</u> credits this semester.
>
> The car <u>only looks</u> old; it's really quite new.
>
> Joe isn't <u>only handsome;</u> he's smart too.
>
> Paul cleans house <u>only on Saturdays.</u>

When you read these sentences you'll find yourself putting nearly equal emphasis on both *only* and the word that follows it.

But there's also a common problem with *only:* It's frequently misplaced—and most of the time we don't even notice!

> I'm only taking twelve credits this semester.
>
> Paul only cleans house on Saturdays.
>
> We're only going to be gone for two or three days.
>
> Jane refuses to watch the Super Bowl; she only likes baseball.

Even songwriters get it wrong:

> I only have eyes for you.

Perhaps the judgments of "wrong" and "misplaced" are inaccurate— too picky perhaps—when we consider how often this placement of *only* occurs both in speech and in the formal prose of respected writers. Nevertheless, in some cases, the reader will get a clear message when the *only* puts emphasis on a specific detail, to strengthen the sentence focus. That message says, "Pay attention! I've crafted this sentence carefully."

FOR GROUP DISCUSSION

How does Richard Ellis control the rhythm in this paragraph from *The Search for the Giant Squid*? (Look closely at the words at the beginning of each sentence.)

There is probably no apparition more terrifying than a gigantic, saucer-eyed creature of the depths with writhing, snakelike, grasping tentacles, a huge gelatinous body, and the powerful beak of a humongous seagoing parrot. Even the man-eating shark pales by comparison to such a horror. In only a few species do octopuses and squids reach the monstrous size required to attack swimmers, but this has not deterred writers and filmmakers from recruiting them when an underwater man-killer is needed.

KEY TERMS

Adverbial of emphasis	Existential *there*	Rhythm
Cleft sentence	Expletive	Stress
Conjunctive adverb	Intonation	*There*-transformation
Correlative	Intonation pattern	Transitional phrase
conjunction	*It*-cleft	*What*-cleft
End focus	Power words	

RHETORICAL REMINDERS

Sentence Rhythm

Have I considered my reader's expectations by putting the new information in line for end focus, unless otherwise marked?

Controlling Rhythm

Have I used the *there*-transformation and cleft sentences effectively—but not too frequently?

Have I placed interrupting words and phrases and clauses where they will be the most effective?

Power Words

Have I considered the impact of power words on the rhythm pattern?

Have I considered the contribution that correlative conjunctions could or do make to the rhythm and the reader's expectations?

Have I placed *only* in its most effective position?

PUNCTUATION REMINDER

In punctuating my sentences, have I taken into consideration that a comma changes the rhythm of the sentence, adding length and stress to the preceding word?

CHAPTER
7

The Writer's Voice

CHAPTER PREVIEW

In the first six chapters we looked at the structure and connection of sentences, including options the writer has for controlling the way the reader reads and interprets those sentences. This chapter continues that discussion, focusing on features of language that affect the writer's **voice** and, thus, the reader's interpretation. Think of your writer's voice as the identity you create through choosing words and arranging them on the page. Just as different facets of your identity appear during the day, depending on whom you're talking to, your writing voice or identity will vary according to your imagined readers. Sometimes your voice will be angry, sometimes friendly, other times meditative. You can easily come up with a list of the various voices you assume on a regular basis. The key in writing is to be able to control your voice so that you convey the message you want to. You can gain this control by understanding certain features of language: **tone,** the writer's stance, or attitude toward the topic; **diction,** the choice of words; **point of view,** the perspective from which the writer views the topic; and **metadiscourse,** the signals that help guide the reader through the text as well as communicate the writer's credibility and authority.

As you would expect, all of these features depend on the writing situation: the audience, the purpose, and the topic. Your writer's voice in a personal letter, for example, will be quite different from the voice in a letter to a prospective employer. Your voice in a personal essay for your composition class will be different from the voice you choose for a history research paper. In all of your writing, however, your writer's voice should be your voice, your **personal voice.**

TONE

In conversation there's nothing very mysterious about tone of voice and its contribution to meaning:

> "He was his usual cheerful self."
> "She's got attitude."
> "I think he was kidding."

In a face-to-face encounter, of course it's not only the voice that communicates the tone: There's the red face, the raised eyebrows, the rolling eyes, the smile, the smirk, the pleased expression.

But even on the telephone, without visual cues, we usually have no trouble drawing conclusions about tone. A person's voice may exude confidence or trepidation, hostility or pleasure, anger, bitterness, indifference. "How did she sound?" is a question someone might ask you about a phone conversation—not only, "What did she say?"

But how does your *writer's* voice sound? What determines its tone? Indeed, what does *tone* mean when there is no sound, only words on paper?

To answer these questions, consider what you read in the Introduction about rhetoric—about the choices we make based not only on the topic we're writing about but also on the audience and purpose. In that discussion we compared your writer's voice in a text message to your best friend with a letter to the dean of your college. Or consider the words you would use in a letter to a prospective employer. You would choose words to convey an earnest and confident and businesslike tone—and of course you'd be careful to dot every *i* and cross every *t,* so to speak.

Clearly, it's the rhetorical situation—the topic, the purpose, and the audience—that determines the tone. For example, newspapers and newsmagazines generally call for a neutral, objective voice. But apparently not always—not in this Associated Press article about rodent fossils discovered in South America:

> Eeek! Imagine a rodent that weighed a ton and was as big as a bull.
>
> Uruguayan scientists say they have uncovered fossil evidence of the biggest species of rodent ever found, one that scurried across wooded areas of South America about 4 million years ago, when the continent was not connected to North America.
>
> A herbivore, the beast may have been a contemporary, and possibly prey, of saber-toothed cats—a prehistoric version of Tom and Jerry.
>
> For those afraid of rodents, forget hopping on a chair. Its huge skull, more than 20 inches long, suggested a beast more

than eight feet long and weighing between 1,700 and 3,000 pounds.

Although British newspapers variously described it as a mouse or a rat, researchers say the animal, named Josephoartigasia monesi, actually was more closely related to a guinea pig or porcupine.

—Raphael G. Satter

The author's tongue-in-cheek tone here is anything but neutral. His opening with the interjection *eek* is a sure way to signal a playful tone. His use of the imperative—*imagine a rodent, forget hopping on a chair*—invites our participation, our agreement; his choice of details—*big as a bull, a prehistoric version of Tom and Jerry*—keeps us interested.

And in the following short piece, one of several in "Parade's Special Intelligence Report," a regular feature of *Parade* magazine, the use of the word *snafu* in the headline sets the reader up to expect that same kind of flippant tone:

Social Security Snafu

The federal government had to cough up cash last month and mail a "letter of explanation" to 51 million Americans who were short-changed on their Social Security checks. It seems the Bureau of Labor Statistics was supposed to give them 2.5% cost-of-living increases but only added 2.4%, due to faulty math. Recipients won't get rich: It's about $12 to $19 more. (We wonder what it cost to calculate the difference, then print and mail all those letters.) But the blunders didn't stop there: Some folks were sent financial data about their neighbors.

As you can see, the writer fulfills the headline's expectations. It's the choice of words that does it: *cough up, short-changed, faulty math, blunders.* You can be quite sure that a news release on the topic sent by the Bureau of Labor Statistics would have used different words.

In each of these examples, the writer's attitude toward the topic, the writer's take on the topic, clearly sets the tone: tongue-in-cheek, flippant, facetious, derisive.

EXERCISE 19

1. Rewrite the "Snafu" paragraph in a neutral tone, as the Bureau of Labor Statistics might have done in a news release. In addition to the informal words mentioned, you'll also want to consider the

appropriateness of *It seems* in the second sentence, the reference to getting rich in the third, and the sentence in parentheses.

2. These five short paragraphs open an article by Jeff Gammage entitled "One Significant Swede" about Carl Linnaeus in the magazine section of the *Philadelphia Inquirer* (June 28, 2005):

> At the Swedish museum in South Philadelphia, the staff is getting ready for a gala, year-long celebration of the 300th birthday of Carl Linnaeus.
>
> They face just one pesky problem: Most people don't know who the heck he is.
>
> And that's a shame, sponsors say. Because Linnaeus is not just another guy in a powdered wig.
>
> The Scandinavian scientist came up with a big, world-changing idea, a way to tidy up the clutter of the natural universe: He invented a system to name and categorize everything that lives, has lived or will live. And then he got people to follow his rules.
>
> Remember your high school biology teacher pounding *kingdom-phylum-class* into your head? You can thank—or blame—Carl Linnaeus

As you can see, the first paragraph covers the standard *who-what-when-where-why* of journalistic reporting in a straightforward way. What has the writer done to change the tone of the last four paragraphs?

A. Revise the last four paragraphs so that they conform to the straight reporting of the first paragraph.

B. Then, revise the opening paragraph so that it conforms in tone to the final four paragraphs.

For the revisions, you might want to combine paragraphs into perhaps just one or two.

DICTION

All of the published examples in the preceding section, besides illustrating tone, show clearly the connection between tone and **diction,** the choice of words: They are two sides of the same coin. Both are connected to the writing situation as well as to the essential sense of the words. And it may take only a few words to change the tone from neutral to ironic or bitter or skeptical or enthusiastic—depending, of course, on their meanings.

Where do those meanings come from? While the dictionary can give the core meaning of a word—its **denotation**—its essential sense resides in the language user and in the written or spoken context in which it is used. This special sense, association, or overtone carried by the word is called its **connotation.** For example, *economical* and *cheap* are synonyms: They both mean "thrifty." However, their connotations differ. While *an economical car* has a positive connotation, suggesting good gas mileage, *a cheap car* has a negative connation, bringing to mind the hassles of needing multiple car repairs. Communication takes place when the essential sense of a word is shared between speaker and listener, writer and reader.

Groups of synonyms can often be organized according to levels of formality. You would no doubt be able to sense that of the three verbs *choose, select,* and *pick out* (a phrasal verb), *pick out* is least formal and *select* is most formal. The words you choose are effective only when they are appropriate in the writing situation, appropriate for the audience and purpose, when they convey your message accurately and comfortably. The idea of comfort may seem out of place in connection with diction, but, in fact, words, especially those with negative connotations, can sometimes cause the reader to feel uncomfortable. You've probably experienced such feelings yourself as a listener—hearing a speaker whose words for one reason or another strike you as inappropriate and make you feel uncomfortable. Writing can provoke those same feelings in a reader.

As a reader yourself, you undoubtedly spot an inappropriate word simply because it commands attention—negative, uncomfortable attention. And when words are inappropriate, they set up communication barriers. As a writer you must learn to spot your own inappropriate words. One of the most common such attention-getters is the word that is too formal for the situation. Sometimes, of course, the opposite problem occurs: a word too informal for its purpose. But student writers are more likely to have the mistaken notion that writing calls for a sophisticated vocabulary. And so they look for words that demonstrate that sophistication.

One consequence of that inappropriate word choice is the loss of a personal voice. If what you've written doesn't sound like something you'd actually say, then you should reconsider your choice of words or style of phrasing. This is not to suggest that writing is exactly like speech; it's not, of course. In our everyday conversation with family and friends, we use informal words and phrases that we rarely see in writing, and we commonly use sentence fragments. Further, in writing we use certain modifiers and connectors, such as the *further* at the beginning of this sentence, that we rarely use in speaking. But even when we include such structures, we should be able to recognize our words as our own.

The following passage is the opening of a law school applicant's short essay in response to the question "Why do you want to study law?"

> It has long been a tenet of my value system that as a capable individual I have a social and moral duty to contribute to the improvement of the society in which I live. It seems that the way to make a valuable contribution is by choosing the means that will best allow me to utilize my abilities and facilitate my interests.

In spite of the **first person** point of view—the use of *I*—there's nothing personal in those lines. Here the writer's voice simply doesn't fit the rhetorical situation. If she had been asked in a face-to-face interview why she wanted to go to law school, she certainly would not have begun her answer with "It has long been a tenet of my value system." Never in her life has she begun a sentence that way. Instead, she would have said "I believe" or "I've always thought." But like many inexperienced writers, she associated formal writing with lofty phrases and uncommon words.

A personal voice does not preclude the use of big words or uncommon words. Nor does the expression "big words" refer to the number of syllables. It means pretentious or fancy words, words that call attention to themselves. Pretentious words send the message that the writer is trying too hard. The word *tenet,* as used in the law school statement, is one such pretentious word; it's out of place. Even the Declaration of Independence, with its formal, ceremonial language, uses the simple word *truths:*

> We hold these truths to be self-evident.

Chances are that Thomas Jefferson didn't consider, even in his first draft,

> We hold these tenets of our value system to be self-evident.

There are times, of course when an uncommon word is called for, a word with the precise meaning you want. All of us have in our passive vocabulary words that we rarely, if ever, use in speaking; and using them when they're called for does not mean giving up our personal voice. The mere fact that a word is infrequent does not make it pretentious. In the opening sentence of the previous paragraph, for example, the verb is *preclude.* It's not a common word, but there's certainly nothing fancy or pretentious about it: It's simply the most precise word for the job.

Another problem with pretentious language is the flabbiness that it produces, such as "utilize my abilities and facilitate my interests." Verbs like *utilize* and *facilitate* may sound impressive, but what do they really mean? *Utilize* simply means *use:* "to use my abilities." And it would probably surprise the law school applicant to learn that *facilitate* does not mean "to carry out," as she apparently assumed; it means "to make easier." So "facilitate my interests" is not only pretentious; it is meaningless.

FOR GROUP DISCUSSION

1. Words are powerful. As a writer you can use to advantage the power that words hold to call up images in the mind of the reader. But to use words effectively, you have to understand the meanings, the associations, they are likely to have for the reader. Consider the following sets of related words: What features do the members have in common? What features separate them? In what context would one be more effective than another?

   companion/friend/buddy   careful/stingy/thrifty/tight
   picky/careful/prudent   slumber/sleep/snooze
   cocky/confident   foolhardy/daring/rash/bold
   slender/skinny/scrawny

2. Bertrand Russell is credited with the following "conjugation of an irregular verb":

   I am firm. You are obstinate. He is pigheaded.

   Using some of the groups of words in Part 1, and adding to them as necessary, try your own conjugations.

   Example: I am slender; you are skinny; he is scrawny.

3. One characteristic of ineffective diction is the overuse of **clichés,** many of which are **similes,** comparisons that transfer the qualities of one thing (or person or animal) to another. Such comparisons become clichés when the reader knows exactly what's coming—that is, when there is no new information involved. Unlike the message of pretentious words, trying too

hard, clichés send the message that the writer isn't trying hard enough. The comparison is much more effective when it evokes a fresh image, when it helps the reader see something or someone in a new way.

Chances are you and most of your classmates can complete the following phrases with identical words:

quiet as a _____	mean as _____
hot as _____	light as _____
cold as _____	pretty as _____
scared as a _____	weak as _____
strong as _____	ugly as _____
fast as _____	tough as _____
avoid like the _____	sell like _____

Now, instead of using the expected word, find one that creates a fresh image. For example, you might say, "Quiet as a sealskin coat."

Note: You'll find it interesting and instructive to compare the answers given by the nonnative speakers of English in the class with those of native speakers.

Verbs and Formality

As you might expect, the level of formality in our prose is determined in large part by our choice of verbs—the pivotal unit in the sentence. Among the verbs that send an informal signal to the reader are **phrasal verbs,** common verbs combined with one or more **particles,** or preposition-like words. Some of the verb-plus-particle combinations form **idioms.** The term *idiom* refers to a set phrase whose meaning cannot be predicted from the separate meanings of the words. The meaning of the idiom *give up,* for example, is different from the combined meanings of *give* and *up:* It means "surrender" or "abandon."

Our language is filled with such idioms: *turn down, bring about, bring on, put up with, stand for, think up, take off, take up, look down on, brush aside, get on with, walk out on, come down with, swear off, write off*—the list goes on and on. As you can see, these are common verbs, part of our everyday speech. They lend an air of familiarity, a conversational tone to the writer's voice.

Idioms are certainly appropriate in informal contexts—for example, in a personal essay or narrative, or for a general audience, such as you might address in a letter to the editor of a newspaper. But for research papers or technical reports—and certainly for résumés and letters to prospective employers—a more formal verb may be called for. One way of adding formality, then, is to look carefully at (*scrutinize*) your sentences and do away with (*eliminate*) or at least cut down on (*reduce*) the number of idioms.

EXERCISE 20

A. Substitute a single word for each of the idioms listed in the second paragraph of the preceding discussion. In some cases there will be more than one possibility.

B. The idioms we have used in writing this book certainly influence its level of formality. Here are some of the sentences you have seen so far. Come up with a more formal version of each.

1. <u>Come up with</u> a more formal version of each.

2. The punctuation convention <u>calls for</u> a comma. . . .

3. There are three steps we follow in <u>turning</u> the active voice <u>into</u> passive.

4. All sentences are <u>made up of</u> one or more independent clauses.

5. The first sentence in a paragraph <u>sets up</u> expectations in the reader about what is coming.

6. We can easily <u>figure out</u> what the sentence means.

7. We can <u>think of</u> it as part of the contract between writer and reader.

8. You can be sure that in reading their own prose, whether silently or aloud, they are <u>paying attention to</u> sentence rhythm.

9. The pronoun <u>stands in for</u> the entire noun phrase.

10. We <u>call on</u> *do* when we need an auxiliary. . . .

Nominalized Verbs and Abstract Subjects

One common feature of formal writing, especially academic writing, is the use of **nominalized verbs**—verbs that have been turned into nouns: *occur →
occurrence, succeed → success, combine → combination, remove → removal.*

Writers take advantage of this feature to link sentences together; they use the verb (actually the entire predicate) to present new information and the nom- inalized verb, often preceded by a demonstrative *this, that, these,* or *those,* to establish known information:

> The grammar of the written language <u>differs</u> greatly from that of the spoken language. <u>This difference</u> is attributable to the con- stant innovations of spoken language.

In this example *differ* and *difference* affirm the known-new contract.

Though nominalized verbs contribute to cohesion, they should be used with care. Because they are so common and so easy to produce, they can become a trap for the unwary writer, introducing abstraction where con- crete ideas belong. It's during the revision stage of writing that you'll want to be on the lookout. Ask yourself, is the **agent**—the initiator of the action—there and, if so, is it functioning as the subject? In other words, does the sentence explain *who is doing what?* If the answer is no, your sen- tence may be a prime candidate for revision. Can you find the agent in the following sentence?

> High student achievement led to the creation of the Gifted Stu- dents Program.

Although *high student achievement* is the subject, it is an abstraction. The agent could be *students,* or it could be the unnamed creators of the pro- gram. Here is one possible revision:

> The School Board created the Gifted Students Program for high achievers.

Another possible source of confusion is the sentence with a verb phrase or a clause as subject, rather than the usual noun phrase. When you study these structures in Chapter 10, you'll see that they are common substi- tutes for noun phrases. But because they are abstractions, they too may be pitfalls for the unwary writer. Again, the source of the problem may be that of the misplaced or missing agent:

> The <u>buying</u> of so many American companies and so much real estate by the Japanese caused concern on Wall Street.
>
> <u>Analyzing</u> the situation in China shows that opportunities for investment are growing.

Although we need context to tell us the best way to revise these sentences, we can see and hear a problem. The sentences seem to be about actions— but they can't show the action in a strong and concrete way because the agents of those actions are not there in subject position. This kind of agentless sentence should send up a red flag—a signal that here's a candidate for revision.

EXERCISE 21

Revise the following passages, paying special attention to unnecessary nominalizations and problems of agency. The first two items are the examples from the preceding discussion. Remember to ask yourself, "Who is doing what?"

1. The buying of so many American companies and so much real estate by the Japanese caused concern on Wall Street.

2. Analyzing the situation in China showed that opportunities for investment were growing.

3. In the biography of Lyndon Johnson by Robert Caro, the account of the Senate election of 1948 is described in great detail.

4. One of the requirements for the completion of the application for a scholarship was the submission of a financial statement by the student's parents.

5. The overuse of salt in the typical American diet has had the result of obscuring the natural taste of many foods. Nutritionists maintain that a reduction in people's dependence on salt would lead to an enhancement of taste and heightened enjoyment of food.

Contractions

Contractions affect the rhythm of sentences and, in doing so, affect the reader's perception of the writer's voice. That voice will probably strike the reader as more conversational, less formal, when contractions are part of the message. Contractions help to close the distance between writer and reader.

Although contractions are often seen as too conversational, most writers, even in formal contexts, will contract the negative *not* in such words as *don't* and *can't*:

> If you use ready-made phrases, you not only <u>don't</u> have to hunt about for words; you also <u>don't</u> have to bother with the rhythms of your sentences, since these phrases are generally so arranged as to be more or less euphonious.
> —George Orwell ("Politics and the English Language")

Other frequent contractions are those with the auxiliary verbs *have, had, will, would, is, am,* and *are.* Here are some common examples:

> Negatives: can't, don't, won't, couldn't, doesn't, isn't
> Auxiliaries: I'd, she'll, they're, we've, he's, it's

The contracted forms of *be* can also occur when they function as the main verb:

> You're happy.
> I'm sad.

The contracted *is* is especially common with *it* and *there:*

> It's a nice day today.
> There's a storm due tomorrow.

If you think about—and listen for—sentence rhythm, you'll understand the contribution that contractions make in eliminating or greatly diminishing a syllable. As you read the following passages, consider how different the sentences would be without the contractions they include:

> Cats, I surmise, seem unsocial to us only because we aren't good at recognizing the signals of other species. We interpret cat signals as telling us, for instance, that the cat doesn't care about us and doesn't miss us when we're gone. If people were giving off similar signals, our interpretation would probably be right. But they're not people, and we're wrong.
> —Elizabeth Marshall Thomas (*The Atlantic Monthly*)

You may have noticed that none of the examples, either in the lists or in the quoted passages, involve nouns—only pronouns. Contractions with nouns—"My dog'll eat anything"; "The Senate's accomplished a lot lately"—are fairly common in conversation and in written quotations and dialogue, but they are rare in most writing situations. However, contractions with pronouns are anything but rare.

The advice against using contractions that you may have heard or read simply does not reflect actual usage. Even fairly formal written prose commonly includes the contracted *not,* as the Orwell passage illustrates. And in negative questions, the contracted form is essentially required:

> Hasn't the winter weather been wonderful?
> Shouldn't the tax laws be revised?

In the uncontracted form, the *not* predominates, changing the intended emphasis, if not the meaning:

> Has the winter weather not been wonderful?
> Should the tax laws not be revised?

An interesting feature in negative statements is that often the writer has more than one contraction to choose from.

> She is not here. → She's not here *or* She isn't here.

Both contracted forms are less formal than the original, but there's also a difference between the two: In the version with the diminished *not (isn't)*, the reader will probably put more emphasis on *here*—and may then expect a different follow-up sentence:

> She isn't here. She's in class.
> She's not here. I don't know where she is.

If you want to ensure that the reader puts strong stress on the negative, you can use the uncontracted *not*—with or without the contracted *is*. Another difference between these two contracted versions is the number of syllables. The sentence with *isn't* has four syllables; the one with *not* has only three—a rhythm difference that in a given situation may be important.

In some cases where there's a choice of contractions, you may also notice a difference in formality, with the uncontracted *not* on the more formal side:

> I won't be there. / I'll not be there.
> I haven't finished. / I've not finished.
> I wouldn't go there if I were you. / I'd not go there if I were you.

Even though the second version in each case includes a contraction, it has a rather formal tone.

It's important to recognize the connection between the level of formality and the use of contractions: In general, the more formal the writing, the fewer contractions you'll find, or want to use, especially contracted auxiliaries. However, in most of the writing you do for school or on the job, the occasional contraction will certainly be appropriate. It's important to recognize the contribution that contractions can make to your personal voice.

FOR GROUP DISCUSSION

Consider the personal voice that you hear in the following advertisements, which appeared during the same week in two different publications. How would you characterize the tone and the diction? In each case the opening paragraph shown is the headline for the ad.

Rewrite each of the ads using the voice and tone of the other one.

1. Looks like this winter will be warmer than the last. Lands' End introduces the newest—and driest—in Polartec outerwear.

    Have you met Polartec yet? If you're into winter sports, betcha you have.

    It's the original man-made fleece. A nubby fabric that weighs nothing—yet keeps you warm when it's umpteen below.

    Well, the folks at Malden Mills who dreamed up Polartec have outdone themselves now.

    They've not only created an even cozier warmer version—they've made it more water repellent, too.

    So much so, that it inspired us at Lands' End to introduce a whole bunch of new Polartec outerwear.

    —*The Atlantic Monthly*

2. A perfect dinner party requires hours of planning and preparation. Having decent appliances doesn't hurt, either.

    Fresh herbs as opposed to dry. Going to the butcher instead of the supermarket. The wedding china, not everyday.

    Her dinner party was that special. Perhaps the brilliant shine of stainless steel inspired her, from a kitchen that was special too. Filled with restaurant-quality appliances—aka the Pro-Style Collection from Jenn-Air.

    From the quintessential cooktop to the matching refrigerator and dishwasher, they're all sleek, gleaming and state-of-the-art. The crème de la crème, as they say.

    True, throwing the perfect dinner party is a major project. But if you've got the perfect kitchen, it's a labor of love.

    —*The New Yorker*

Metaphor

As you have seen, the choice of words affects the reader's response to the message and no doubt to the writer as well. The use of contractions tends to close the distance between writer and reader. Another technique for closing that distance is the use of *metaphor,* the application of words from one sphere to another.

You were introduced to the grammar of metaphor in Chapter 2 when you read about the linking-*be* followed by a noun phrase as subject complement. A "something is something" sentence becomes metaphor when that equation is figurative rather than literal—in other words, when the two "somethings" belong to different spheres or domains. Shakespeare's

All the world's a stage

and Charlie Brown's (Charles Schulz's)

Happiness is a warm puppy

illustrate the wide range of possibilities—from the profound to the commonplace.

But *be* sentences, like these examples, are by no means the only form of metaphor, or even the most common. In our everyday language we apply words from one domain to another, creating metaphor with just a simple modifier. Language itself is often described metaphorically: flowery prose, gutter journalism, bathroom words, hard-boiled detective novels. Newsmagazines abound with metaphors, many of them overworked. *Time* reported on "an industrial dinosaur like General Motors" the same week that *Newsweek* described the company as "a sinking ship." In *Time*'s story the head of the company "doesn't like sitting in the back seat"; in *Newsweek*'s he's helping to steer "a treasure galleon."

Metaphor can often illuminate and lighten a serious or technical discussion. In the following extended metaphor, *New York Times* writers explain the issue of class. This paragraph is from an article by Janny Scott and David Leonhardt called "The Shadowy Lines That Still Divide," the first installment of an eleven-part series called "Class in America":

> One way to think of a person's position in society is to imagine a hand of cards. Everyone is dealt four cards, one from each suit: education, income, occupation and wealth, the four commonly used criteria for gauging class. Face cards in a few categories may land a player in the upper middle class. At first, a person's class is his parents' class. Later, he may pick up a new hand of his own; it is likely to resemble that of his parents, but not always.

The following passage opens the third paragraph of a long article by Lauren Resnick and Chris Zurawsky in *American Education,* a publication

of the American Federation of Teachers, describing the standards movement in American schools. The two preceding paragraphs introduce the
topic in straightforward academic prose.

> At about fifteen years of age, the standards movement is in its
> adolescence, and many are already preparing to kick it out of
> the house. Before we give up on our unruly teen, however, let's
> take a clear look at what we have to be proud of, what flaws we
> need to address, and what might be the benefits of pressing
> ahead.

After just two sentences of the teenager metaphor, however, the reader is
back to serious business, with the questions that the article goes on to
address. Undoubtedly, though, in both of these examples, the metaphor
has made the reader stop and think about the topic in a new way.

METADISCOURSE

Metadiscourse refers to certain signals that help the reader understand
the writer's message. The word *metadiscourse* actually means discourse
about discourse—signals that clarify the purpose or direction of a particular passage, acting as guideposts for the reader. For example, a word like
thus tells the reader that what follows is a summary. And when a sentence
opens with *for example*, as the previous one does, you know the sentence
will discuss an example of the concept just mentioned. The phrase may
not be necessary—many examples go unmarked—but sometimes that
help is very important.

Some of our most common and useful metadiscourse signals are the
conjunctive adverbs you read about in Chapter 4: *however, so, nevertheless*,
and prepositional phrases such as *in other words, in addition*, and *in fact*
(see the list on pages 65 and 67). Other text connectors you're familiar
with, such as *first, in the first place, second, next, finally*, and *in conclusion*,
clearly add to the ease of reading, the flow of the text. Those that signal
contrasting pairs of ideas—*on the one hand/on the other hand*—are especially
helpful. Signals like these contribute to the sense of cohesion, the flow of
the paragraph—and sometimes to its accurate interpretation—by keeping
the reader informed of the writer's intentions.

We can think of these text connectors as primarily informational, to
help the reader understand the message.

Other structures that we label as metadiscourse have a different purpose and a different effect: They offer guidance for reading the text,
informing the reader of the writer's own attitude about the content of the
message.

As you read the following passages, think about the role played by the underlined words. If the sentences look familiar, it's because they have all appeared in earlier sections of this book.

1. <u>The point is</u> that we, as readers, shouldn't have to do the figuring.
2. Parallelism is usually thought of as a device for enhancing a writer's style—<u>and indeed it is that</u>—as you learned in Chapter 4.
3. You've <u>probably</u> been told at one time or another to avoid *I* or *you* or the passive voice—and, <u>very possibly</u>, the *it*-cleft as well.

All of these underlined structures qualify as metadiscourse.

The opener, *the point is,* in (1) emphasizes our take on the importance and validity of the proposition. The inserted sentence in (2) calls attention to the truth of the statement about parallelism that could be taken wrong, given the wording "is usually thought of." The paragraph goes on to emphasize the importance of parallelism to cohesion.

The use of *probably* and *very possibly* in (3) is called hedging: There's no way we could know for sure that you've been told those things, so we don't want to sound too positive. We don't want you, the reader, to be stopped by a bold statement when it may not be valid in your case. And we certainly don't want you to lose confidence in our authority to write on this topic. Other hedging terms are words like *perhaps,* verbs like *seem* or *indicate* or *suggest* and phrases like *to a certain extent,* as well as the modal auxiliaries *might* and *may* and *could.*

Although you might think that using words like *perhaps* and *probably* would communicate doubt about the author's authority and the reliability of the information, such **hedges** actually have the opposite effect on the reader. In *Constructing Texts,* George Dillon maintains that they "certify the writer as a modest, careful scholar whose tentative conclusions are probably of wider application and greater likelihood than he feels he can claim" (p. 91).[1]

There are many other kinds of metadiscourse markers that affect the writer's personal voice: Some of them comment on the content of the sentence; some of them allow the writer to address the reader directly; some comment on what is coming next—or what the reader has already learned. Here are some further examples, also taken from earlier sections of the book:

<u>As you probably noticed,</u> the only difference between the two passages is in the rhythm pattern of the last sentence in each.

---

[1]Dillon's book is listed in the Bibliography under "Composition Theory."

The following passive sentence, <u>which may look familiar,</u> closes the
first paragraph of the section in Chapter 2 called "Sentence
Patterns". . . .

<u>It is important to recognize</u> that pronouns without antecedents are
in violation of the known–new contract.

<u>And you can be sure</u> that in reading their own prose, whether
silently or aloud, they are paying attention to sentence rhythm.

In the following paragraph, from *Saga of Chief Joseph* by Helen Addison
Howard, the author translates "Nez Perce" in a parenthetical comment, a
type of metadiscourse called a **code gloss,** a term applied when the writer
clarifies the meaning of a word or phrase. You'll see other obvious
metadiscourse signals as well:

> After Lewis and Clark passed through their country (about
> which more later), French-Canadian trappers came to trade the
> white man's guns, cloth, metal articles, and trinkets for their
> pelts of beaver. The French traders, it is claimed, applied the
> name "Nez Perce" (Pierced Nose) to these Indians because
> a few members of the tribe used to pierce their noses to insert a
> shell for ornament. This habit was not a tribal custom, but the
> name clung to them.

Still another example of metadiscourse appears in the first sentence of the
paragraph introducing the previous quotation: The sentence beginning
"In the following paragraph" is called an **attributor,** the source of the
quoted information. Attributors add authority to the text. In the previous
discussion of Dillon's comment about hedges, the attributor phrase begins
"In *Constructing Texts*"; the opening "According to" is another common
lead-in for an attributor.

All of these metadiscourse markers send messages to the reader from
and about the writer. They say, in effect, "I'm helping you out here, trying
to make your job of reading and understanding easier."

The Overuse of Metadiscourse

It can happen, as you would expect, that inexperienced writers sometimes
get carried away with metadiscourse, with those helpful messages, to the
detriment of their primary message. The following paragraph is from a
paper written by a student participating in a research study on the

effectiveness of teaching metadiscourse. The underlined segments were identified as metadiscourse by the researchers:

> In the beginning the television <u>was posed</u> as a real asset for families with children because it would be a big influence in the home. <u>Basically this is what Marie Winn discussed in her article "The Plug-In Drug." As a young adult today</u> I can safely say that the hours one person sits in front of the television has greatly increased from what it was forty years ago. <u>So yes Winn is correct in stating</u> that the television is a major influence on children these days.[2]

FOR GROUP DISCUSSION

Consider the use of metadiscourse in the following paragraph, the first paragraph in Chapter 9 of Thomas S. Kuhn's *The Structure of Scientific Revolutions*. This chapter is entitled "The Nature and Necessity of Scientific Revolutions."

> These remarks permit us at last to consider the problems that provide this essay with its title. What are scientific revolutions, and what is their function in scientific development? Much of the answer to these questions has been anticipated in earlier sections. In particular, the preceding discussion has indicated that scientific revolutions are here taken to be those non-cumulative developmental episodes in which an older paradigm is replaced in whole or in part by an incompatible new one. There is more to be said, however, and an essential part of it can be introduced by asking one further question. Why should a change of paradigm be called a revolution? In the face of the vast and essential differences between political and scientific development, what parallelism can justify the metaphor that finds revolutions in both?

Identify all the uses of metadiscourse in the paragraph; characterize their purpose and their effect on the reader.

---

[2]Quoted in the article by Chang and Steffensen listed in the Bibliography under "Metadiscourse."

EXERCISE 22

A. Continue the survey of your writing style.

	Professional	Student
1. Number of sentences with first person pronouns	_____	_____
2. Number with second person: *you* or *your*	_____	_____
3. Number of transitional phrases	_____	_____
4. Number of hedging words	_____	_____
5. Number of code glosses	_____	_____
6. Number of attributors	_____	_____

B. What do your statistics tell you? Do they tell you anything about the kinds of metadiscourse expected in a specific writing situation? Do they suggest any types of metadiscourse that you might consider using in the future? If they do, what is it about your writing situation that makes you think these metadiscourse signals would be appropriate?

POINT OF VIEW

In discussing **point of view**—the perspective from which the writer views the topic—we again take up the discussion of **personal pronouns.** In Chapter 1 we saw personal pronouns as stand-ins for noun phrases and used them to determine those phrase boundaries; in Chapter 5 we recognized their role as cohesive devices. Here we look at their relationship to point of view. The writer's decision about point of view is essentially a choice about **person,** a feature of personal pronouns: Shall I write in **first person**? **Second person**? A combination? Or shall I stick strictly to **third person**?

In the following chart, the first forms shown are **subjective case,** the form used when the pronoun functions as the subject or subject complement in its sentence. The forms shown in parentheses are variations of case (**possessive, objective**): The possessive case is used when the pronoun functions as a determiner; the objective case is used in three complement positions (direct object, indirect object, object complement) and as the object of a preposition.

PERSON	NUMBER	
	Singular	**Plural**
1st	I (my, me)	we (our, us)
2nd	you (your, you)	you (your, you)
3rd	he (his, him) she (her, her) it (its, it)	they (their, them)

(The case of personal pronouns is discussed further on pages 249–251.)

Many kinds of essays are written in first person—more than you might think. Personal narratives, of course, are nearly always first person, but so are many other essays. In fact, it would probably be accurate to say that most essay writers use first person somewhere in their text—an occasional *we* or *our* or *us*. The exceptions are business and scientific reports and historical essays, which are often strictly third person. Newspapers and newsmagazines also stick to third person when they report the news. But writers of editorials and syndicated columns and feature stories regularly use both first and second person. And in textbooks it's certainly common to see both first and second person. In this one you'll find sentences with *we* or *our* or *you* or *your* on every page.

If it's true that first person is a common point of view, then why do teachers so often rule it unacceptable in the essays they assign? You may have had an English teacher in high school or college who required you to stick to third person. One reason for that proscription against first person is undoubtedly the bad writing that so often results, with *I* turning up as the subject of almost every sentence—as if the writer, the "I," were the topic being discussed.

The most common use of first person in professional writing is the plural—*we* and *us* and *our* rather that *I* and *me* and *my*. The result is a kind of collective first person (sometimes referred to as the "royal *we*" or the "editorial *we*"). You'll find that collective first person in the preamble to the Constitution: "We the people . . . for ourselves and our posterity . . . ." The *we* in this book is also often that collective *we*, though at times it refers just to the two authors of this book. Following is another example of the collective *we*, a first-person passage from *A Brief History of Time* by Stephen W. Hawking:

> Now at first sight, all this evidence that the universe looks the same whichever direction <u>we</u> look in might seem to suggest there is something special about <u>our</u> place in the universe. In particular, it might seem that if <u>we</u> observe all other galaxies to

be moving away from <u>us,</u> then <u>we</u> must be at the center of the universe.

Here the first-person plural is especially effective, where the writer wants the reader to be included in his description of the universe.

Another point of view that teachers sometimes rule out is the second person, the use of *you*. But it too is common for many writing occasions. You'll notice that many of the sentences in the foregoing paragraphs, as well as the sentence you're reading now, include *you* as the subject. This use of *you* not only gets the attention of the reader, it actually involves the reader in the subject matter.

But *you* does not always address the reader; it is often used in a more general sense, with a meaning more like that of the third person. Notice the use of *you* in this passage from *Broca's Brain* by Carl Sagan, describing an excursion into the back rooms of the Museum of Man in Paris:

> Most of the rooms were evidently used for storage of anthropological items, collected from decades to more than a century ago. <u>You</u> had the sense of a museum of the second order, in which were stored not so much materials that might be of interest as materials that had once been of interest. <u>You</u> could feel the presence of nineteenth-century museum directors engaged, in their frock coats, in goniometrie and craniologie, busily collecting and measuring everything, in the pious hope that mere quantification would lead to understanding.

Here *you* takes the place of "one" or "a person"; it is not "you the reader." Some teachers, however, prefer *one* to this general *you:*

> When <u>one</u> sees the Golden Gate Bridge for the first time, the sight is simply breathtaking.

The use of *one* adds a formality, a distance that *you* does not have. The sentence sounds formal and British, like something Prince Charles would say. In American English, we're more likely to use *you* rather than *one* to convey that third-person indefinite sense:

> When <u>you</u> see the Golden Gate Bridge for the first time, the sight is simply breathtaking.

This use of *you* is technically second person, but the meaning is closer to the indefinite third-person *one*.

It is not at all unusual to mix the point of view. A first- or second-person passage always includes pronouns in the third person. And many essays that are essentially third person have an occasional *we* or *our* or *you*. There is no rule that says good writing should not have that versatility of view.

FOR GROUP DISCUSSION

1. Revise the point of view in the paragraph by Carl Sagan. What version—first-person, second-person, or third-person—do you prefer? Why?

2. Next, revise the point of view in the paragraph by Stephen H. Hawking. Which version sounds better to you? Why?

3. Now, change the point of view of one of your own paragraphs and discuss the differences you find.

KEY TERMS

Abstract subject	Hedge	Phrasal verb
Agent	Idiom	Point of view
Attributor	Metadiscourse	Possessive case
Cliché	Metaphor	Second person
Code gloss	Nominalized verb	Simile
Connotation	Objective cass	Subjective case
Contraction	Particle	Third person
Denotation	Person	Tone
Diction	Personal pronoun	Voice
First person	Personal voice	

RHETORICAL REMINDERS

What is there in my sentence structure and word choice that has established my tone? Have I avoided words that contradict my tone?

Can I hear my personal voice in the words I've written? Have I avoided unusual words that don't really sound like me—words I probably wouldn't use in speech?

Have I been accurate and complete in attributing the ideas and words of outside sources and in using quotation marks for passages that are not my own?

Are my contractions appropriate, given the level of formality I want to achieve? Are my contractions attached only to pronouns (*she's*) and auxiliaries (*can't*)—not to nouns (*John'll go with us; The teacher's talking*)?

Have I used hedging words appropriately, where I need to hedge? Emphatic words where I want to show emphasis? Have I guided the reader where such guidance would help?

PUNCTUATION REMINDERS

Have I set off metadiscourse markers with commas where an emphasis on the marker would be useful?

Have I included apostrophes in contractions to indicate where a letter or letters have been left out?

Have I used quotation marks correctly (e.g., outside the period at the end of a sentence)? (*Note:* See pages 278–279 in the Glossary of Punctuation.)

PART III

Making Choices: Form and Function

Proper words in proper places make the true definition of Style.
—JONATHAN SWIFT

We hope that the first seven chapters have helped you recognize your knowledge of language structure as your writer's toolbox, with tools that can help you make good decisions as you write and revise—or, as Jonathan Swift put it, decisions that help you find the proper words for proper places. By "proper," Swift is referring to appropriateness, words that are suitable to the occasion: the grammatical choices that produce the desired rhetorical effects.

The four chapters in this section pull together and expand on some of the details of sentence structure you have studied in earlier chapters:

Chapter 8: Choosing Adverbials
Chapter 9: Choosing Adjectivals
Chapter 10: Choosing Nominals
Chapter 11: Other Stylistic Variations

In Chapter 1 you were introduced to the *-al* forms of *adverb* and *adjective*. There, and in subsequent chapters, you learned that forms other than adverbs and adjectives, such as prepositional phrases and dependent clauses, can modify verbs and nouns. You saw the term *nominal,* the *-al* form of *noun,* in the description of a dependent clause functioning as a direct object.

In the first three chapters of this section, then, you will learn to think about the basic sentence units and their modifiers in terms of both **form** and **function.** The following chart will help you organize this two-sided analysis. You'll discover that all of the general **functions** listed on the right—adverbial, adjectival, and nominal—can be carried out by all of the general **forms** listed on the left—words, phrases, and clauses.

FORM	FUNCTION
Word	***Adverbial***
noun	modifier of verb
verb	
adjective	***Adjectival***
adverb	subject complement
	object complement
Phrase	modifier of noun
noun phrase	
verb phrase	***Nominal***
gerund	subject
infinitive	subject complement
participle	direct object
prepositional phrase	indirect object
	object complement
Clause	object of preposition
independent clause (sentence)	appositive
dependent clause	
adverbial clause	
adjectival clause	
nominal clause	

The last chapter in this section, Chapter 11, focuses on ways in which you can endow your sentences with special effects through punctuation and placement and other stylistic choices.

CHAPTER
8

Choosing Adverbials

CHAPTER PREVIEW

In this chapter we focus on two features that make adverbials such power-ful tools for writers: the variety of their forms and, equally important, their movability. In previous chapters, unless the adverbials were specifi-cally mentioned, you probably didn't pay much attention to them in the sentences and paragraphs and exercises you were examining for other purposes. In this chapter they will get all of our attention. In terms of grammatical choices and rhetorical effects, adverbials probably have more to offer the writer than any other unit in the sentence.

As you study this chapter, let the Form/Function chart on the previous page serve as your mental organizer for the words and phrases and clauses in their role as adverbials. We'll begin with a consideration of that impor-tant feature, movability.

THE MOVABLE ADVERBIALS

The Glossary of Terms, beginning on page 280, defines *adverbial* as

Any structure, no matter what its form, that functions as a modifier of a verb—that is, that functions as an adverb normally functions.

You'll recall that the word *adverb* is the name of a word class, one of the four form classes—not the name of a function. But as our definition of adverbial makes clear, we generally think of adverbs as modifiers of the verb—in other words, part of the predicate. Likewise, all the other forms that function as adverbs—in other words, all the adverbials—are considered part of the predicate as well. However, one of the adverbial's most versatile features is its ability to be placed elsewhere in the sentence. For example, consider how often in a story or essay the opening adverbial sets the scene:

> When in the course of human events . . .
>
> Four score and seven years ago . . .
>
> Once upon a time . . .

Many of the Chapter Previews in this book begin with that scene-setting adverbial:

> In this chapter . . .

Another important function of the opening adverbial is to provide cohesion, the tie that connects a sentence to what has gone before. Opening adverbials can also provide road signs that connect the sentences in special ways—for example, to orient the reader in terms of time or place. Notice in the following paragraph from *The Sea Around Us* how Rachel Carson opens her sentences with adverbials:

> <u>Sometimes</u> the disintegration [of islands] takes abrupt and violent form. The greatest explosion of historic time was the literal evisceration of the island of Krakatoa. <u>In 1680</u> there had been a premonitory eruption on this small island in Sunda Strait, between Java and Sumatra in the Netherlands Indies. <u>Two hundred years later</u> there had been a series of earthquakes. <u>In the spring of 1883,</u> smoke and steam began to ascend from fissures in the volcanic cone. The ground became noticeably warm, and warning rumblings and hissings came from the volcano. <u>Then, on 27 August,</u> Krakatoa literally exploded. <u>In an appalling series of eruptions, that lasted two days,</u> the whole northern half of the cone was carried away. The sudden inrush of ocean water added to the fury of superheated steam to the cauldron. <u>When the inferno of white-hot lava, molten rock, steam, and smoke had finally subsided,</u> the island that had stood 1,400 feet above the sea had become a cavity a thousand feet below sea level. <u>Only along one edge of the former crater</u> did a remnant of the island remain.

Opening adverbials like these are especially common in narrative writing, the story or explanation of events through time. You'll notice that most of

Carson's adverbial openers provide information of time. And she has used a variety of forms:

Adverbs: *Sometimes, Then*

Prepositional phrases: *In 1680, In an appalling series of eruptions . . .*

Dependent clause: *When the inferno . . . subsided*

FOR GROUP DISCUSSION

Carson's opening adverbials are clearly there for the purpose of cohesion, for guiding the reader through the events in time, introducing the details in sequence. It is at the end of each sentence where we find the new information, the reason for the sentence, as in this dramatic main clause:

Then, on 27 August, Krakatoa literally exploded.

The paragraph's last sentence opens with an adverbial prepositional phrase telling *where:*

Only along one edge of the former crater did a remnant of the island remain.

The time adverbials in the other sentences are clearly there to create cohesion. Why has Carson used this information of place to open the sentence? In spite of its length, this opener is not set off by a comma. What else do you notice about this final sentence?

ADVERBS

As we have seen, many of our adverbs provide information of time and place and frequency: *sometimes, then, soon, often, tomorrow.* You read about their meaning and movability in Chapter 1 (pages 15–16). Some of the adverbs included in that discussion are the adverbs of manner, which are produced by adding *-ly* to adjectives: *quickly, slowly, carefully, gracefully,* and literally thousands more—given the thousands of adjectives available. They are also among our most movable adverbs, appearing not only at the beginning and end of the sentence, but also between the subject and the predicate, even within the main verb:

My roommate *is seriously thinking* about changing her major.

The movability of adverbs allows the writer to take charge of the way the reader reads and interprets the sentence. Read the roommate sentence aloud; then compare your reading with this version:

> My roommate *is thinking <u>seriously</u>* about changing her major.

You will probably hear more stress given to the adverb when it follows the verb.

We should note that if you open the sentence with an adverb set off by a comma, it will often become a **sentence modifier,** saying something about the sentence as a whole, rather than as simply modifying the verb. Bear in mind as well what you learned in Chapter 5 about the effect a comma can have: The word preceding it will get strong stress:

> <u>Seriously,</u> my roommate is thinking about changing her major.

In this case, it's not the thinking that is serious. This shift in meaning does not generally occur with the time and place adverbs, like those we saw earlier: *sometimes, then, now, here, there, everywhere.* Single-word sentence modifiers are more commonly the *-ly* adverbs:

> *Clearly,* something has to be done about the health system.
>
> *Luckily,* we survived the accident with only minor injuries.

PREPOSITIONAL PHRASES

No doubt our most common adverbial—perhaps even more common than the adverb—is the prepositional phrase, introduced in Chapter 1, where you saw both adverbial and adjectival prepositional phrases. Following are examples of adverbial information that prepositional phrases provide:

Direction:	*toward the pond, beyond the ridge, across the field*
Place:	*near the marina, on the expressway, along the path*
Time:	*on Tuesday afternoon, at noon, in modern times, in the spring of 1883*
Duration:	*until three o'clock, for several days, during spring break, throughout the summer months*
Manner:	*in an appalling series of eruptions, without complaint, with dignity, by myself, in a frenzy*
Cause:	*because of the storm, for a good reason*

The Proliferating Prepositional Phrase

Our two most common prepositions, *of* and *to,* are especially vulnerable to proliferation. Both occur in countless idioms and set phrases. For example, we regularly use *of* phrases with numbers and with such pronouns as *all, each, some,* and *most:*

> one of the guests, all of the people, some of the students, most of the problems, the rest of the time, half of the food, each of the parts

Of is also used to indicate possessive case, as an alternative to *'s:*

> the capacity of the trunk, the base of the lamp, the opening night of the new show, the noise of the crowd

And we use it to show direction and position and time:

> the front of the house, the top of the bookcase, the back of the page, the end of the play

Because there are so many such situations that call for prepositions, it's not at all unusual to find yourself writing sentences with prepositional phrases strung together in chains. You can undoubtedly find many such sentences in the pages of this book. In fact, the sentence you just read ended with two: "*in* the pages *of* this book." It would be easy to add even more: "in the pages of this book about the grammar of English for writers." As you edit what you have written, it's important to tune in to the rhythm of the sentence: A long string of short phrases is a clue that suggests revision. Ask yourself if those prepositional phrases are proliferating awkwardly.

Awkwardness is not the only problem—nor is it the most serious. The sentence that ends with a long string of prepositional phrases often loses its focus. Our usual rhythm pattern follows the principle of end focus; it calls for the new information to be the last or next-to-the-last structural unit. Notice, for example, what happened to that altered sentence in the previous paragraph. Here's the original; read it aloud and listen to the stress:

> You can undoubtedly find many such sentences in the pages of this book.

Chances are you put stress on *many* and on *this book.* Now read the altered version:

> You can undoubtedly find many such sentences in the pages of this book about the grammar of English for writers.

Because you expected the sentence to have end focus, you probably found yourself putting off the main stress until you got to *writers.* But that last unit (starting with *about*), consisting of three prepositional phrases, is known information. Not only should it get no stress, *it shouldn't be there at all.* That kind of unwanted repetition of known information is what we call **redundancy.**

Here's another illustration of this common source of redundancy—an edited version of the opening sentences from the previous paragraph:

> Awkwardness is not the only problem with those extra preposi-
> tional phrases in our sentences—nor is it the most serious of the
> writer's problems. The sentence that ends with a long string of
> prepositional phrases often loses its focus on the main point of
> the sentence that the writer intended it to have.

Those redundant modifiers add to the total number of words—and that's about all they add. Clearly, they have added no new information. And they have obliterated the original focus.

EXERCISE 23

The problem with proliferating prepositional phrases lies not only in their ungraceful rhythm but also in the resulting lack of focus—a more serious error. The following are altered versions of paragraphs you read in Chapter 6. Read them aloud, paying particular attention to the intonation, including the points of main stress. Remember that redundant information may be the culprit that keeps the sentence from having a clear focus. Think about new information as you revise these sentences to give them a clearer focus. (You may compare your edited version with the originals on page 109. They are items 1 and 2 of Exercise 17.)

1. Never be an investor in something you don't understand or in the dream of an artful salesperson of some product. Be a buyer, not a sellee. Figure out for yourself what you want to buy (be it life insurance, mutual funds or a vacuum cleaner for the home) and then shop for a good buy before making up your mind. Don't let someone else tell you what the necessities for your life are—at least not if he happens to be the salesman who wants to sell it to you.

2. Plaque has almost become a household word in this country. It is certainly a household problem for most people. But even though everyone is affected by it every day few people really understand

the seriousness of plaque in their daily lives or the importance of controlling it. Plaque is an almost invisible sticky film of bacteria that in the case of all of us continuously forms throughout the day and night. Plaque germs are constantly multiplying and building up on the teeth. Any dentist will tell you that controlling plaque from forming is the single most important step to better oral health for people everywhere.

NOUN PHRASES

The nouns and noun phrases that function adverbially constitute a fairly small category, compared with the other adverbials. Many of them resemble objects of prepositions—that is, prepositional phrases with their prepositions missing:

> I studied [for] *five solid hours* yesterday.
> My vacation begins [on] *Friday* at 5:00 p.m.
> I sent the package [via] *airmail.*

In some cases, the noun or noun phrase following an intransitive verb may look surprisingly like a direct object rather than an adverbial:

> The hikers walked *single file* up the steep trail.
> I study *every night* until 1:00 a.m.
> The children ran *home* as fast as their legs would carry them.

While the referents of these noun phrases are different from those of their subjects, as with transitive, Pattern 5 sentences, their information, the questions they answer, are the adverbial *where* or *when* or *how,* not the *what* or *whom* of the direct object. As a further test that these noun phases are not direct objects, when we try to make the sentences passive, the revision simply won't work:

> *Single file was walked by the hikers.

VERB PHRASES

Another kind of phrase that functions as an adverbial is the verb phrase—in this case, the **infinitive phrase:**

> I got up early this morning <u>to study for my Spanish test.</u>

The infinitive is usually easy to recognize: the base form of the verb preceded by *to,* sometimes called the *infinitive marker.* There's an understood "in order to" meaning underlying most adverbial infinitives:

I got up early this morning in order to study.

The problem known as "dangling" sometimes occurs with the adverbial infinitive phrase. As with other verbs, the infinitive needs a subject; the reader assumes that its subject will be the subject of the main clause, as it is in the example with *study.*

When the subject of the infinitive is not included, the infinitive dangles:

*To keep your grades up, a regular study schedule is important.

*For decades the Superstition Mountains in Arizona have
been explored in order to find the fabled Lost Dutchman
Mine.

Certainly the problem with these sentences is not a problem of communication; the reader is not likely to misinterpret their meaning. But in both cases a kind of fuzziness exists that can be cleared up with the addition of a subject for the infinitive:

To keep your grades up, you ought to follow a regular study
schedule.

For decades people [or adventurers or prospectors] have explored
the Superstition Mountains in Arizona to find the fabled Lost
Dutchman Mine.

The dangling infinitive, which is fairly obvious at the beginning of the sentence, is not quite so obvious at the end, but the sentence is equally fuzzy:

*A regular study schedule is important to keep your grades up.

Two rules will help you use infinitives effectively:

**The subject of the adverbial infinitive is also the subject of the
sentence or clause in which the infinitive appears.**

**An infinitive phrase that opens the sentence is always set off by
a comma.**

DEPENDENT CLAUSES

One of the most important adverbial forms is the dependent clause, which you saw briefly in Chapter 4:

> <u>Because the weasel is wild,</u> it should be approached with great caution.
>
> Yesterday the teacher called the students lazy <u>when they complained about their assignment.</u>

Its importance lies in the information-bearing potential of its subject—predicate structure; it has the information-bearing quality of a complete sentence. As you can see in our two examples, without their opening conjunctions, the dependent clauses are, in fact, complete sentences:

> The weasel is wild.
>
> They complained about their assignment.

The subordinating conjunction indicates the relationship of the dependent adverbial clause to the independent sentence, the main clause. The clause introduced by *because* adds a reason; *when* adds time information. We have many such subordinating conjunctions, words and phrases that connect the clause for a specific purpose:

Time:	*when, whenever, after, as, before, once, since, till, until, now that, while, as long as, as soon as*
Concession:	*though, although, even though, if, while*
Contingency:	*if, once*
Condition:	*if, in case, as long as, unless, provided that*
Reason:	*because, since, as long as*
Result:	*so, so that*
Comparison:	*as, just as, as if*
Contrast:	*while, whereas*

Adverbial clauses are certainly common structures in our language. We use them automatically and often in conversation. But in writing they are not automatic, nor are they always used as effectively as they could be. Two problems that show up fairly often are related to the meaning of the sentence:

1. The wrong idea gets subordinated.
2. The meaning of the subordinating conjunction is imprecise.

Here, for example, are two related ideas that a writer might want to combine into a single sentence:

> We worked hard for our candidates.
>
> We suspected that our candidates didn't stand a chance.

Here are two possibilities for connecting them:

> *Although* we worked hard for our candidates, we suspected they didn't stand a chance.
>
> We worked hard for our candidates, *even though* we suspected they didn't stand a chance.

We need context, of course, to know precisely how the relationship between hard work and the chances of winning should be expressed; but given no other information, the second version expresses what would appear to be the logical relationship.

Perhaps an even more common problem than the imprecise subordinating conjunction is the compound sentence with no subordination—the sentence with two independent clauses, two equal focuses, that might be more accurate and effective with a single focus. The most common culprit is the compound sentence with *but* as the connector. Here, for example, is a paragraph opener in a *New York Times Magazine* article about sleep. The paragraph preceding this one gives examples of accidents on the job connected with work schedules:

> The biological clock is flexible enough to adjust to slight changes in a person's work schedule, *but* in many industries rotations in shift work are so drastic that they play havoc with body rhythms, leaving employees unable to sleep at home and impairing their productivity at work. [Italics added]
>
> —Eric Eckholm

Here the two clauses are clearly not equal: The main idea is the second clause. The idea in the first one, although it has not previously appeared in the article, is presented as understood, the known information. The new information is in the second clause. Revising the sentence to make the first clause dependent, or subordinate—a way of identifying it as background information—will help the reader focus on the new idea:

> *Although* the biological clock is flexible enough . . .

Subordination of the first clause signals the reader that the main idea—the foreground—is coming later. Quite frequently *while*-clauses and *since*-clauses communicate this same kind of message, telling the reader that the information in the dependent clause is already known, knowledge that the reader and writer share.

EXERCISE 24

Turn the following complete sentences into dependent clauses by (1) adding a subordinating conjunction in the opening position and (2) adding the resulting clause to another sentence as a modifier, either at the beginning or at the end. You will have to supply the main clause. See page 157 for a list of subordinators; use at least six different ones in your sentences; try for ten.

Example: The party ended at midnight.

We got home earlier than expected because the party ended at midnight.

or

If the party ended at midnight, why did you get home at 3:00 a.m.?

1. The stock market continued to decline during the last quarter.

2. Myra has lost her fortune in the stock market.

3. Cleo couldn't pay her phone bill last month.

4. There is simply no way to avoid the problem.

5. There were several ways we could have solved the computer problem.

6. Ben couldn't decide which SUV to buy.

7. NCAA recruiting violations have been in the news again.

8. The building across the street burned to the ground last weekend.

9. A great many new teachers will be needed when school starts in the fall.

10. The service sector is a large part of the economy.

Punctuation of Adverbial Clauses

There is one standard punctuation rule that applies to the adverbial clause:

> **An adverbial clause that opens the sentence is always set off by a comma.**

This rule applies no matter how short that clause may be:

<u>If you go to the party,</u> I'll go too.
<u>Even though I'll be bored,</u> I guess I'll go to the party.
<u>When Eric calls,</u> ask him to bring some pizza.

When the adverbial clause closes the sentence, the punctuation will vary, depending on the relationship of the information in the dependent clause to that of the main clause. As a general rule, when the idea in the main clause is conditional upon or dependent upon the idea in the adverbial clause, there is no comma. For example, the idea of the main clause—the opening clause—in the following sentence will be realized only if the idea in the adverbial clause is carried out; thus, the main clause depends on the *if*-clause:

Pat will go to Sue's party if you promise to be there.

In other words, Pat may or may not go to the party. But in the next sentence the dependent clause does not affect Pat's behavior. The comma confirms that lack of effect.

Pat is going to the party at Sue's on Saturday night, <u>even though</u> she knows she'll be bored.

Here's another pair of sentences that illustrates this distinction:

I think that Shawn left the office because he felt sick.
I think that Shawn left the office, because I was just there.

Without the comma, the second sentence would have a different meaning.
The use of the comma with a final adverbial clause is probably one of the least standardized of our punctuation rules. It is one situation where you can use your voice to help you decide about the punctuation: If you put extra stress on the last word in the main clause, or if you detect a slight change in the pitch of your voice at the end of the main clause, you probably need a comma.

The Movability of Adverbial Clauses

The movability of adverbial clauses is especially important from a rhetorical point of view. As a sentence opener, the clause often supplies the transition from the previous sentence or paragraph, usually with a cohesive link of known information. The old standard rule of putting subordinate ideas in dependent clauses and main ideas in main clauses is probably more accurately stated as "known information in the opening clause, new information in the closing clause." And certainly that closing clause could be an adverbial clause, depending on the context. For example, the reason for an action or decision as stated in a *because* clause could easily be the new information.

Although most adverbial clauses occupy either the opening or closing slots of the sentence, they can also occur in the middle, between the subject and predicate or between the verb and complement. In this position the clause will be set off by commas, one before and one after:

> I learn later that night, <u>when ties are loosened during a coffee break,</u> that I am wrong.
>
> —James R. Chiles *(Smithsonian)*

> My brother, <u>when he was only four years old,</u> actually drove the family car for about a block.

That interruption in the usual flow of the sentence slows the reader down. Notice also that it adds stress and length to the word just preceding the clause, and it changes the rhythm pattern. We saw the same principle at work in Chapter 6, when we manipulated the intonation contour of the sentence by shifting word order and changing the punctuation. Ordinarily the subject is in an unstressed valley; it is old information. But a parenthetical comment following it, a word or a phrase or a clause set off by commas, as in our example, puts the subject in a position of stress; the reader will give it extra length and emphasis. Compare the stress given to *brother* in the previous example with the following revisions, where the adverbial clause either opens or closes the sentence:

> When he was only four years old, my brother actually drove the family car for about a block.

> My brother actually drove the family car for about a block when he was four years old.

And it's not only a difference in the stress on *brother* that makes the inserted *when*-clause noteworthy. That internal positioning of the adverbial clause is unusual; it sends a message to the reader that says, "Pay attention. I did this on purpose."

The Because-*Clause Myth*

Because a dependent clause looks so much like a full sentence (remember, it consists of a sentence preceded by a subordinator), it is a prime candidate for fragmenthood—that is, a part of a sentence punctuated as a full sentence. One of the most common such fragments is, apparently, the *because*-clause:

> Everyone agreed that our midterm was unfair. Because our professor included questions about cases we hadn't discussed in class. It turns out she hadn't even assigned them.

It appears that some teachers have discovered a sure-fire way to prevent such fragments: Ban *because* as a sentence opener. As a result, many student writers don't understand that *because* can, indeed, open a sentence, just as all the other subordinating conjunctions can; however, if that *because*-clause is new information, it belongs at the end of the sentence. In the previous example, the *because*-clause should be added to the previous sentence:

> Everyone agreed that our midterm was unfair because our professor included questions we hadn't discussed in class.

It's possible that the *because*-clause is frequently punctuated as a full sentence on the basis of speech. In answer to a spoken question of cause, the natural answer is a dependent clause:

> Why are you late? *Because I missed the bus.*

In this speech situation, the respondent has simply omitted the known information, the information in the question. The response in the following exchange, which includes the known information, is much less likely to occur:

> Why are you late? *I'm late because I missed the bus.*

EXERCISE 25

Combine each of the following groups of sentences into a single sentence, using coordination and subordination. In some cases you may have to reword the sentence to make it sound natural. You can probably come up with more than one possibility for each.

1. The famous Gateway Arch is in St. Louis.
   Kansas City claims the title "Gateway to the West."

2. Our spring semester doesn't end until the second week of June.
   Many students have a hard time finding summer jobs.

3. Thomas Jefferson acquired the Ozark Mountains for the United States in 1803.
   That was the year of the Louisiana Purchase.
   We bought the Louisiana Territory from Napoleon.

4. Auto companies offered enticing cash rebates to buyers of new cars last January.
   Car sales increased dramatically.

5. The neighbors added a pit bull to their pet population, which now numbers three unfriendly four-legged creatures.
   We have decided to fence in our backyard.

6. The human circulatory system is a marvel of efficiency.
   It is still subject to a wide variety of degenerative diseases.

7. Carbohydrates—starches—are the body's prime source of energy.
   Fad diets that severely restrict the intake of starches are nearly always ineffective.
   Such diets can also be dangerous.

8. By 1890 the buffalo population of the West had been nearly wiped out.
   It now numbers more than 60,000.
   About 400 ranchers in Colorado are raising buffalo for meat.

The Elliptical Adverbial Clause

One common variation of the adverbial clause is the **elliptical clause,** one in which something is deleted. Elliptical clauses introduced by the time connectors *while* and *when* are especially common:

> While waiting for the bus, we saw the police arrest a pickpocket at the edge of the crowd.
> When stripped of its trees, the land becomes inhospitable.

Here the deletions of the subject and part of the verb have produced tighter structures, and there is certainly no problem in interpreting the meaning. The understood subject in the elliptical clause is also the subject of the main clause:

> While we were waiting for the bus
> When the land is stripped of its trees

This feature of elliptical clauses—let's call it a rule—is an important one for the writer to recognize:

> **The subject of the main clause is always the understood subject of the elliptical clause as well.**

This rule simply reflects the interpretation that the reader expects. Unfortunately, it is not always followed. Note what has happened in the following sentence:

> *While waiting for the bus, the police arrested a pickpocket at the edge of the crowd.

This sentence reports—no doubt inadvertently—that it is the police who were waiting for the bus. We call that a dangling elliptical clause. The writer should not expect the reader to give the sentence any other interpretation.

◀ FOR GROUP DISCUSSION

Sometimes the information left out of elliptical clauses produces ambiguity— that is, more than one possible meaning.

1. Rewrite the following sentences in two ways to show their two possibilities:

   Joe likes Tracy better than Pat.
   The Lions beat the Badgers worse than the Hawkeyes.

2. Explain how it's possible for both of these sentences to be grammatical:

   My little sister likes our cat better than me.
   My little sister likes our cat better than I.

EXERCISE 26

(1) Underline all of the adverbial structures in the following sentences. (2) Identify the form of each: adverb, noun (or noun phrase), prepositional phrase, verb phrase, or dependent clause. (3) Identify the kind of information it provides: time, frequency, duration, place, reason, manner, condition, direction.

1. To save money, I often eat lunch at my desk.

2. After breakfast let's take the bus to the shopping center.

3. After my dad retired from the navy, he started his own business.

4. We furiously cleaned house to get ready for the party.

5. As soon as the guests left, we collapsed in a heap on the couch.

6. The legislature held a special session last week to consider a new tax bill.

7. When October came, the tourists left.

8. Victoria was crowned queen of England when she was only eighteen years old.

9. African killer bees are slowly making their way northward.

10. At last report, they had reached the southern border of Texas.

11. We stayed home last night because of the snowstorm.

12. If there is no further business, the meeting stands adjourned.

For further practice with adverbials, change the form of the adverbial while retaining the information.

....

FOR GROUP DISCUSSION

In *Notes Toward a New Rhetoric,* Francis Christensen reports a study undertaken by his students in an English class to discover the kinds of structures other than the subject that professional writers use in the opening sentence slot. They selected works (ten fiction, ten nonfiction) of twenty American authors and counted the first 200 sentences. (They omitted quotations, dialogue, fragments, questions, and sentences with postponed subjects—that is, cleft sentences and *there-* transformations. Here are the findings, based on 4,000 sentences counted:

979 (24.5%) had a sentence opener other than subject;

919—in other words, all but 60—were adverbials, including adverbs, prepositional phrases, clauses, and nouns (adverbial infinitives were counted with the verbal group, listed next);

47 were verbal phrases (including infinitives and *-ing* verbs);

13 were other constructions, including adjective phrases and inverted subjects and predicates.

In addition to the 979 sentence openers, there were 266 sentences (6.65%) that opened with coordinating conjunctions (*and, but, or, nor, so, yet, for*).

Examine the sentence openers in your own writing; then compare your percentages with those of your classmates and with the professionals.

(*Note:* One of the works included in the study was Rachel Carson's *The Sea Around Us,* quoted on page 150. Her numbers were the highest among the twenty writers: 79 nonsubject openers in her 200 sentences, 74 of which were adverbials; and 29 conjunctions as sentence openers.)

KEY TERMS

Adverb	Elliptical clause	Sentence modifier
Adverbial	Infinitive phrase	Subordinating
Adverbial clause	Movability	conjunction
Adverb of manner	Prepositional phrase	
Dependent clause	Redundancy	

RHETORICAL REMINDERS

Placement of Adverbials

Have I considered transition and cohesion and the known-new contract in using adverbials?

Proliferating Prepositional Phrases

Have I avoided strings of prepositional phrases that obscure the focus of the sentence and add no new information?

Understood Subjects

Is the understood subject in every elliptical clause also the subject of the main clause?

Is the subject of every adverbial infinitive also the subject of the main clause?

PUNCTUATION REMINDERS

Have I used a comma to set off an adverbial clause that opens the sentence?

Have I used a comma to set off an infinitive phrase that opens the sentence?

CHAPTER 9

Choosing Adjectivals

CHAPTER PREVIEW

The traditional definition of *adjective* is "a word that modifies a noun." Like the word *adverb,* however, *adjective* refers to a word class with particular characteristics, not to a grammatical function. That traditional definition, then, turns out to be a definition not of *adjective* but rather of **adjectival,** the topic of this chapter. And as you saw on the Form and Function chart on page 148, there are many forms that do the work of adjectives, a variety of words, phrases, and clauses that add information to nouns. Given the diversity of forms available for expanding noun phrases, along with the number of roles in the sentence that noun phrases play, you can see that opportunities abound for writers to enhance and enrich their prose in choosing adjectivals.

THE NOUN PHRASE

As you learn about the various forms that function as adjectivals, it is useful to put them in the context of the noun phrase, to picture them in relation to the noun headword. Each of the forms has its designated place, with the headword noun occupying the central position; the single-word modifiers—determiners, adjectives, and nouns—come before the noun headword; the phrases and clauses follow:

determiner   adjective   noun   HEADWORD   phrase   clause

We will take up each of these positions, beginning with the determiners.

PREHEADWORD MODIFIERS

Determiners

Most nouns require a **determiner,** the noun signaler that occupies the opening position in the noun phrase. The determiner class includes articles, possessive nouns, possessive pronouns, demonstrative pronouns, and numbers, as well as a variety of other common words. In both speech and writing you select most determiners automatically. But sometimes in your writing you will want to give that selection deliberate thought.

As the first word in the noun phrase, and thus frequently the first word of the sentence and even of the paragraph, the determiner can provide a bridge between ideas. The selection of that bridge can make subtle but important differences in emphasis, providing transition for the reader—and it can certainly change the rhythm of the sentence:

> <u>The</u> decision that Ben made was the right one.
>
> <u>That</u> decision of Ben's was the right one.
>
> <u>Ben's</u> decision was the right one.
>
> <u>Every such</u> decision Ben made . . .
>
> <u>His</u> decision . . .
>
> <u>Such a</u> decision might have been questionable . . .
>
> <u>A</u> decision like that . . .

In selecting determiners, then, writers have the opportunity to make subtle distinctions and to help their readers move easily from one idea to the next in a meaningful way.

In Chapter 5 we looked at the special problem of the demonstrative pronouns used as subjects when they would be better used as determiners. As with other pronouns, the four demonstratives—*this, that, these, those*—always refer to known information. Any pronoun can become a problem when it has no clear referent—that is, when the information it represents is not, in fact, known. In the case of demonstratives, the problem can be solved by providing a headword and using the pronoun as a determiner. Here is a sentence from Chapter 5 that illustrates the problem:

> My roommate told me she has decided to drop out of school.
>
> *This* took me completely by surprise.

The problem is easily solved:

> *This decision* took me completely by surprise.

We probably don't give much thought to determiners, either as readers or as writers. But with all the choices available, as writers we certainly should. And sometimes determiners need our special attention.

FOR GROUP DISCUSSION

In Chapter 12 we look briefly at the semantic features of nouns that regulate our selection of determiners. For example, the indefinite article *a* signals only countable nouns, while the definite *the* can signal both countables and noncountables.

All the determiners are missing from the following passages. Add them to all the nouns that need them. You'll discover, when you compare your versions with those of your classmates, that for some nouns there are choices—not only a choice of determiner but in some cases a choice of whether or not to use a determiner.

A. Dorothy was little girl who lived on farm in Kansas. Tornado struck farm and carried her over rainbow to land of Munchkins. Soon afterwards she met scarecrow who wanted brain, tin man who wanted heart, and lion who wanted courage. On way to Emerald City four friends met wicked witch who cast spell on them in field of flowers. Witch wanted magic shoes that Dorothy was wearing. When they reached city, as you recall, they met wizard. Story has happy ending.

B. Planet has wrong name. Ancestors named it Earth, after land they found all around them. So far as they thought about planet as whole, they believed for centuries that surface consisted almost entirely of rocks and soil, except for smallish bodies of water like Mediterranean Sea and Black Sea. They knew about Atlantic, of course, but they regarded it as relatively narrow river running around rim of world. If ancients had known what earth was really like they undoubtedly would have named it Ocean after tremendous areas of water that cover 70.8 percent of surface.

—adapted from *The Sea* (Time-Life Books)

There were several nouns in those passages that you left bare, without determiners. Why? How do they differ from the nouns that needed them? In how many cases did you have a choice of adding a determiner or not?

Did you notice a relationship between your use of the articles (*a* vs. *the*) and information—that is, whether known or new information? Which article did you use when a noun was mentioned for the first time? Which for subsequent mentions? What conclusions can you draw about the indefinite *a* and the definite *the?*

Adjectives and Nouns

Adjectives and nouns fill the position between the determiner and the headword. When the noun phrase includes both, they appear in that order:

Determiner	Adjective	Noun	Headword
a	dismal	weather	forecast
the	new	pizza	shop
your	important	career	decision

We frequently use more than one adjective:

You'll notice that there are no commas in the preceding noun phrases, even though there are several modifiers in a row. But sometimes commas are called for. A good rule of thumb is to use a comma if it's possible to insert *and* between the modifiers. We would not say *a recent and covert and military operation* or *an unusual and financial arrangement.* However, we would say *an exciting and innovative concept,* so in writing that phrase without *and,* we would use a comma: *an exciting, innovative concept.*

In general, our punctuation system calls for a comma between two adjectives when they are of the same class—for instance, when they are both subjective qualities like "festive" and "exciting" and "innovative." However, in the noun phrases we saw without commas—*covert military operation* and *unusual financial arrangement*—the two adjectives in each pair are different kinds of qualities. The easiest way to decide on punctuation is to remember *and:*

> **Use a comma between prenoun modifiers if it's possible to use** ***and.***

Sometimes prenoun modifiers are themselves modified or qualified:

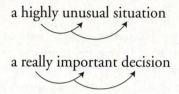

When the first modifier is an *-ly* adverb, as in these two examples, we do not connect it with a hyphen. With other adverbs, however, and with nouns and adjectives as modifiers, we do use a hyphen for these prenoun compound modifiers:

> the English-speaking world
> a four-door minivan

Here the hyphen makes clear that *English* modifies *speaking* rather than *world* and that *four* modifies *door,* not *minivan.*

Here are some other examples of hyphens with prenoun modifiers:

a problem-solving approach	a bases-loaded home run
a poor inner-city neighborhood	a small-town high school teacher
a fuel-injected engine	a well-developed paragraph

Another occasion for hyphens in preheadword position occurs when we use a complete phrase in the adjective slot:

an off-the-wall idea	the end-of-the-term party

Modifier Noun Proliferation. There's a pitfall for writers in this system of prenoun modifiers: the temptation to string together too many adjectives or nouns. It's easy to do. For example, the curriculum committee of the faculty is known as the "faculty curriculum committee." And when the committee meets, it has a "faculty curriculum committee meeting." The minutes of that meeting then become the "faculty curriculum committee meeting minutes." And so on. Such strings are not ungrammatical, but they easily become unreadable.

You can make such noun phrases somewhat easier to read by using an *of* phrase in place of the last modifier in the string:

> a meeting of the faculty curriculum committee
> the minutes of the faculty curriculum committee meeting

EXERCISE 27

Punctuate the following sentences, paying particular attention to commas and hyphens that might be needed in prenoun position. Remember the rule about those commas: If you can add *and*, you probably need a comma. Remember also to apply what you know about punctuating compound sentences and compounds within sentences. You may also have to correct some fused sentences.

1. The administration's recent clean air proposals have been criticized as inadequate not only by environmental groups but also by highly placed government officials from several states.

2. A high ranking federal employee testified at a Congressional hearing on Monday.

3. The stock market reached an all time high last week and will probably keep going up.

4. There was a splendid old table for sale at the auction.

5. A big yellow delivery truck is blocking the driveway and its driver is nowhere to be seen.

6. There was not enough firefighting equipment available this summer for the widespread devastating forest fires in the Northwest.

7. I found an expensive looking copper colored bracelet in the locker room and immediately turned it in to the coach.

8. A commonly held notion among my cynical friends is that big business lobbyists run the country they could be right.

9. I have back to back exams on Wednesday.

10. The highly publicized paper recycling program has finally become a reality on our campus this fall after a year long surprisingly acrimonious discussion.

POSTHEADWORD MODIFIERS

Prepositional Phrases

The adjectival prepositional phrase, which follows the headword noun, is our most frequently occurring postnoun modifier. It is identical in form to the adverbial prepositional phrase we saw in Chapter 7; only its function is different. It's there to add a distinguishing feature to the noun, often defining "which one":

> The security guard <u>in our building</u> knows every tenant personally.
> We had delicious fish and chips at the new seafood restaurant <u>near the marina</u>.
> The meeting <u>during our lunch hour</u> was a waste of time.
> Ed finally found an occasion to meet that beautiful girl <u>with the long red hair</u> <u>in our math class.</u>

Because prepositional phrases are so common, both as adverbials and as adjectivals, they can easily get out of hand. In Chapter 8, you may recall, we pointed out the problem of the proliferating prepositional phrase: the tendency for writers to string them together. Such proliferation can easily obscure the sentence focus. One of the examples in that discussion included a string of five prepositional phrases at the end of the sentence, four of which are adjectival:

> You can undoubtedly find many such sentences in the pages <u>of this book</u> <u>about the grammar</u> <u>of English</u> <u>for writers</u>.

The last three of those four adjectival phrases are not only unnecessary, they obscure the focus of the sentence, which was intended to be on "this book." Those three superfluous phrases add nothing but words—no new information at all.

In place of certain adjectival prepositional phrases, the writer may have the option of using a prenoun modifier:

> an elderly lady with white hair = an elderly white-haired lady
> guests for dinner = dinner guests
> the soliloquy in the second act = the second-act soliloquy
> the problems with the budget = the budget problems
> the final exam in calculus = the calculus final

And sometimes revision may be just a matter of choosing a more precise word:

> a bunch of flowers = a bouquet
> the main character of the story = the protagonist
> birds that fly south in the winter = migratory birds

Adjective Phrases

We have described the usual position for an adjective: between the determiner and the noun headword. However when the adjective is expanded into a phrase with qualifiers or is compounded, it will occupy a position following the headword, where it will be set off by commas:

> The hot, tired Boy Scouts trudged the last mile to their campsite.
> The Boy Scouts, <u>hot and tired,</u> trudged the last mile to their campsite.
> This highly unusual banking crisis calls for extraordinary measures.
> This banking crisis, <u>highly unusual,</u> calls for extraordinary measures.

And in one of the weasel sentences in Chapter 2, we saw an opening adjective phrase when the subject was a personal pronoun:

> Obedient to instinct, he bites his prey at the neck.

In this case, the opening position is the only one that sounds natural; personal pronouns rarely have modifiers in postheadword position.

Unlike the previous examples of adjective phrases, which simply comment on the subject, in the following sentence the adjective phrase in postnoun position clarifies the referent of the noun:

> The students <u>unable to attend the audition</u> will have to make special arrangements with the play director.

Here the modifier tells which students will have to make arrangements.

The punctuation of postnoun modifiers is taken up later in this chapter.

Participial Phrases

One of our most versatile adjectivals is the **participial phrase,** a verb phrase headed by the present or past participle form of the verb.

> The **<u>helicopter</u>** <u>hovering over the roof</u> frightened the dogs.
> We were shocked to see all the homeless **<u>people</u>** <u>living on the streets of Los Angeles.</u>
> The **<u>travelers</u>** <u>going through airport security</u> do not look happy.

You'll notice that these noun phrases with participial modifiers resemble sentences; the only thing missing is an auxiliary:

> the helicopter [is] hovering over the roof
> the homeless people [are] living on the streets of Los Angeles
> the travelers [are] going through airport security

In other words, the noun and the participle that modifies it have a subject–predicate relationship. This is an important feature of participial phrases for you to understand, as you will see later in the discussion of dangling participles.

Why do we use participles? Like adjectives and prepositional phrases, participles add information about the noun headword; and because they are verb phrases in form, they add a whole verbal idea, just as the predicate does. In the first example, the subject, *helicopter,* is the subject of two verb phrases: *hovering over the roof* and *frightened the dogs.* The two verb phrases could have been expressed with a compound predicate:

> The helicopter hovered over the roof and frightened the dogs.

or with a main clause and a dependent clause:

> The helicopter frightened the dogs as it hovered over the roof.

The participial phrase, however, allows the writer to include both verbal ideas in a more concise way. Even more important than conciseness is the clear focus of the sentence with a single predicating verb.

The Prenoun Participle. When the participle is a single word—the verb with no complements or modifiers—it usually occupies the adjective pre-headword position:

> Our <u>snoring</u> visitor kept the household awake.
>
> The <u>barking</u> dog next door drives us crazy.
>
> I should replace that <u>broken</u> hinge.
>
> The old hound growled at every <u>passing</u> stranger.

And, as we saw in the earlier discussion of hyphens, an adverb sometimes modifies the participle:

> a <u>fast-moving</u> object
>
> a <u>well-developed</u> paragraph

Remember, too, that if the adverb in that prenoun modifier is an *-ly* adverb, there will be no hyphen:

> a carefully conceived plan
>
> a fully grown dog

The Movable Participle. We can think of the position following the headword in the noun phrase as the home base of the participial phrase, as it is of the adjectival prepositional phrase. However, the participial phrase can be moved to the beginning of the sentence—*but only if it modifies the subject and if it is set off by commas:*

> Looking out the window, my mother waved to me.
>
> Carrying all of their supplies, the Boy Scouts trudged up the mountain in search of a campsite.
>
> Laughing uproariously, the audience stood and applauded.
>
> Shifting his weight from one foot to the other, the man looked impatient as he waited by the fountain.
>
> Pressured by Congress, the president agreed to support an increase in the minimum wage.

Only those participial phrases that are set off by commas can undergo this shift—that is, only those that are nonrestrictive. (Punctuation of phrases and clauses is discussed on pages 185–187.)

While the single-word participle generally fills the preheadword adjective position, it too can sometimes open the sentence—and with considerable drama:

> Exasperated, she made the decision to leave immediately.
>
> Outraged, the entire committee resigned.

You'll note that both of these openers are past participles, rather than the *-ing* present participle form; they are, in fact, the passive voice. The last participial phrase in the previous set of examples, "*Pressured by Congress,*" is also passive. There the *by* phrase offers a clue. (Underlying it is the sentence "*Congress pressured the president.*") In the case of the single-word participles here, the *by* phrase is understood.

That same participial phrase—the nonrestrictive phrase that modifies the subject—can also come at the end of the sentence:

> The Boy Scouts trudged up the mountain in search of a campsite, carrying all of their supplies on their backs.
>
> The audience stood and applauded, laughing uproariously.
>
> The man looked impatient as he waited by the fountain, shifting his weight from one foot to the other.

The reason for choosing one position over another has to do with sentence rhythm and focus. At the end of the sentence the participle gets much more attention than it would at the beginning or in the home-base position. At sentence end, participial phrases have great flexibility; there's room to spread out and expand, so it's not unusual to see more than one and to see them with embedded modifiers of their own. In opening and closing position they are sometimes called **free modifiers.**

The first two examples are from Jeff Shaara's Civil War story *The Last Full Measure:*

> He [Robert E. Lee]'d been awake even before that, staring up at the dark and thinking of Jackson.
>
> He [Grant]'d been up front again this morning, correcting one officer's mistake, adjusting lines of infantry that had dug in too close to the mouths of their own big guns. The men on the front lines had become wary of the rebel sharp-shooters, stayed low, flinching from the small bits of lead whistling overhead, sent at them from a hidden enemy very far away.

The following passage is from J. M. Coetzee's *Waiting for the Barbarians:*

> They live in settlements of two or three families along the banks of the river, fishing and trapping for most of the year, paddling to the remote southern shores of the lake in the autumn to catch redworms and dry them, building flimsy reed shelters, groaning with cold through the winter, dressing in skins.

And many of the details we learned about weasels in Chapter 2 came by way of participial phrases:

> Outside, he stalks rabbits, mice, muskrats, and birds, killing more bodies than he can eat warm, and often dragging the carcasses home. Obedient to instinct he bites his prey at the neck, either splitting the jugular vein at the throat or crunching the brain at the base of the skull, and he does not let go.

The Dangling Participle. The participial phrase provides a good way to change the focus of the sentence, as we have seen in these variations—but it carries an important restriction:

> **The participle can open or close the sentence *only* if it modifies the subject—that is, when the subject of the participle is also the subject of the sentence and is in regular subject position. Otherwise, the participle will dangle.**

Remember, a participle modifies its own subject. Simply stated, a dangling participle is a verb without a subject:

> *Carrying all of our supplies for miles, the campground was a welcome sight.
>
> *Having swung his five-iron too far to the left, Joe's ball landed precisely in the middle of a sand trap.
>
> * Furiously filling in the bubbles on the answer sheet, the time was up before I could finish the test.

The campground, of course, did not do the carrying; nor did Joe's ball swing the five-iron; and I was the one filling in those bubbles, not "the time." You can fix such sentences (and avoid them in the first place) by making sure that the subject of the sentence is also the subject of the participle:

> Having carried all of our supplies for miles, *we* were exhausted by the time we reached the campground.
>
> Having swung his five-iron too far to the left, *Joe* once again hit the ball into the sand trap.
>
> Furiously filling in the bubbles on the answer sheet, *I* still wasn't able to finish the test before time was up.

Another common source of the dangling participle, and other dangling modifiers as well, is the sentence with a delayed subject—a *there*-transformation, for example, or an *it*-cleft:

> *Having moved all the outdoor furniture into the garage, there was no room left for the car.
>
> *Knowing how much work I had to do, it was good of you to come and help.

In the second sentence, *you* is the subject of the participle, so it's there in the sentence, but it's not in the usual subject position. Sometimes the most efficient way to revise such sentences is to expand the participial phrase into a complete clause. That expansion adds the missing subject:

> <u>After we moved all the outdoor furniture into the garage,</u> there was no room left for the car.
>
> It was good of you to come and help <u>when you learned how much work I had to do.</u>

Even though there is often no problem of communication with dangling and misplaced modifiers—that is, the reader probably knows what you mean—you may in fact be communicating something you hadn't intended: You may be sending a message that says, "Fuzzy thinking."

Our language includes a few participial phrases that we use in sentence-opening position that are not dangling, even though the subject of the sentence is not their subject. They function as sentence modifiers rather than as noun modifiers. The most common are the "speaking of" phrases:

<u>Speaking of</u> old movies, have you seen *Gaslight?*

<u>Speaking of</u> the weather, we should probably cancel the picnic.

There are other *-ing* words that have the status of prepositions. They often open a sentence in order to set up the topic:

<u>Regarding</u> your job interview, the supervisor called to change the time.

<u>Concerning</u> the recent book about the Kennedys, several reviewers have doubted its credibility.

Because of their common use, such expressions have achieved the status of set phrases. Nevertheless, they may be regarded by some readers as too casual or informal for certain writing situations.

EXERCISE 28

Rewrite the following sentences to eliminate the dangling participles. In some cases you may want to expand the participles into full clauses.

1. Having endured rain all week, the miserable weather on Saturday didn't surprise us.

2. Hoping for the sixth win in a row, there was great excitement in the stands when the band finally played "The Star Spangled Banner."

3. Known for her conservative views on taxes and the role of government, we were not at all surprised when the Republican county commissioner announced her candidacy for the General Assembly.

4. Exhausted by the heat and humidity, it was wonderful to do nothing but lie in the shade and drink iced tea.

5. Having spent nearly all day in the kitchen, everyone agreed that my superb gourmet meal was worth the effort.

6. Feeling pressure from the environmentalists, the Clean Air Act was immediately put on the committee's agenda.

7. Obviously intimidated by a long history of defeats in Morgantown, there seems to be no way that our basketball team can beat the West Virginia Mountaineers on their home court.

8. Arriving unexpectedly on a weekend when I had two papers to finish and a big exam coming up, I didn't feel exactly overjoyed at seeing my parents.

Relative Clauses

Another modifier in the noun phrase following the noun is the adjectival dependent clause called the **relative clause,** also called the *adjective clause.* Because it is a clause—that is, a structure with a subject and a predicate—this adjectival modifier is a powerful tool; it enables the writer to embed a complete subject–predicate idea into a noun phrase.

In many respects, the relative clause and the participial phrase are alike. The participial phrase, in fact, is actually a shortened version of the relative clause. All of the examples we saw earlier could easily be expanded into clauses with no change in their meaning:

> The helicopter <u>that is hovering over the roof</u> frightened the dogs.
>
> We were shocked to see all the homeless people <u>who are living on the streets of Los Angeles.</u>
>
> The travelers <u>who are going through airport security</u> do not look happy.

One feature the participle has that the clause does not is its movability: The clause rarely moves out of the noun phrase; it almost always follows the noun it modifies.

The Relatives.   The relative clause is introduced by either a **relative pronoun** (*that, who,* or *which*) or a **relative adverb** (*where, when,* or *why*); the relative plays a part in the clause it introduces. In the case of the relative pronoun (the most common introducer), the part will be that of a noun: a subject, direct object, indirect object, subject complement, object of the preposition, or, as possessive nouns generally function, a determiner.

The relative pronoun *who* has different forms depending on its **case,** its role in the clause—*who* (**subjective**), *whose* (**possessive**), and *whom* (**objective**):

> The man <u>who called last night</u> wouldn't leave his name.

Here *who* is the subject in its clause.

> The student <u>whose notes I borrowed</u> was absent today.

Here the possessive relative, *whose,* is the determiner for *notes.* (You'll recall that "determiner" is a common role for possessive pronouns.) The clause, in normal left-to-right fashion, is "I borrowed whose notes."

> Our dog, Rusty, <u>whom we all dearly loved</u>, was recently killed on the highway.

Here the objective relative, *whom,* is the direct object in its clause: "We all dearly loved whom."

When the relative pronoun is an object in its clause, it can be deleted if the clause is **restrictive**—that is, if the clause is not set off by commas. In the previous example, the clause is **nonrestrictive,** so the relative *whom* cannot be deleted. And you'll notice also that *whom* makes the sentence sound formal, not like something you would say. But in the following example, the *whom* can be omitted, and in speech it certainly would be. Most writers too would probably omit it.

> King Edward VIII gave up the throne of England for the woman <u>(whom)</u> <u>he loved.</u>

The relative pronoun *that* always introduces restrictive clauses; in other words, *that* clauses are never set off by commas:

> You choose a color <u>that you like.</u>
> A boy <u>that I knew in junior high</u> called me last week.
> A truck <u>that was going too fast for road conditions</u> hit our dog.

In the first two preceding sentences, *that* can be omitted. Some writers, in fact, would insist on leaving it out in the second one because it refers to a person; some writers insist on *who* and *whom* in reference to people—not *that.* The easiest and smoothest solution is simply to omit the relative:

> A boy <u>I knew in junior high</u> called me last week.

However, the relative *cannot* be omitted when it functions as the subject in its clause, as in the sentence about the truck. Nor can it be omitted if the clause is nonrestrictive—no matter what role the pronoun fills:

> Rob Miller, <u>whom I knew in junior high,</u> called me last week.

We should note, too, that in speaking this sentence we are more likely to say *who,* even though the objective case of the pronoun is called for; most listeners wouldn't notice the difference. (*Who* actually sounds correct because it's at the beginning of the clause, where the subjective case is found.)

The relative pronoun *which* is generally reserved for nonrestrictive clauses—those set off by commas:

> My roommate's financial problems, <u>which he finally told me about,</u> have caused him a lot of stress this semester.

The relative adverbs *where, when,* and *why* also introduce adjectival clauses, modifiers of nouns denoting place (*where* clauses), time (*when* clauses), and of the noun *reason* (*why* clauses):

> Newsworthy events rarely happen in the small *town* <u>where I lived as a child.</u>
>
> We will all feel nervous until next *Tuesday,* <u>when results of the auditions will be posted.</u>
>
> I understand the *reason* <u>why Margo got the lead.</u>

THE BROAD-REFERENCE CLAUSE

As we have seen, the relative clause is part of a noun phrase—and the antecedent of the relative pronoun that introduces it is the headword of that noun phrase:

> The **students** <u>who live across the hall</u> are quiet today.

> I came to see the **dress** <u>that you bought for the prom.</u>

> Joe's **car,** <u>which he bought last week,</u> looks like a gas guzzler to me.

However, the relative clause introduced by *which,* instead of referring to a particular noun, sometimes has what is called **broad reference:**

> Joe bought a gas guzzler, <u>which surprised me.</u>
>
> Tom cleaned up the garage without being asked, <u>which made me suspect that he wanted to borrow the car.</u>

Here the antecedent of *which* in both cases is the idea of the entire main clause, not a specific noun.

One way to revise this vague broad-reference clause is to furnish a noun that sums up the idea of the main clause, so that the clause will have specific, rather than broad, reference. Note in the revisions that the relative *that* has replaced *which,* and the clauses now have nouns to modify:

> Joe bought a gas guzzler, <u>a decision</u> that surprised me.
>
> Tom cleaned up the garage without being asked, <u>a rare event</u> that made me suspect he wanted to borrow the car.

This solution to the vague antecedent is sometimes called a **summative modifier.**

There are other solutions to the broad-reference *which* clause besides the summative modifier. For example, we could revise the following sentence,

> I broke out in a rash, which really bothered me,

in at least three ways. The first is the summative modifier:

> I broke out in a rash, a problem that really bothered me.
>
> Breaking out in a rash really bothered me.
>
> The rash I got last week really bothered me.

The earlier example about the clean garage also has other possibilities:

> When Tom cleaned up the garage without being asked, I suspected that he wanted to borrow the car.
>
> Tom's cleaning of the garage without being asked made me suspect that he wanted to borrow the car.

While it's true that broad-reference clauses often have a vague quality, sending a message of carelessness, there are times when a *which* in reference to the whole clause makes the point clearly—and, in fact, may be preferred:

> The men my two sisters married are brothers, which makes their children double cousins.

EXERCISE 29

Revise the following sentences to eliminate any instances of the broad-reference *which.*

1. My roommate told me she was planning to withdraw from school, which came as a complete surprise.

2. The first snowstorm of the season in Denver was both early and severe, which was not what the weather service had predicted.

3. The college library has finally converted the central card catalog to a computer system, which took over four years to complete.

4. The president had some harsh words for Congress in his recent press conference, which some observers considered quite inappropriate.

5. Wendell didn't want to stay for the second half of the game, which made Harriet rather unhappy.

6. We're having company for dinner three times this week, which probably means hot dogs for the rest of the month.

7. In his State of the Union message, the president characterized the last two years as a period of "unprecedented prosperity," which one economist immediately labeled "sheer hype and hyperbole."

8. The Brazilian government has grudgingly agreed to consider new policies regarding the rain forests, which should come as good news to everyone concerned about the environment.

FOR GROUP DISCUSSION

The following paragraph, the first one in "Revival Road," a short story by Louise Erdrich, contains nine sentences, with a total of sixteen clauses, seven of which are either adjectival or adverbial. You'll notice, however, that there are many more than sixteen verbs in the sentence. List all the verbs that you find; name their function. Then consider their effect on the overall description.

From the air, our road must look like a length of rope flung down haphazardly, a thing of inscrutable loops and half-finished question marks. But there is a design to Revival Road. The beginning of the road is paved, though with a material inferior to that of the main highway, which snakes south from our college town into the villages and factory cities of New Hampshire. When the town has the money, the road is also coated with light gravel. Over the course of a summer, those bits of stone are pressed into the softened tar, making a smooth surface on which the cars pick up speed. By midwinter, though, the frost has crept beneath the road and flexed, creating heaves that force the cars to slow again. I'm glad when that happens, for children walk down this road to the bus stop below. They walk past our house with their dogs, wearing puffy jackets of saturated brilliance—hot pink, hot yellow, hot blue. They change shape and grow before my eyes, becoming the young drivers of fast cars that barely miss the smaller children, who, in their turn, grow up and drive away from here.

PUNCTUATION OF PHRASES AND CLAUSES

Does this modifier need to be set off by commas? That's the question to be answered about the punctuation of participial phrases and relative clauses in the noun phrase. The question also comes up in the case of certain appositives, which are discussed in Chapter 10.

The answer to the question has to do with the purpose of the modifier: Is it there to identify the referent of the noun being modified—that is, to restrict its meaning—or simply to comment on it. (The traditional terms for the difference are *restrictive* and *nonrestrictive*.)

You may recall back in Chapter 2 you saw the word *referent* in the discussion of sentence patterns: When the subject complement in the *be*-pattern or the linking-verb pattern is a noun or noun phrase, it has the same referent as the subject (*Mary is my sister*). *Referent* means the thing (or person, event, concept, and so on) that the noun or noun phrase stands for: *Mary* and *my sister* refer to the same person. The term *referent* is useful here, too, in thinking about the purpose of the modifier as well as the knowledge of the reader: Is the referent of the noun clear to the reader without the modifier?

In the following sentence, with no other context, the relative clause is needed to identify the referent of the noun phrase *the president:*

> The president <u>who was elected in 1932</u> faced problems that would have overwhelmed the average person.

Ordinarily we would say that the noun phrase *the president* has many possible referents; the *who* clause is needed to make the referent clear; it defines and restricts *the president* to a particular man, the one elected in 1932. But what if the reader already knows the referent from previous context?

> Franklin Delano Roosevelt took office at a time when the outlook for the nation was bleak indeed. The president, <u>who was elected in 1932,</u> faced decisions that would have overwhelmed the average person.

In this context the referent of *the president* is already defined by the time the reader gets to it: The clause is simply commenting, so it needs to be set off by commas. In other words, the commas are sending the message that the *who* clause is extra information, just a comment. You don't need this information to know who is being discussed here. In contrast, the lack of commas in the earlier sentence without context sends the message that the *who* clause is needed to identify the referent of *president*. In other words,

> Restrictive (no commas) = identifying
>
> Nonrestrictive (commas) = commenting[1]

---

[1]*Comment* and *identify* are terms that Francis Christensen introduced in his book *Notes Toward a New Rhetoric*. It is listed under "Punctuation" in the Bibliography.

Punctuation of participial phrases works the same way. When the participial phrase provides information for identifying, or defining the referent, there are no commas:

The merchants <u>holding the sidewalk sales</u> are hoping for good weather.

This lack of commas, then, implies that not all merchants are concerned about the weather—only those who are holding the sidewalk sales. The *holding* phrase is there to tell which merchants are hoping for good weather. In other words, there's another group of merchants who may or may not be concerned about the weather. The lack of commas identifies a particular subgroup of merchants—in this case, those concerned about the weather.

> **Use commas around a nonrestrictive modifier when the modifier is only commenting on the noun rather than identifying it—when the reader already knows the referent or if there is only one possible referent.**

In the punctuation of relative clauses, the relative pronoun provides clues:

1. The *that* clause is always restrictive; it is never set off by commas.
2. The *which* clause is generally nonrestrictive; it is set off by commas. If you want to figure out if your *which* clause needs commas, try substituting *that*. If you can do so without changing the meaning, then the commas can, and perhaps should, be omitted.
3. If the relative pronoun can be deleted, the clause is restrictive:

   The bus (that) I ride to work is always late.
   The woman (whom) I work with is always early.

The next two rules of thumb apply to both clauses and phrases:

4. After any proper noun, the modifier is nonrestrictive:

   Willamette University, which was established seven years before the Gold Rush of 1849, is within walking distance of Oregon's capitol.
   In Alaska, where the distance between some cities is vast, many businesses and individuals own private planes.

5. After any common noun that has only one possible referent, the modifier will be nonrestrictive:

The highest mountain in the world, which resisted the
    efforts of climbers until 1953, looks truly forbidding
    from the air.
Mike's twin brother, who lives in Austin, has a personality
    just like Mike's.
My mother, sitting by the window, is talking to herself.

EXERCISE 30

Decide whether the participial phrases in the following sentences are restrictive
(defining) or nonrestrictive (commenting) and punctuate them accordingly.

1. Many coal miners in West Virginia refused to approve two sections
   of the contract offered by management last week. They maintain
   that the sections covering wages and safety represent no improvement over their present contract expiring on Friday at midnight.

2. A group of students held a protest rally in front of the administration building yesterday. The students hoping for a meeting with
   the provost were demonstrating against the tuition hike recently
   approved by the trustees. The increase expected to take effect in
   September will raise tuition almost 15 percent.

3. The senator and her husband sitting next to her on the speaker's
   platform both looked calm as they waited for the mayor to finish the
   introduction. Then the mayor turning to look directly at the senator
   shocked both the audience and the listeners on the platform.

EXERCISE 31

Combine the following groups of sentences into single sentences by
embedding some of the ideas as modifiers. You will probably want to use
adverbial modifiers as well as adjectivals—participial phrases and relative
clauses you have just been studying in this chapter. In some cases you may
have to make other changes in the wording as well.

1. In many parts of the country, citizens are mobilizing against
   crime and drugs.
   They are driving drug dealers out of their neighborhoods.

2. More and more public officials are supporting the legalization of
   certain drugs.
   They argue that there is no other way to win the drug war.

3. Fingerprints have been used for criminal identification since 1891.
   A police officer in Argentina introduced the method.

The computer has revolutionized the storage and retrieval of fingerprints.

4. The leaning tower of Pisa is 179 feet high.
   It is over 800 years old.
   It leans 17 feet off the perpendicular.

5. In 1997 an earthquake struck the Assisi region of Italy.
   Many priceless mosaics from the 14th century were destroyed.
   The mosaics decorated the walls and ceiling of the Basilica of St. Francis.

6. The highest incidence of colon cancer in the United States occurs in the Northeast.
   The Northeast also has the highest levels of acid rain.
   Cancer researchers suspect that there is a causal link between the two.

7. The rate of colon cancer is related to the amount of carbon dioxide in the air.
   Carbon dioxide absorbs ultraviolet light.
   Ultraviolet light fuels the body's production of vitamin D.

8. Influenza, or flu, is a viral infection.
   It begins as an upper respiratory infection and then spreads to other parts of the body.
   Flu causes aches and pains in the joints.

9. Flu viruses mutate constantly.
   We cannot build up our immunity.
   New varieties spread from person to person and from place to place.

10. The sodium intake of the average American is far higher than necessary.
    The recommended level is 400 to 3,300 mg per day.
    The average American consumes over 4,000 mg per day.

A Punctuation Rule Revisited

The very first punctuation lesson you learned in this book, back in Chapter 2, concerned the boundaries between parts of the sentence:

> Do not use a single comma to separate the required units in the basic sentence.

The punctuation lessons in this chapter perhaps explain why the word *single* was included in that rule. In this chapter you have seen sentences in which a modifier that falls between two units is set off with two commas:

> My mother, sitting by the window, is talking to herself.

You may be tempted to think that here the subject and predicate are separated by a single comma, the comma after *window.* But they are not. It's important to recognize that the second comma has a partner and that the purpose of these commas is to allow the participial phrase into the noun phrase as a modifier. *That particular participle wouldn't be allowed without its two commas.* In other words, that comma is not *between* sentence units: It is part of the subject.

You have learned a great many punctuation rules so far in this book—and there are more to come in the next chapter! Learning those rules in connection with the expansion of sentences, as you are doing, should help you recognize their purposes and use them well. And you can be sure that using punctuation well—using it to help the reader and doing so according to the standard conventions—will go a long way in establishing your authority.

EXERCISE 32

Continue your style inventory. This time count the kinds of sentences you have used in your essay, whether simple, compound, or complex. (The latter refers to a sentence that includes a dependent clause—that is, a clause that functions as an adjectival or adverbial or one that fills a nominal position.) Compare your essay with one written by a professional—perhaps an essay that you've read in your English class or one that your instructor suggests.

	Your Essay	Professional
1. Total number of simple sentences	_____	_____
2. Total number of compound sentences	_____	_____
a. number connected with *and*	_____	_____
b. number connected with *but*	_____	_____
c. number with other conjunctions	_____	_____
d. number with semicolons	_____	_____
3. Number of complex sentences	_____	_____
4. Number with adjectival clauses	_____	_____
5. Number with participial phrases	_____	_____
a. at sentence opening	_____	_____
b. at sentence end	_____	_____
6. Number of opening adverbial clauses	_____	_____
7. Number of other adverbial openers	_____	_____

KEY TERMS

Adjectival
Adjective
Adjective phrase
Broad-reference clause
Commenting modifier
Dangling participle
Defining modifier

Determiner
Free modifier
Headword
Nonrestrictive
    modifier
Noun phrase
Participial phrase

Participle
Prepositional phrase
Relative adverb
Relative clause
Relative pronoun
Restrictive modifier
Summative modifier

RHETORICAL REMINDERS

Prenoun Modifiers

Have I paid attention to commas and hyphens in the noun phrase?

Have I avoided strings of nouns as modifiers?

Postnoun Modifiers

Do opening and closing participles modify the subject of the sentence?

Have I thought about sentence focus in placing the participles?

Does the punctuation distinguish between restrictive (defining) and nonrestrictive (commenting) phrases and clauses?

Have I made a conscious choice in my use of participles and clauses?

Have I avoided fuzzy broad-reference *which* clauses?

PUNCTUATION REMINDERS

Have I used a comma between prenoun modifers where it's possible to use *and?*

Have I used commas around a nonrestrictive modifier when the modifier is only commenting on the noun rather than defining it— when the reader already knows its referent or if it has only one possible referent?

Have I used a comma to set off a verb phrase that opens the sentence? And have I made sure that the subject of the sentence is also the subject of the verb in that verb phrase?

CHAPTER 10

Choosing Nominals

CHAPTER PREVIEW

In the Form/Function chart on page 148, one of the general functions listed on the right is that of **nominal**—the *-al* form of the word *noun.* Up to this point, we've been using the term *noun phrase* for those various NP functions in the sentence patterns that are listed there. You've seen pronouns act as nominals, of course, taking the place of noun phrases; in fact, back in Chapter 1 we encouraged you to discover the beginning and ending of the noun phrase by substituting a personal pronoun. In this chapter, however, you'll see structures other than noun phrases and pronouns as subjects and as direct objects and in the other NP positions—in other words, as nominals.

Before taking up the other forms that fill the noun phrase positions, we will introduce one more nominal function, one that does not show up in the sentence patterns—a nominal position called the **appositive.** It will probably turn out to be very familiar.

APPOSITIVES

We'll begin with some examples of appositives:

Tim, <u>the deli manager at Giant Foods,</u> used to own a restaurant.

<u>An ex-Marine who once played professional football,</u> the security guard at our school makes us feel very secure indeed.

Jack London's novel <u>*The Call of the Wild*</u> was serialized in *The Saturday Evening Post* in the summer of 1903.

Here's an appositive you saw in the previous chapter:

> Most nouns require a determiner, <u>the noun signaler that occupies the opening position in the noun phrase.</u>

Note that when the appositive renames the subject, it can open the sentence, as the second sample sentence illustrates.

You might be tempted to label these underlined structures as adjectivals rather than nominals. While they are noun phrases in form, they do appear to function like other noun modifiers. And that can certainly be a useful way to think of them as you consider adding layers of modification to your sentences. But there is one important difference: the fact that the appositive not only adds information about the noun, it actually *renames* the noun phrase. It could, in fact, take its place:

> The deli manager at Giant Foods used to own a restaurant.

> An ex-Marine who once played professional football makes us feel very secure indeed.

> *The Call of the Wild* was serialized in *The Saturday Evening Post* in the summer of 1903.

> Most nouns require the noun signaler that occupies the opening position in the noun phrase.

Clearly, we've lost some information in these revisions; but as you can see, the appositive could fill the noun phrase position on its own.

Often the appositive is simply a name:

> (1) Our friend <u>Blane</u> drives a snazzy red Miata.

Sometimes that name is set off by commas:

> (2) The judge's husband, <u>Morrie,</u> stays home with the kids.

Because the judge has only one husband (she wouldn't have been elected otherwise!), the purpose of adding the name in sentence (2) is different from the purpose in (1): We would know who stays home with the kids even if the sentence didn't include the husband's name. But in sentence (1), without a name, the reader doesn't know who the Miata driver is: The appositive is there to identify, to define, the referent of the noun phrase "our friend." As you can see, the distinction between restrictive (identifying) and nonrestrictive (commenting) modifiers that you studied in connection with adjectivals applies to appositives as well. In other words, *Blane* restricts the meaning of "our friend." In (2), however, *Morrie* simply comments; the noun phrase, *the judge's husband,* needs no restriction: It has only one possible referent.

There's another important attribute of the appositive to consider. Here's one we used in the discussion of commas and sentence rhythm:

> This role for the comma, <u>to shift the peak of stress,</u> is probably one you hadn't thought about before.

This appositive is an infinitive phrase, a verb phrase, in form. While appositives are nominals, they need not be noun phrases. As you will see later in this chapter, verb phrases, both *-ing* verbs and infinitives, commonly fill nominal roles—and that includes the role of appositive.

FOR GROUP DISCUSSION

The relationship between the appositive and the noun it renames is very much like the relationship between the two NP (nominal) positions in Pattern 2 sentences where "something is something":

> Tim **is** the deli manager at Giant Foods.
>
> The security guard at our school **is** an ex-Marine.
>
> The determiner **is** a noun signaler.

As you can see, we have turned these appositive examples into linking-*be* sentences. But like most writers, you probably don't need instruction for adding *be* to your prose. However, you might want to perform the opposite kind of revision: turning the subject complement of a Pattern 2 sentence into an appositive. This kind of sentence-combining technique can often solve the problem of choppy sentences, as well as the overuse of *be*.

You and your classmates will undoubtedly come up with more than one way to revise the following passages to eliminate the "something is something" opener:

1. *The Lost Colony* is an outdoor symphonic drama that tells the story of the British settlement on Roanoke Island. It has been performed in Manteo, North Carolina, every summer since 1937.

2. Alan B. Shepard was the first American to fly in space. He was launched on a 302-mile suborbital shot over the Atlantic in 1961.

3. The Gateway Arch in St. Louis is the nation's tallest memorial. It commemorates the westward expansion of the United States. It was designed by architect Eero Saarinen. It is made of stainless steel and rises 630 feet high from its foundation.

EXERCISE 33

Underline the noun phrases that are functioning as appositives. Remember, an appositive noun phrase has the same referent as the nominal it renames.

1. Folk songs, simple ballads sung to guitar music, became very popular in the 1960s.

2. One of the best-known folk singers of that period was Arlo Guthrie, son of the legendary songwriter Woody Guthrie.

3. An offbeat film about illegal trash dumping, *Alice's Restaurant* was inspired by Arlo's song of the same name.

4. The theme of many Arlo Guthrie songs, the search for personal freedom, is still appealing today.

5. Gillian Welch, a contemporary folk singer and songwriter, combines simple ballad-like melodies with topical lyrics in two very popular CDs, *Soul Journey* and *Time (The Revelator)*.

6. I went to the concert with my friend Casey, who is Gillian Welch's biggest fan.

The Colon with Appositives

In Chapter 4 we saw the colon in its role as a connector of clauses in compound sentences. Here we see it in its more common role, as a signal for an appositive:

> I'll never forget the birthday present my dad bought me when I was ten: a new three-speed bike.

This sentence can also be written with a comma or a dash instead of a colon:

> I'll never forget the birthday present my dad bought me when I was ten—a new three-speed bike.

Like the dash, the colon is a strong signal, putting emphasis on the appositive; you can think of the dash as an informal colon.

One of the most common uses of the colon is to signal a list:

> Three committees were set up to plan the convention: program, finance, and local arrangements.

Here the list is actually a list of appositives renaming the noun *committees*. The colon is a way of saying, "Here it comes, the list I promised." Sometimes the separate structures in the list have internal punctuation of their own, in which case you will want to separate them with semicolons:

> The study of our grammar system includes three areas: phonology, the study of sounds; morphology, the study of meaningful combinations of sounds; and syntax, the study of sentence structure.

Here each of the three noun phrases in the list has a modifier of its own, set off by a comma; the semicolons signal the reader that the series has three items, not six. This is one of the two occasions in our writing system that call for the semicolon. (The other, you will recall, is the semicolon that joins the clauses in a compound sentence.)

When an appositive series is in the middle of the sentence, we use a pair of dashes to set it off:

> Three committees—program, finance, and local arrangements— were set up to plan the convention.

> All three areas of our grammar system—phonology, morphology, and syntax—will be covered in the grammar course.

If we had used commas instead of dashes, the reader might have been confused:

> *All three areas of our grammar system, phonology, morphology, and syntax, will be covered in the grammar course.

We need the two different marks of punctuation—the dashes as well as the commas—to differentiate the two levels of boundaries we are marking. You'll read more about this issue, the hierarchies of punctuation, in Chapter 13.

Avoiding Punctuation Errors

The use of the colon with appositives is the source of a common punctuation error, but one simple rule can resolve it:

> **The colon that introduces an appositive is preceded by a complete independent clause.**

Notice in the earlier examples that the structure preceding the colon is a complete sentence pattern, with every position filled:

Three committees   **were set up**   **to plan the convention.**
    SUBJECT   VERB   ADVERBIAL

The study of our grammar system   **includes**   **three areas.**
             SUBJECT   VERB   DIRECT OBJECT

Because the colon so often precedes a list, the writer may assume that all lists require colons, but that's not the case. In the following sentences, the colons are misused:

> *The committees that were set up to plan the convention are: program, finance, and local arrangements.
>
> *The three areas of the grammar system are: phonology, morphology, and syntax.

Your understanding of the sentence patterns will tell you that a subject complement is needed to complete a sentence that has a form of *be* (here it's *are*) as the main verb. (You can review the patterns in Chapter 2.)

One common variation for the sentence with a list includes the noun phrase *the following*:

> The committees that were set up to plan the convention are the following: program, finance, and local arrangements.

That noun phrase *the following* functions as the subject complement, so the sentence is indeed grammatical. But it's not necessarily the most effective version of the sentence. When you read the sentence aloud, you'll hear yourself putting main stress on the word *following*—a word with no information. If you want to use a colon in such a sentence for purposes of emphasis, the earlier version is smoother and more efficient:

> Three committees were set up to plan the convention: program, finance, and local arrangements.

It certainly makes more sense for the word *convention* to be emphasized rather than *following*.

The Sentence Appositive

Another effective—and dramatic—stylistic device is the **sentence appositive,** a noun phrase that renames or, more accurately, encapsulates the idea in the sentence as a whole. It is usually punctuated with the dash:

> The musical opened to rave reviews and standing-room-only crowds—<u>a smashing success.</u>

Compare that tight sentence with a compound sentence that has the same information:

> The musical opened to rave reviews and standing-room-only crowds; it was a smashing success.

Here are two other examples, in which the reader's attention will be focused on the final sentence appositive:

> A pair of cardinals has set up housekeeping in our pine tree—<u>an unexpected but welcome event.</u>
>
> In August of 2005 Hurricane Katrina hit the Gulf Coast with winds that clocked 150 mph—<u>the worst natural disaster in the nation's history in over 100 years.</u>

The sentence appositive is similar to the appositives we saw earlier, except that instead of simply renaming a noun, the sentence appositive offers a conclusion about the sentence as a whole in the form of a noun phrase.

The sentence appositive also resembles the summative modifier, which you saw in Chapter 9. You may recall that the summative modifier serves as an alternative to the broad-reference *which*-clause:

> Joe bought a gas guzzler, <u>a decision that surprised me.</u>
>
> Tom cleaned up the garage without being asked, <u>a rare event that made me suspect he wanted to borrow the car.</u>

NOMINAL VERB PHRASES

Gerunds

In Chapter 9 you saw the *-ing* verb functioning as a noun modifier, called the participle:

> The travelers <u>going through airport security</u> do not look happy.

In this chapter we use the same *-ing* form as a nominal, to fill an NP slot. In this function, it is called a **gerund:**

> <u>Going through airport security</u> takes the fun out of air travel.

Here the gerund phrase is the subject of the sentence. We can think of gerunds as names, the way we sometimes think of nouns. But rather than naming persons or places and such, gerunds name actions or behaviors. And like noun phrases, the gerund can be replaced by a pronoun:

> <u>It</u> takes the fun out of air travel.

Gerunds can fill all of the NP positions in the sentence:

> The worst part of the security system is <u>taking off your shoes</u>. (subject complement)
>
> I enjoy <u>jogging early in the morning</u>. (direct object)
>
> My biology professor often begins class by <u>telling weird jokes</u>. (object of preposition)
>
> My dad's hobby, <u>collecting stamps</u>, can be time consuming. (appositive)

The Dangling Gerund. You may recall from the discussions of infinitives and participles that when a verb phrase opens the sentence, the subject of the main clause in the sentence is also the subject of the verb in that opening phrase:

> <u>To do well in school</u>, **a student** should set aside study time on a regular basis.
>
> <u>Having finished the decorations</u>, **the homecoming committee** celebrated with a keg of root beer.

Remember that an opening verb phrase sets up an expectation in the reader that the subject of that verb will follow. When something else follows, the opening verb phrase dangles:

> *<u>Having finished the decorations</u>, the ballroom looked beautiful.

The problem of this dangling participle is obvious: It seems to be saying that the ballroom did the decorating. Remember that a participle modifies its own subject. In this sentence the participle has no subject.

This same kind of dangler, this thwarted expectation, can occur when the sentence opens with a prepositional phrase in which the object of the preposition is a gerund:

> *After finishing the decorations, the ballroom looked beautiful.
>
> *Since cutting down on fats, my cholesterol level has dropped.

The rule about opening verb phrases is straightforward:

> **When a verb phrase opens the sentence (whether an infinitive, a participle, or a gerund in a prepositional phrase), the subject of that verb will be the subject of the sentence.**

Shifting the prepositional phrase to the end of the sentence does not solve the problem. The error may not seem quite as obvious, but the dangling nature of the phrase is still there:

> The ballroom looked beautiful after finishing the decorations.
>
> My cholesterol level has dropped since cutting down on fats.

So whether that verb phrase opens the sentence or simply *could* open the sentence, the subject–verb relationship must be there. A good way to fix these dangling gerunds is to expand the prepositional phrase into an adverbial clause:

> The ballroom looked beautiful after we finished the decorations.
>
> My cholesterol level has dropped since I cut down on fats.

The Subject of the Gerund.   Another feature of gerunds that you'll want to be aware of is the form that their subjects sometimes take. In many cases the subject of the gerund does not appear in the sentence, especially when the gerund names a general activity:

> Jogging is good exercise.
>
> Raising orchids requires patience.

However, when the subject of the gerund appears in the gerund phrase itself, it is usually in the possessive case, especially when the subject is a pronoun:

> I objected to **their** arriving in the middle of the meeting.
>
> **My** objecting didn't make any difference.
>
> There is no point in **your** coming if you're going to be so late.

When the subject is a simple noun, such as a person's name, it too is possessive:

> I was surprised at **Terry's** refusing the job offer.

The possessive noun or pronoun fills the role of determiner. However, when the noun has modifiers, or when it is compound, then the possessive is generally not used:

> I was surprised at **Bill and Terry** turning down that beautiful apartment.

An alternative structure, which may sound more natural, is the use of a clause instead of the gerund:

> I was surprised when Bill and Terry turned down that beautiful apartment.

Infinitives

Another form of the verb that functions as a nominal is the **infinitive**—the base form of the verb with *to*. Like the gerund, the nominal infinitive names an action or behavior or state of being. In fact, the infinitive closely parallels the gerund and is often an alternative to it:

> *Gerund:* Remaining neutral on this issue is unconscionable.
>
> *Infinitive:* To remain neutral on this issue is unconscionable.

Like gerunds, the nominal infinitives can function in all the NP positions:

> My cousin wants to be a farmer. (direct object)
>
> His ambition is to raise organic vegetables. (subject complement)
>
> My sister achieved her goal: to graduate in three years. (appositive)

EXERCISE 34

Underline the nominal verb phrases—both gerunds and infinitives—in the following sentences. Identify the function of each nominal verb phrase. You might want to refer to the sentence patterns in Chapter 2 to refresh your memory.

1. The best thing would be to tell the truth.

2. By remaining silent, you are merely making the situation worse.

3. To ignore the judge's order would be foolhardy.

4. Ms. Graham chose to welcome the new investor into the company.

5. This invitation thwarted his latest plan, to buy up a controlling number of stocks.

6. Our composition teacher instructed us to write three drafts of every assignment.

7. Raising the company's national profile was the new owner's long-term goal.

8. The class finally persuaded the instructor to extend the deadline.

9. I appreciate your proofreading this final version for me.

10. The baby's crying upset the rest of the passengers.

NOMINAL CLAUSES

One of the most common nominal clauses is the one introduced by *that*, known in this role as a **nominalizer:**

> I suspect <u>that our history exam will be tough.</u>
>
> The president recently announced <u>that he will ask Congress for tax cuts for the middle class.</u>

You can see in these examples that we have taken a complete sentence and used it as the direct object in another sentence:

> Our history exam will be tough.
>
> He will ask Congress for tax cuts for the middle class.

In the following sentence, the *that* clause fills the subject position:

> <u>That the common cold is caused by a virus</u> has been clearly established by science.

Any declarative sentence can be turned into a nominal clause in this way. And you'll discover that sometimes we don't even need *that*:

> I suspect [_____] our history exam will be tough.
>
> Derek said [_____] he would be late.

In some cases, however, the *that* may be necessary as a signal to the reader that a clause is coming; its omission may cause the reader momentary confusion:

> Last week I suspected my friend Kim, who never goes to class, was getting into academic trouble.

My uncle knows the stockbroker handling his retirement funds never takes unnecessary risks.

In both of these sentences, the addition of *that* would be helpful to signal the reader that *my friend* and *the stockbroker* are subjects, not objects.

When the *that* clause functions as the subject, the nominalizer cannot be omitted:

> *The common cold is caused by a virus has been clearly established by science.

The nominalizer *that* also allows us to turn a direct quotation into indirect discourse:

> *Direct:* He said, "For the past two years the economy has experienced a serious recession."
>
> *Indirect:* He said that for the past two years the economy had experienced a serious recession.

Many of our nominal clauses are introduced by **interrogatives,** the same words we use for questions:

> I wonder <u>why the students are protesting.</u>
>
> <u>Who will be at the party</u> remains a mystery.
>
> I wonder <u>which brand of yogurt has the least fat</u>

Nominal clauses introduced by interrogatives can also function as objects of prepositions and as appositives:

> *Object of preposition:* These days even kindergartners know a lot about <u>how computers work.</u>
>
> *Appositive:* The students' question, <u>why the summer schedule was changed</u>, has not been answered.

Unlike the nominalizer *that,* the interrogatives cannot be omitted from the clauses they introduce; these clauses are essentially questions under discussion.

NOMINALS AS DELAYED SUBJECTS

The nominal *that* clauses functioning as subjects have a formal quality more characteristic of writing than speech; in fact, such sentences are uncommon in speech:

> That the common cold is caused by a virus has been clearly established.
>
> That Sherry dropped out of school was a shock to us all.

In conversation we are more likely to delay the information in the opening clause by substituting the pronoun *it* for the subject—called the **anticipatory *it*:**

> It has been clearly established that the common cold is caused by a virus.
>
> It was a shock to us all that Sherry dropped out of school.

The infinitive phrase as subject can also be delayed in this way:

> To remain neutral on this issue is unconscionable.
>
> It is unconscionable to remain neutral on this issue.

As you can see, the anticipatory *it* allows us to change the rhythm and stress of the sentence in much the same way that we saw with the *it*-cleft in the discussion of rhythm in Chapter 6 (pages 110–111).

EXERCISE 35

Underline the nominal clauses, gerund phrases, and nominal infinitives in the following sentences. Identify the function that each performs in its sentence.

1. The neighbors never suspected that we had a pet boa constrictor in our house.

2. The guest speaker's e-mail message informed us when he would arrive.

3. Mark's complaining about his grades is getting tiresome.

4. My roommate wants to go to law school.

5. His problem is getting accepted.

6. The worst solitude is to be destitute of sincere friendship. [Francis Bacon]

7. The knowledge that spring break is almost here makes me happy.

8. When I saw the questions that were on the exam, I realized I had studied the wrong chapters.

9. It's almost impossible to predict what will be on the final exam.

10. Why reality shows are so popular simply mystifies me.

KEY TERMS

Anticipatory *it*

Appositive

Dangling gerund

Gerund

Infinitive

Interrogative

Nominal

Nominal clause

Nominalizer

Sentence appositive

RHETORICAL REMINDERS

Have I taken advantage of appositives to tighten my prose, especially where I have used the linking-*be?*

Have I made sure that when opening prepositional phrases have gerunds as objects, the subject of the gerund is also the subject of the sentence?

PUNCTUATION REMINDERS

Have I remembered that a complete independent clause precedes a colon?

Have I set off with commas an appositive that simply comments on, rather than identifies or defines, the referent of the noun it renames?

CHAPTER 11

Other Stylistic Variations

CHAPTER PREVIEW

Everything we say, we say "with **style,**" in one sense of the word—when the word refers simply to an individual's way of writing. You have your own style of writing, just as you have your own style of walking and whistling and wearing your hair. We also use the word *style* to characterize the overall impression of a piece of writing, such as the plain style, the pompous style, the grand style, the official style. When you follow advice about being brief and using simple words, the outcome will be a plain style; words that are too fancy will probably result in a pompous style.

The word *style* is also used in connection with variations in sentence structure, with the structural and punctuation choices that you as a writer can use to advantage. For example, in the second sentence of the previous paragraph, three verb phrases in a series are connected with two *and*s and no commas:

> walking and whistling and wearing your hair

It could have been written with two commas and only one *and:*

> walking, whistling, and wearing your hair

Or only commas:

> walking, whistling, wearing your hair

Such stylistic variations have traditionally occupied an important place in the study of rhetoric. In fact, the Greeks had names for every deviation from ordinary word order or usage, and Greek orators practiced using them. Some of the more common ones, you're familiar with, such **figures of speech** as simile, metaphor, and personification. But many of them, you probably don't even notice—such as the shift, in both this sentence and the previous one, of the direct object to opening position. The Greeks called this inversion of usual word order **anastrophe** (pronounced a-NAS-tro-fee).

In studying this chapter you will use your understanding of grammar as you study stylistic choices. You'll look more closely at variations in the series, along with repetition, ellipsis, antithesis, and sentence fragments.

For some of these variations you'll learn the term the Greeks used. But is that important—to learn their labels? Yes and no. Yes, it's important to know, simply, that they have labels. It's important to know that stylistic choices like these are used deliberately by good speakers and writers. But no, it's not really important that you remember their names. It's enough that you make their acquaintance, that you recognize them when you see them again, and feel comfortable using them.

We begin this chapter with a description of a structure you saw way back on the first page of Chapter 2, but one you haven't seen often since then in these pages: the **absolute phrase.** Rather than an adverbial or adjectival, the absolute is considered a sentence modifier because it functions as a kind of loner, standing beyond the sentence. It has a familiar form—that of noun phrase—but it fills none of the noun phrase positions. We include it here in the discussion of stylistic variations not only because it lends a special flair to a descriptive or narrative passage but also because the well-chosen absolute phrase sends the reader a message, a message about the writer's craftsmanship and ability and style.

The purpose of this chapter, then, is to raise your consciousness about style, to encourage you to make the kinds of stylistic choices that send a message to your reader: "Pay attention! Read this carefully. It's important."

ABSOLUTE PHRASES

You saw two absolute phrases on the first page of Chapter 2 in our old familiar weasel paragraph:

> A weasel is wild. Who knows what he thinks? He sleeps in his underground den, <u>his tail draped over his nose</u>.... One naturalist refused to kill a weasel who was socketed into his hand deeply as a rattlesnake. The man could in no way pry the tiny weasel off, and he had to walk half a mile to water, <u>the weasel dangling from his palm,</u> and soak him off like a stubborn label.

If you recall the formula for the noun phrase that opened Chapter 9, you'll recognize that both of these examples follow the pattern:

determiner + noun headword + participial phrase

Absolute phrases are, indeed, noun phrases. This pattern, with a participial phrase as the postheadword modifier, is our most common form of the absolute, although sometimes that modifier is itself a noun phrase, sometimes a prepositional phrase.

Our two weasel examples illustrate one of the two styles of absolutes, the phrase that adds a detail or point of focus to the idea stated in the main clause. Notice in the third sentence how the main clause describes the overall scene, the weasel asleep in his underground den; the absolute phrase moves the reader in for a close-up view, focusing on a detail, just as a filmmaker uses the camera. The example in the last sentence works the same way: The main clause gives us the long shot of the man walking; the absolute focuses on the weasel dangling from his palm.

With only one small addition to these absolutes, the relationship of the noun headword and its modifier becomes clear:

His tail (is) draped over his nose.

The weasel (is) dangling from his palm.

In other words, the absolute actually adds a subject–predicate relationship to its sentence, but does so without actually adding another clause. That third sentence,

The weasel sleeps in his underground den, his tail draped over his nose,

is neither "compound" nor "complex"; in fact, it would be classified as "simple" in traditional grammar, since it has only one clause. However, you can see that it has the impact of a complex sentence, given that it includes what is essentially a subordinate subject–predicate construction.

As you read the sentences containing these two examples, you can probably hear your voice giving emphasis to the noun headword of the absolute phrase. The absolute invariably calls attention to itself, sending a "Pay attention!" message to the reader. For that reason, writers often reserve the absolute for important details. It also sends a more subtle message: "I have crafted this sentence carefully; I know what I'm doing." Even though a reader may not be able to name, perhaps not even to consciously recognize, the absolute phrase, that reader will certainly recognize a writer in control. The well-chosen absolute can add to the writer's authority.

The absolute phrase that adds a focusing detail is especially common in fiction writing, much more common than in expository writing—such as the prose in this textbook and probably your texts for other classes. In the following passages, all from works of fiction, some have a participle as the postnoun modifier, just as Annie Dillard has in her weasel description; however, you'll also see some with noun phrases, others with prepositional phrases.

> There was no bus in sight and Julian, <u>his hands still jammed in his pockets and his head thrust forward,</u> scowled down the empty street.
>
> —Flannery O'Connor
("Everything That Rises Must Converge")

> He smiled a little to himself as he ran, holding the ball lightly in front of him with his two hands, <u>his knees pumping high, his hips twisting in the almost girlish run of a back in a broken field.</u>
>
> —Irwin Shaw ("The Eighty-Yard Run")

In this series of three absolutes, the first and third have noun phrases as the postnoun modifiers: tiny ribbons of light; a purple hollow. . . :

> He saw the city spread below like a glittering golden ocean, <u>the streets tiny ribbons of light, the planet curving away at the edges, the sky a purple hollow extending to infinity.</u>
>
> —Anne Tyler (*The Accidental Tourist*)

And these two examples have prepositional phrases:

> Silently they ambled down Tenth Street until they reached a stone bench that jutted from the sidewalk near the curb. They stopped there and sat down, <u>their backs to the eyes of the two men in white smocks who were watching them.</u>
>
> —Toni Morrison (*Song of Solomon*)

> The man stood laughing, <u>his weapons at his hips.</u>
> —Stephen Crane ("The Bride Comes to Yellow Sky")

In this example, the first absolute phrase adds a detail to the dining event with a prepositional phrase as the modifier; the second, rather than focusing on a detail, explains the significance of the scene described:

> Most days she left the adding machine set up on the kitchen table, so we cleared space around it when we ate, <u>usually just</u>

<u>one or two of us at a time,</u> <u>family dinners long since a thing</u>
<u>of the past.</u>

—Richard Russo (*Bridge of Sighs*)

A second style of absolute phrase, rather than focusing on a detail, explains a cause or condition:

<u>Our car having developed engine trouble,</u> we stopped for the night at a roadside rest area.

We decided to have our picnic, <u>the weather being warm and clear.</u>

<u>Victory assured,</u> the fans stood and cheered during the last five minutes of the game.

The first example could be rewritten as a *because-* or *when-* clause:

<u>When our car developed engine trouble,</u> we stopped . . .

or

<u>Because our car developed engine trouble,</u> we stopped . . .

The absolute allows the writer to include the information without the explicitness of the complete clause; the absolute, then, can be thought of as containing both meanings, both *when* and *because.* The absolute about the weather in the second example suggests an attendant condition rather than a cause.

Here's a familiar (and hotly debated) absolute of this style:

A well-regulated militia being necessary to the security of a free state, the right of the people to keep and bear arms shall not be infringed.

This rendering of the Second Amendment does not include two commas that appear in the original: one following *militia* and one following *arms.* Punctuation conventions have changed in the past two centuries.

As you can probably hear, this second style of absolute adds a formal tone to the sentence, formal almost to the point of stiffness. It's certainly not a structure that's used in speech. In fact, neither of these two styles of absolute phrases is used in speech—in speeches, perhaps, but certainly not in everyday speech.

FOR GROUP DISCUSSION

We could add *with* to most, if not all, of the examples, thus turning the absolute phrases into prepositional phrases:

The man stood laughing, <u>with his weapons at his hips.</u>

There was no bus in sight and Julian, <u>with his hands still jammed in his pockets and his head thrust forward,</u> scowled down the empty street.

Try the other examples as well, with the added *with*.

How would you characterize the difference in the two styles? Has the meaning changed at all?

EXERCISE 36

Expand the following sentences by adding the modifiers called for. (You might want to review participial phrases and relative clauses in Chapter 9.)

1. Add a *who-* clause that tells what one of your relatives is usually like: My cousin (aunt, uncle, sister, etc.), who _____

_____,

surprised everyone at the family reunion.

Now add a dependent clause that explains what your relative did that was so surprising. Now add an absolute phrase at the end of the sentence—a close-up detail.

2. Add a series of participial phrases that tell what the cyclists were doing: From the window we watched the cyclists _____

_____.

Now add an appositive at the end of the sentence as a comment on the whole scene.

3. Use an appositive to describe the trucker: At the far end of the counter sat a trucker, _____

_____.

Now add two prenoun modifiers to explain what sort of counter it is so that the reader will be better able to picture the scene—and an absolute at the end that provides a close-up detail.

4. Start this sentence with an adverbial clause or phrase that tells when: _____

_____,

endless cars jammed the freeway.

Now add a series of absolute phrases that describe the cars.

> 5. Write a sentence or paragraph describing your classroom or campus. Use the modifiers you have been practicing with.

THE COORDINATE SERIES

Many of the variations that writers use for special effects occur in connection with coordinate structures—pairs and series of sentences and their parts. One of those changes is a deviation in the use of conjunctions. Let's go back to the variations possible for the second sentence in the Chapter Preview:

> You have your own style of writing, just as you have your own style of walking and whistling and wearing your hair.

This style, with that extra *and,* was labeled **polysyndeton** by the Greek rhetoricians. You'll recall from the discussion of the serial comma in Chapter 4 that the usual punctuation for the series includes commas until the final *and:*

> walking, whistling, and wearing your hair

Opposite of the extra *and* is the series with no conjunction at all, just commas, a style called **asyndeton:**

> walking, whistling, wearing your hair

The differences are subtle but meaningful. Polysyndeton puts emphasis on each element of the series with a fairly equal beat: _____ and _____ and _____. As Arthur Quinn notes in *Figures of Speech* (see the Bibliography), polysyndeton slows us down, perhaps adds a sense of formality, while asyndeton speeds us up. And asyndeton, the variation with no *ands,* also suggests that the list is open-ended. It seems to suggest, "I could go on and on; I could tell you much more."

In the following passage, Winston Churchill describes Stonewall Jackson using asyndeton in both series; he has embedded one such series within another:

> His character was stern, his manner reserved and unusually forbidding, his temper Calvinistic, his mode of life strict, frugal, austere.

The omission of the conjunctions contributes to the strictness and frugality of style that echo the words themselves. With conjunctions, the sentence would lose that echo:

> His mode of life was strict and frugal and austere.

In the following sentence from *A Not Entirely Benign Procedure: Four Years as a Medical Student,* Perri Klass uses asyndeton to help convey the pressure of medical school:

> The general pressure in medical school is to push yourself ahead into professionalism, to start feeling at home in the hospital, in the operating room, to make medical jargon your native tongue—it's all part of becoming efficient, knowledgeable, competent.

And in the following sentence by Annie Dillard, this one from her memoir, *An American Childhood,* she uses both stylistic variations: asyndeton in the opening and the final series; polysyndeton in the series with *or:*

> As for loss, as for parting, as for bidding farewell, so long, thanks, to love or a land or a time—what did I know of parting, of grieving, mourning, loss?

Perhaps the series is not a feature of language that you've thought much about in your writing. But as these examples illustrate, a well-constructed series can add a great deal of stylistic flair. And while it's not important that you remember their labels, now that you know about polysyndeton and asyndeton, you can add these devices to your collection of writers' tools with the assurance that using them will make the reader pay attention and, what's even more important, recognize your competence and authority as a writer.

REPETITION

Repetition has come up before in these pages—in both a positive and a negative sense. On the positive side, repetition gives our sentences cohesion: The known–new contract calls for the repetition, if not of words, then of ideas. It is part of the glue that holds paragraphs together. But we also have a negative label for repetition when it has no purpose, when it gets in the reader's way: Then we call it *redundancy.* You may recall the discussion of redundancy in connection with flabby prepositional phrases that added nothing but words to the sentence and kept the reader from focusing on the new information.

If you've heard warnings about redundancy, if you've seen "red" in the margins of your essays, you might hesitate to use repetition deliberately. But don't hesitate. It's easy to distinguish redundancy from good repetition, from repetition as a stylistic tool. You saw examples of good repetition in the discussion of parallelism as a cohesive device in Chapter 5.

In an essay on redundancy and ellipsis as writing strategies, listed in the Bibliography, Keith Grant-Davie reports that redundancy "is widely seen as a kind of linguistic cholesterol, clogging the arteries of our prose and impeding the efficient circulation of knowledge" (455). On the other hand, effective redundancy contributes "good cholesterol," especially in the field of technical writing.

While "good cholesterol" was not a term they used, the Greek rhetoricians had a label for every conceivable kind of good repetition—from the repetition of sounds and syllables to that of words and phrases in various locations in the sentence. We confine our discussion to repetition in coordinate structures that make the reader sit up and take notice. Again, to emphasize their importance as tools, we use their ancient labels.

Consider the Gettysburg Address. Which of Lincoln's words, other than "Fourscore and seven years ago," do you remember? Probably "government of the people, by the people, and for the people." It's hard to imagine those words without the repetition: "Of, by, and for the people" just wouldn't have the same effect. Lincoln's repetition of the same grammatical form is called **isocolon.** And think about President Kennedy's stirring words, with his repetition of *any* to signal five noun phrases:

> [We] shall pay any price, bear any burden, meet any hardship, support any friend, oppose any foe to assure the survival and the success of liberty.

Notice, too, Kennedy's use of asyndeton. He seems to be saying, "I could go on and on with my list."

You don't have to be a president to use that kind of repetition, nor do you have to reserve it for formal occasions. Whenever you use a coordinate structure, there's an opportunity for you to add to its impact with repetition, simply by including words that wouldn't have to be included. The following sentence, from an essay in *Time* by Charles Krauthammer, could have been more concise, but it would have lost its drama:

> There is not a single Western standard, there are two: what we demand of Western countries at peace and what we demand of Western countries at war.

The following example of isocolon, the repetitions in the *of*- phrases, is part of a paragraph from Virginia Woolf's essay "How Should One Read a Book?" Notice also the asyndeton in the paragraph's opening sentence:

> It is simple enough to say that since books have classes— fiction, biography, poetry—we should separate them and take from each what it is right that each should give us. Yet few people ask from books what books can give us. Most commonly we come to books with blurred and divided minds,

asking of fiction that it shall be true, of poetry that it shall be false, of biography that it shall be flattering, of history that it shall enforce our own prejudices. If we could banish all such preconceptions when we read, that would be an admirable beginning.

A series of clauses too can be dramatized by repetition. The following sentence by Terrence Rafferty is from a review of the movie *Mountains of the Moon,* which appeared in the *New Yorker.* Here too the repetition helps to persuade the reader of the accuracy of the description "an intellectual adventurer":

> He [Sir Richard Burton] had travelled widely, in Europe, Asia, and Africa; he had mastered a couple of dozen languages; he had written seven books; and he had made a reputation as an intellectual adventurer, a man whose joy was to immerse himself in other cultures, to experience everything—even (or perhaps especially) things that his countrymen loathed and feared.

The Greeks called this repetition of clause openings **anaphora.**

The repetitions we have seen so far are contained within sentences, in compound structures—verb phrases in Kennedy's speech, clauses in the Krauthammer and Rafferty sentences, prepositional phrases in the Woolf passage. But whole sentences with obvious repeated elements not only add a stylistic flair beyond the sentence level, they contribute a great deal to the cohesion of a paragraph and beyond. We saw a number of examples in Chapter 5. You may recall the paragraph about Portland (page 94) where one sentence begins with *Its eastern border is* and the following one with *Its western border is.* In a paragraph illustrating parallelism on page 102, four successive sentences begin with *It can be.* These are both examples of anaphora, the repetition of clause openings.

These kinds of repetition are obviously not the artery-clogging kind of redundancy. Rather than hindering the flow of the sentence or paragraph, they enhance it. And they certainly send a message to the reader that the writer has crafted the work with care.

◀ FOR GROUP DISCUSSION

Shakespeare, of course, was a master of all kinds of stylistic variations. If you've read *The Merchant of Venice,* you may remember these well-known words, spoken by Shylock in Act III, Scene I:

> He hath disgrac'd me, and hind'red me half a million, laugh'd at my losses, mock'd at my gains, scorn'd my nation, thwarted

my bargains, cool'd my friends, heated mine enemies; and what's his reason? I am a Jew. Hath not a Jew eyes? Hath not a Jew hands, organs, dimensions, senses, affections, passions? Fed with the same food, hurt with the same weapons, subject to the same diseases, heal'd by the same means, warm'd and cool'd by the same winter and summer, as a Christian is? If you prick us, do we not bleed? If you tickle us, do we not laugh? If you poison us, do we not die? And if you wrong us, shall we not revenge?

A. Identify the various rhetorical figures that Shakespeare has used here. In what ways does the sentence style enhance the meaning of Shylock's words?

B. Examine your own use of compound structures or those of a class-mate in a peer review session. Look for places where one or more of the stylistic variations you have read about here—polysyndeton, asyndeton, isocolon, and anaphora—would enhance the effective-ness of the writing. For example, you might add details by turning a compound structure into a series. You'll want to bear in mind that these variations can affect the focus and rhythm.

WORD-ORDER VARIATION

A number of the classical rhetorical schemes have to do with variation in normal subject-verb-complement word order, as we saw in the examples of *anastrophe* in the Chapter Preview. Such deviations are especially common in poetry. In reading poetry, we're always on the lookout for subjects and predicates in unexpected places. Here, for example, is the opening of Robert Frost's famous poem "Stopping by Woods on a Snowy Evening":

Whose woods these are, I think I know.

In this line the opening clause is the direct object of *know*:

I think I know *something*.

This inversion of word order can also be effective in prose, mainly because we're not looking for it. It can put stress on the verb, just as it did in Frost's line. In one of the earlier examples cited from this chapter,

But many of them, you probably don't even notice,

the verb is in line for end focus. And in the following sentence, Charles Dickens made sure that the reader would hear the contrast between *has* and *has not:*

> Talent, Mr. Micawber has; money, Mr. Micawber has not.

Another variation in word order occurs with certain adverbs in opening position, when a shift of subject and auxiliary is required:

> Never before <u>had I seen</u> such an eerie glow in the night sky.
>
> Rarely <u>do I hear</u> such words of praise.

You'll notice that the opening adverbial is a peak of stress. The reader will focus on that opening negative—and will pay attention.

The following sentence, written by Winston Churchill, illustrates yet another kind of shift in word order. Here the very last noun phrase in the sentence is the grammatical subject:

> Against Lee and his great Lieutenant [Stonewall Jackson], united for a year of intense action in a comradeship which recalls that of Marlborough and Eugene, were now to be marshalled the overwhelming forces of the Union.

When you read this sentence aloud, you can hear your voice building to a crescendo on *overwhelming forces,* just as Churchill planned. In fact, it's hard to read the sentence without sounding Churchillian. The sentence leaves the reader in suspense until the end.

The inversion in this passage, from *The Templars* by Piers Paul Read, produces something of that same Churchillian effect:

> The conversion of Constantine was of momentous consequence for Christianity. Equally significant for the future of the Empire was his decision to move its capital from Rome to Byzantium on the Bosphorus.

In Chapter 9 we saw another variation in the expected word order when we shifted adjective phrases from their usual preheadword position:

> <u>Hot and tired,</u> the Boy Scouts trudged the last mile to their campsite.
>
> The Boy Scouts, <u>hot and tired,</u> trudged the last mile to their campsite.

> <u>Highly unusual,</u> the situation called for extraordinary measures.
>
> The situation, <u>highly unusual,</u> called for extraordinary measures.

These shifts are less dramatic than Churchill's, but they do change the emphasis and call attention to themselves. In both versions, they put the strong stress on the subject, rather than on the predicate, its usual place. The reader of the Boy Scout sentence will not be surprised to read on about the physical condition of the boys. If the writer had not called attention to the adjectives, the reader might have expected to read about the campsite in the next sentence. Likewise, in the other example, both versions put strong stress on the subject. Read them aloud, then compare your reading with this version:

The highly unusual situation called for extraordinary measures.

You probably heard the highest peak of stress on the word *extraordinary* rather than on the subject. The reader of this version will expect to learn more about those measures; in the other two versions the reader probably expects to read more about the situation and what makes it unusual.

All of these word order variations change the rhythm patterns and thus the messages that the reader will get. As a writer, you will want to construct your sentences with the reader and the reader's expectations in mind.

FOR GROUP DISCUSSION

In the following paragraph, the opening paragraph of Chapter 5 in Daniel J. Boorstin's *The Discoverers,* you'll find two sentences that illustrate anastrophe:

> While man allowed his time to be parsed by the changing cycles of daylight, he remained a slave to the sun. To become the master of his time, to assimilate night into the day, to slice his life into neat, usable portions, he had to find a way to mark off precise small portions—not only equal hours, but even minutes and seconds and parts of seconds. He would have to make a machine. It is surprising that machines to measure time were so long in coming. Not until the fourteenth century did Europeans devise mechanical timepieces. Until then, as we have seen, the measuring of time was left to the shadow clock, the water clock, the sandglass, and the miscellaneous candle clocks and scent clocks. While there was remarkable progress five thousand years ago in measuring the year, and useful week clusters of days were long in use, the subdivided day was another matter. Only in modern times did we begin to live by the hour, much less by the minute.

A. You'll notice that the two sentences illustrating anastrophe also include the shift of the subject and the auxiliary verb. What do they have in common with those examples with *never before* and *rarely* in the discussion? Note as well other figures of speech that Boorstin uses here.

B. Note the variation in sentence length. Where do you find the topic sentence in this paragraph?

C. In Chapter 7 you read about metadiscourse; you'll find two examples in this paragraph. What effect do they have on you as a reader?

ELLIPSIS

Another fairly common stylistic variation—another that the Greeks used in their oratory—is **ellipsis,** which refers to a sentence in which a part is simply left out, or understood. As you might expect, they had many names for this variation, depending on the kind of structure deleted. We use the umbrella term *ellipsis* for all of them.

One example we've already seen is Churchill's description of Stonewall Jackson:

> His character was stern, his manner reserved and unusually forbidding, his temper Calvinistic, his mode of life strict, frugal, and austere.

And you saw this sentence as an illustration of the series without conjunctions, asyndeton; however, it's also a good example of ellipsis, where all the clauses except the first are missing the verb: "his manner [was] reserved . . . his temper [was] Calvinistic," and so on. Here are some other, similar, examples, where part of the second clause or phrase is left out to avoid repetition:

> The first day of our vacation was wonderful; the second, miserable.
>
> For breakfast we had eggs; for lunch, eggs; and for dinner, eggs again.
>
> Some of our games this season were awesome; others awful.
>
> Percy always orders the extra-large latte for himself; for me, the medium. He gets his with sugar; I get mine without.

Note that within the sentence a comma sometimes signals the omission, depending on the rhythm, where the pause produced by the comma may be needed to help the reader. As you can hear when you read these sentences, this use of ellipsis gives them a tight, controlled quality that would be missing if the clauses were complete.

In some clauses of comparison, the ellipsis is required by our grammar:

I'm a week older than Terry [is old].
My sister isn't as tall as I [am tall].

or

I'm a week older than Terry is [old].
My sister isn't as tall as I am [tall].

These structures are not a problem for native speakers; we use them automatically. But some elliptical clauses are not quite as obvious; they can be left dangling, as we saw in the discussion on pages 163–164.

*While waiting for the bus, the police arrested a pickpocket at the edge of the crowd.

As you may recall from Chapter 8, the subject of that *while-* clause must be the same as the subject of the main clause:

While [we were] waiting for the bus, we saw the police arrest a pickpocket at the edge of the crowd.

In this case, if you prefer to stay with *the police* as the subject of the main clause, there's an easy solution: Simply get rid of the ellipsis; write out the clause in full:

While we were waiting for the bus, the police arrested . . .

When well used, ellipsis can create a bond of sorts between the writer and the reader. The writer is saying, in effect, I needn't spell everything out for you; I know you'll understand.

You may be thinking at this point that if you actually used such sentences in your essays your teacher would mark them as sentence fragments and ask you to correct them. But that's not likely. Clearly, these elliptical sentences are not accidental; in fact, the opposite message will get through to the reader: "Pay attention. I crafted this sentence carefully."

We should note that *ellipsis* is also the term we use to refer to the string of periods, or *ellipsis points,* that indicate to the reader that we have left something out of quoted material. You can read more about this punctuation convention on page 276 in the Glossary of Punctuation.

ANTITHESIS

In his book on classical rhetoric, referred to in an earlier chapter (also listed in the Bibliography), Edward P. J. Corbett defines **antithesis** as "the juxtaposition of contrasting ideas, often in parallel" (464); among his examples illustrating this figure of speech are the words of Neil Armstrong as he stepped on the moon in 1969:

> That's one <u>small step for a man,</u> one <u>giant leap for mankind.</u>

This example is from George W. Bush's second inaugural address:

> Across the generations we have proclaimed the imperative of self-government because <u>no one is fit to be a master</u> and <u>no one deserves to be a slave.</u>

Benjamin Franklin included this example of antithesis in a letter he wrote in 1783:

> There never was <u>a good war,</u> or <u>a bad peace.</u>

Don't get the idea that world-changing events and presidential speeches are the only occasions for antithesis. Advertisers often use the same kind of juxtaposition of contrasting ideas. Here are some headlines from magazine ads published in *Atlantic* and *Harper's* :

> Before our <u>engineers design our cars,</u> our <u>racing programs design our engineers.</u>
>
> <u>Felt</u> but <u>not seen.</u> Because our miracle is on the inside . . . [mattress ad]
>
> We only <u>live once.</u> But we <u>sit many, many times.</u> [chair ad]
>
> You <u>can't see</u> the innovative technology. But you <u>can certainly hear</u> it. [sound system]

The first one is a clever play on words; in the last three, the negative comment is there to contrast with, and thus enhance, the positive quality being promoted. Earlier we saw an example of antithesis in a quotation from Dickens used to illustrate word order variation:

> Talent, Mr. Micawber <u>has;</u> money, Mr. Micawber <u>has not.</u>

The following example is a portion of the paragraph that follows the Boorstin paragraph about clocks quoted in the Group Discussion activity on page 217. It includes the kind of antithesis that you are likely to see in works you are reading—and also to use—where contrasts are included to emphasize the point:

> The first steps toward the mechanical measurement of time, the beginnings of the modern clock in Europe, <u>came not from</u> farmers or shepherds, <u>nor from</u> merchants or craftsmen, <u>but from</u> religious persons anxious to perform promptly and regularly their duties to God. Monks needed to know the times for their appointed prayers. In Europe the first mechanical clocks were designed <u>not to *show*</u> the time <u>but to *sound*</u> it. . . . [author's emphasis]

In his autobiography, *Long Walk to Freedom,* Nelson Mandela uses antithesis to explain the importance of education:

> Education is the great engine of personal development. It is through education that <u>the daughter of a peasant can become a doctor,</u> that <u>the son of a mineworker can become the head of the mine,</u> that <u>a child of farmworkers can become the president of a great nation.</u> It is what we make out of <u>what we have, not what we are given,</u> that separates one person from another.

In the discussion of cohesion in Chapter 5 we also saw antithesis, where Stephen Jay Gould contrasts "violence, sexism, and general nastiness" with "peacefulness, equality, and kindness." And the Virginia Woolf example of anaphora we saw earlier also illustrates antithesis: "asking of fiction that it shall be true, of poetry that it shall be false. . . ."

THE DELIBERATE FRAGMENT

The sentence fragments used for their stylistic effect are not the kind that teachers mark with a marginal "frag"; those are usually the result of punctuation errors, often a dependent clause punctuated as a full sentence. But experienced writers know how to use fragments deliberately and effectively—noun phrases or verb phrases that add a detail without a full sentence and invariably call attention to themselves. Here are two examples from the novels of John le Carré:

> Our Candidate begins speaking. <u>A deliberate, unimpressive opening.</u>
>
> —*A Perfect Spy*

> He began packing up his desk. <u>Precisely.</u> <u>Packing to leave.</u> <u>Opening and shutting drawers.</u> <u>Putting his file trays into his steel cupboard and locking it.</u> <u>Absently smoothing back his hair between moves, a tic that Woodrow had always found particularly irritating in him.</u>
>
> —*The Constant Gardener*

Barack Obama opens Chapter 5 of his memoir, *Dreams from My Father,* with three sentence fragments in two sentences. The second sentence has two fragments, an absolute phrase and a noun phrase:

> Three o'clock in the morning. The moon-washed streets empty, the growl of a car picking up speed down a distant road.

In the following paragraph from *Love Medicine* by Louise Erdrich, we are hearing fragmented thoughts—ideal candidates for sentence fragments. You'll notice that some are simple noun phrases, some are absolutes—a noun with a modifier following—and some are dependent clauses. But, obviously, all are deliberate:

> <u>Northern lights.</u> Something in the cold, wet atmosphere brought them out. I grabbed Lipsha's arm. We floated into the field and sank down, crushing green wheat. We chewed the sweet kernels and stared up and were lost. Everything seemed to be one piece. <u>The air, our faces, all cool, moist, and dark, and the ghostly sky.</u> Pale green licks of light pulsed and faded across it. <u>Living lights.</u> Their fires lobbed over, higher, higher, then died out in blackness. At times the whole sky was ringed in shooting points and puckers of light gathering and falling, pulsing, fading, rhythmical as breathing. <u>All of a piece.</u> <u>As if the sky were a pattern of nerves and our thought and memories traveled across it.</u> <u>As if the sky were one gigantic memory for us all.</u> <u>Or a dance hall.</u> And all the world's wandering souls were dancing there. I thought of June. She would be dancing if there was a dance hall in space. She would be dancing a two-step for wandering souls. <u>Her long legs lifting and falling.</u> <u>Her laugh an ace.</u> <u>Her sweet perfume the way all grown-up women were supposed to smell.</u> <u>Her amusement at both the bad and the good.</u> <u>Her defeat.</u> <u>Her reckless victory.</u> <u>Her sons.</u>

And in the following passage from *The Shipping News,* E. Annie Proulx conveys a tentative quality of the characters' feelings:

> Wavey came down the steps pulling at the sleeves of her home-made coat, the color of slushy snow. She got in, glanced at him. <u>A slight smile.</u> <u>Looked away.</u>
>   <u>Their silence comfortable.</u> <u>Something unfolding.</u> But what? <u>Not love, which wrenched and wounded.</u> <u>Not love, which came only once.</u>

Both ellipsis and sentence fragments contribute to that tentativeness.

EXERCISE 37

Examine the style of one of your essays or, if working in groups, an essay written by a classmate.

1. Calculate the average length of the sentences. Then count the number that surpass the average length by at least ten words and the number at least five words below the average.

2. Note any series of three or more structures. Do they follow the order of climax, with the longest and/or most important member last in the string? Do any have variations in their punctuation, either asyndeton or polysyndeton?

3. Are there any places where a compound structure could be expanded into a series to add stylistic interest or further information?

4. Is there any clause-level punctuation other than commas and periods—semicolons, colons, dashes? Are there places where alternative punctuation might enhance the effectiveness?

5. How many sentences begin with opening phrases or clauses that precede the subject? Check for other word-order variation, such as subject–verb shifts.

6. Count the instances of any repetition, ellipsis, and antithesis.

7. Count the number of appositive and absolute phrases.

Write an evaluation of the essay based on these findings.

FOR GROUP DISCUSSION

The writers of the following passages have used a great many stylistic tools to good advantage. Identify the places where they have sent that special message to the reader: "Pay attention! I've crafted this sentence carefully."

[George Caleb] Bingham's greatest paintings depend upon an open rhetoric, an uncannily frank relation to their audience. We view his subjects from a perspective that includes us within the painting, and the direct looks we meet there usually recall the openness of Bingham's own disposition, itself characteristically American. Looking at *Fur Traders Descending the Missouri* as if from a canoe or from the Missouri's bank, we are obliged to remember that rivers have mouths and sources. *Fur Traders* can certainly be read as a painting in which the wilderness is brought into the frame of civilization, tending ever downriver. But it is more ambiguous than that, and ambiguity is an important source of its effect. Backlit by the diffuse light of the rising sun, offset by an island still in shadow, barely accented by a line of ducks wheeling over the far shore, these exotic figures are just as redolent of where they have been as of where they are going. And as time moves the viewer farther and farther downstream from the wilderness, it seems more and more as if this painting leads us upstream in imagination to the wilder country from which this man and boy have just descended.

—Verlyn Klinkenborg
(*Smithsonian*)

The general pressure in medical school is to push yourself ahead into professionalism, to start feeling at home in the hospital, in the operating room, to make medical jargon your native tongue—it's all part of becoming efficient, knowledgeable, competent. You want to leave behind that green, terrified medical student who stood awkwardly on the edge of the action, terrified of revealing limitless ignorance, terrified of killing a patient. You want to identify with the people ahead of you, the ones who know what they're doing. And instead, I have found it necessary to retain some of the greenness, so I could explain the hospital to people for whom it was not familiar turf.

—Perri Klass (*A Not Entirely Benign Procedure*)

(*Note:* You saw the opening sentence of this paragraph in the discussion of asyndeton)

It is so known through the length and breadth of its watershed. The Bay. There is no possible confusion with any other body of water, no need for more precise description. It is, after all, the continent's largest estuary. Its waters are rich, the main supply of oysters, crabs, clams and other seafoods for much of the Atlantic seaboard. Its shorelines cradled our first settlements. It is the Chesapeake.

—William W. Warner (*Beautiful Swimmers*)

(*Note*: This paragraph opens the book's first chapter, "The Bay.")

On two occasions, the contractor hired a group of Mexican aliens. They were employed to cut down some trees and haul off debris. In all, there were six men of varying age. The youngest in his late twenties; the oldest (his father?) perhaps sixty years old. They came and they left in a single old truck. Anonymous men. They were never introduced to the other men at the site. Immediately upon their arrival they would follow the contractor's directions, starting working—rarely resting—seemingly driven by a fatalistic sense that work which had to be done was best done as quickly as possible.

I watched them sometimes. Perhaps they watched me. The only time I saw them pay me much notice was one day at lunchtime when I was laughing with the other men. The

Mexicans sat apart when they ate, just as they worked by themselves. Quiet. I rarely heard them say much to each other. All I could hear were their voices calling out sharply to one another, giving directions. Otherwise, when they stood briefly resting, they talked among themselves in voices too hard to overhear.

—Richard Rodriguez (*Hunger of Memory*)

Thornton's command cracked out like a pistol shot. Buck threw himself forward, tightening the traces with a jarring lunge. His whole body was gathered compactly together in the tremendous effort, the muscles writhing and knotting like live things under the silky fur. His great chest was low to the ground, his head forward and down, while his feet were flying like mad, the claws scarring the hard-packed snow in parallel grooves. The sled swayed and trembled, half-started forward. One of his feet slipped, and one man groaned aloud. The sled lurched ahead in what appeared a rapid succession of jerks, though it never really came to a dead stop again . . . half an inch . . . an inch . . . two inches . . . The jerks perceptibly diminished; as the sled gained momentum, he caught them up, till it was moving steadily along.

—Jack London (*The Call of the Wild*)

The mass movement of the Scandinavian peoples between the years AD 750 and 1050, one of the great migrations of European history, began as plunder-raids and ended as conquest and settlement. People from what is now known as Sweden established a kingdom in part of European Russia. Adventurers from Norway colonized parts of the British Isles, the Faroes, and Iceland, pushed on to Greenland and eventually the coast of Labrador. And the Danes—also called Norsemen— conquered northern France (which became Normandy) and finally England. Collectively, these peoples are referred to as the Vikings, a name which is thought to come either from the Norse *vik* (a bay, indicating "one who frequents inlets of the sea") or from the Old English *wic,* a camp, the formation of temporary encampments being a prominent feature of Viking raids. In the past, the Vikings have been described as daring pirates but, while there is obviously much truth to the stereotype, recent scholarship likes to emphasize the long-term peaceful benefits of the Norse landings. It has been suggested, too, that the native Anglo-Saxons took advantage of the Viking raids to settle old scores with each other. Unlike the

Anglo-Saxon race war against the Celts, which preserved virtually no trace of the Celtic languages in English, the Danish settlers had a profound influence on the development of Old English.

—Robert McCrum, Robert MacNeil,
and William Cran *(The Story of English)*

KEY TERMS

Absolute phrase	Ellipsis	Redundancy
Anaphora	Figures of speech	Repetition
Anastrophe	Fragment	Style
Antithesis	Isocolon	Word-order variation
Asyndeton	Polysyndeton	

RHETORICAL REMINDERS

Have I taken advantage of the stylistic possibilities of absolute phrases and of various kinds of repetition, word-order variation, antithesis, and ellipsis to heighten the drama and/or call attention to particular passages?

In my series of three or more structures, have I considered order of importance and/or length?

PUNCTUATION REMINDERS

Have I used any punctuation variations for any series, such as asyndeton or polysyndeton?

Do my punctuation choices help the reader, especially in long sentences with internal punctuation?

Have I used colons, semicolons, and dashes accurately and effectively?

PART IV

Your Way with Words

Whate'er you think, good words, I think, were best.
—WILLIAM SHAKESPEARE

Your intuitive understanding of sentences in your native language is more than matched by your remarkable way with words. The sentences that you automatically generate whenever the need arises are, of course, strings of individual words, which you select from an inventory, or **lexicon,** of many thousands of entries—an internal dictionary of sorts.

In reality, however, individual entries in our lexicon and their definitions are quite different from those in a standard dictionary. Our definitions are bound up with experience and memory, so they include all the associations that the word holds for us, negative and positive. For example, think about your own personal definition of *mother* and *kindergarten* and *picnic* and *summer;* it's obvious that no dictionary can describe the pictures that those words conjure up for you. But despite the differences in our mental word pictures, our desire to communicate demands that the words of our lexicon have referents in common with those of the larger community.

Like the grammatical choices we make, the words we choose contribute greatly to the rhetorical effect of our prose. Our words are indeed powerful tools in our writer's toolkit. In this chapter, we will look more closely at our lexical choices and the rules that govern their use in three major sections: form class words, structure words, and pronouns.

CHAPTER 12

Words and Word Classes

LEXICAL RULES

The number of words and their associations stored in our **lexicon** (the inventory of words in our memory) are indeed impressive; equally impressive are the grammatical rules and restrictions that determine how we put our words together into sentences. The following pairs of sentences illustrate how those subconscious rules and restrictions work—or fail to work:

> Kevin had some trouble last night with his homework.
> Paul had a trouble last night with his homeworks.
>
> Sue is being funny.
> Rob is being tall.
>
> Pam walked to school.
> Kate walked to home.

You probably recognized that in each case the second sentence is ungrammatical—that is, it is not a sentence that a native speaker would say. A comparison of the two sentences in each pair illuminates the kinds of **lexical rules** that operate in English.

The first pair illustrates the restriction that prevents us from saying "homeworks," a distinction we make between the **countable** and **noncountable nouns** of in our lexicon: *Homework* is noncountable; it's a kind of **mass noun;** others in the class are *sugar* and *water* and *oil* and *cotton.* Another noncountable class is that of **abstract nouns,** such as *happiness* and *peace.* The first pair of sentences also demonstrates the restriction built into the **indefinite article,** *a* (or *an*), one of our **determiners,** or noun signalers. Noncountable nouns, such as *homework* and *happiness,*

228

cannot be signaled by *a,* nor do they have a plural form: Native speakers simply do not say "homeworks" or "a happiness."

The second pair of sentences illustrates the semantic qualities of adjectives: *Tall* describes an unchanging condition, or state, so it cannot be used with the progressive "is being," which suggests a dynamic, or changeable, quality. The adjective *funny* includes both possible meanings: "Sue is funny" suggests a permanent characteristic of Sue's personality; "Sue is being funny" suggests a condition of the present moment. The two sentences with *walked* in the list of pairs illustrate how arbitrary, or unsystematic, some of our rules are. There is something in our lexicon that restricts us from using the preposition *to* with *home,* although we do, of course, say "to school."

The grammar rules illustrated here are obviously not the kind that you studied in your grammar classes; chances are, you were not even aware that you follow rules like these when you speak and write. And certainly you don't want to worry about such rules—or even try to remember them. You couldn't remember them all even if you wanted to; in fact, no one has ever described them all. With these few we have just scratched the surface. We are looking at these rules simply to illustrate the kinds of information that our internal lexicon includes and to help you recognize and appreciate that your way with words is truly remarkable.

It is obvious that for a native speaker the restrictions illustrated by these pairs of sentences have somehow become internalized. Linguists sometimes describe such features as a built-in hierarchy, much like the taxonomy that scientists use in classifying plants and animals. Each level—phylum, class, order, family, genus, and species—includes features that differentiate it from the other levels. The farther down the hierarchy, the more specific the details that distinguish the classes. The following scheme illustrates certain features of nouns:

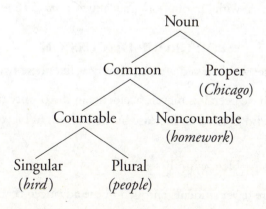

The restrictions built into the word determine its place in the hierarchy; each word carries with it only those features in the higher intersections (or nodes) that it is connected with: *Homework* is a noncountable, common noun; *bird* is a singular, countable, common noun. Determiners, too, have such built-in features: The indefinite article, *a* (or *an*), includes "singular" and "countable," so we are restricted from using it with *homework;* it signals only those nouns that fit in the lowest, left-hand branch, like *bird.* The **definite article,** *the,* is much more versatile as a determiner: It can signal nearly all nouns, even noncountables:

> Have you finished <u>the</u> homework?
>
> <u>The happiness</u> I felt at that moment is beyond description.

Many words in our lexicon can appear in both branches of a node, depending on their context. For example, some nouns can be both countable and noncountable:

> I had <u>a</u> strange <u>experience</u> yesterday.
>
> I've had <u>experience</u> working with animals.

> Ron had <u>two beers</u> today already.
>
> He drinks <u>beer</u> often.

The countable/noncountable feature applies also to certain signalers of nouns, such as *less/fewer, amount of/number of,* and *much/many.* The commercial that advertises a certain brand of soft drink as having "less calories" than another brand has failed to make the countable/noncountable distinction: *Calories* is a countable noun; the fact that it's plural tells us that. We generally reserve *less* for noncountables; the description of that soft drink should be "*fewer* calories." We would also talk about the "number of calories," not the "amount of calories," just as we would say "many calories," not "much calories." Such noncountables as *water* and *cotton* and *love* and *homework* pattern with "amount of" and "much"; *calories* does not.

◀ FOR GROUP DISCUSSION

A careful writer would avoid writing sentences like these two:

> *There have been less bicycle accidents in the county this year.
>
> *I have also noticed an increase in the amount of bicycles on the roads.

But there's no problem with these:

> There are fewer students enrolled in the advanced ceramics class this year.

There is an increase in the number of students enrolled in the
  beginning course.

Think about where in the noun hierarchy you would find *accidents, bicy-
cles,* and *students.* How would a careful writer revise those first two sentences? If you were helping a nonnative speaker revise those sentences,
how would you explain the changes?
  Would that careful writer avoid any of these?

> There were less than a dozen bicycle accidents in the county this year.
>
> We had fewer accidents than last year.
>
> We have less dollars than we need.
>
> We have less money than we need.
>
> We have less than ten dollars to last until payday.

You probably gave that nonnative speaker some advice about the use of
less and *fewer.* Should you revise your explanation? In what way?

PARTS OF SPEECH

Books about grammar commonly open with the classification of words
into "parts of speech." You perhaps remember your own language arts
classes from junior high, where you began your study of grammar by
defining *noun* and *verb* and *adjective* and *adverb* and such. As you learned
in the discussion of the lexicon, our internalized grammar includes rules
and restrictions that determine how we use our words. In a sense, those
rules constitute definitions of a sort for our word classes; so in this study
of the parts of speech we look at those internalized definitions.
  We begin by classifying the words of our lexicon into the two broad
groups introduced in Chapter 1: **form classes** and **structure classes.** To
understand the difference between the two groups, imagine an inexperienced speaker of English saying a sentence such as,

> Strange dog standing porch.

Even though it doesn't sound exactly like English, the sentence certainly
communicates. Now imagine the same sentence spoken by an experienced speaker:

> A strange dog is standing on the porch.

or, perhaps,

> That strange dog is standing near the porch.

The added words make the message more explicit, of course, but the nouns and verb the first speaker used are adequate to get the gist of the message across. Those are the *form-class words;* the missing ones are the *structure-class words,* those that provide the grammatical connections.

In general, the form-class words—nouns, verbs, adjectives, and adverbs—provide the primary lexical content; the structure classes—determiners, pronouns, auxiliaries, qualifiers, prepositions, conjunctions—explain the grammatical or structural relationships. Using a metaphor, we can think of form-class words as the bricks of the language and structure words as the mortar that holds them together.

Although **pronouns** are commonly listed as members of the structure class, they actually straddle the line between the form and structure classes. Many pronouns are like the form classes, insofar as they have variations in form; and they function as nouns, as substitutes for nouns and noun phrases. But they also belong with the structure classes: The possessive and demonstrative pronouns also function as determiners (*my* house, *that* boat). Also, like the structure classes, pronouns are a small, closed class, admitting no new members.

Probably the most striking difference between the form classes and the structure classes is characterized by their numbers. Of the approximately half-million words in our language, the structure words number only in the hundreds. The form classes, however, are large, open classes; new nouns and verbs and adjectives and adverbs regularly enter the language as new technology and new ideas require them. They are sometimes abandoned, too, as the dictionary's "obsolete" and "archaic" labels testify. But with few exceptions, the structure classes remain constant—and limited. We have managed with the same small store of prepositions and conjunctions for generations, with few changes. It's true that we don't hear *whilst* and *betwixt* anymore, nor do we see them in modern prose and poetry, but most of our structure words are identical to those that Shakespeare and his contemporaries used.

THE FORM CLASSES

Nouns, verbs, adjectives, and adverbs are called the form classes because each class has specific forms, a set of inflectional endings, or **inflections,** that distinguishes it from all other classes. As we emphasized in Chapter 1, the feature of form is very useful in defining the class. For example, instead of defining *noun* in its traditional way, as "the name of a person, place, or thing," you can define it according to its form: "A noun is a word that can be made plural and/or possessive." And instead of defining *verb* as a word that shows action, which isn't very accurate, you can use the criterion of form, which applies to every verb, without exception: "A verb is a word that has an *-s* and an *-ing* form." These are the definitions built into your internal grammar system.

Nouns

Recall from your study of Chapter 1 that **nouns** have an inflection for plural (*-s* or *-es*) and for **possessive case:**

Singular	**Plural**	**Singular Possessive**	**Plural Possessive**
cat	cats	cat's	cats'
treasure	treasures	treasure's	treasures'
fortress	fortresses	fortress's	fortresses'

Not every noun fits into the entire set. For example, noncountable nouns have no plural form: mass nouns, such as *homework* and *milk;* abstract nouns, such as *peace* and *tranquility;* and proper nouns. And some nouns have irregular plurals, an inflection other than *-s* or *-es: children, men, feet, mice, crises.* But certainly the vast majority of our nouns are inflected in this regular way, with *-s* (or *-es*) for those that have a plural form, with *-'s* for singular possessive and *-s'* or (*-es'*) for plural possessive.

It's easy to make mistakes in writing the plural and possessive of some nouns; read aloud the three inflected forms in the set of nouns—*cats, cat's, cats'* —and you'll understand why. In speech we make no distinction; they sound identical. The apostrophe is strictly an orthographic signal, a signal in the written language.

As you may know, the apostrophe is easy to misuse. It's not unusual to see it used mistakenly in plurals, especially if the plural looks a bit strange:

> *Fishing license's sold here.

This sign was spotted in the window of a sporting goods store; clearly, someone goofed. And the use of the apostrophe on this poster announcing the schedule of a musical group is also wrong:

> Now playing Tuesday's at The Lounge.

We use the apostrophe with the *s* in the possessive case, not in the plural: *Joe's Bar & Grill, Tuesday's meeting.* The only exception to that rule occurs in the case of letters or numbers that would be unreadable without the apostrophe:

> There are three t's in my name.

Probably the best rule of thumb to remember is that when you add an *s* sound, you add the letter *s*—in both plural and possessive: *cat, cat's, cats, cats'.* Words that end with an *s* (or an *s*-like sound), such as *fortress* or *church* or *dish*, require a whole syllable for the plural, an *-es: fortress/fortresses, church/churches, dish/dishes.* But we write the singular possessive just as we do with words like *cat:* We simply add *'s: fortress's, church's, dish's.* For the plural possessive, we simply add the apostrophe to the plural, as we do with *cats': fortresses', churches', dishes'.*

Even with nouns that already end in an *s* sound, we add another when we make it possessive. For example, the last name *Jones* ends in an *s* sound. To form the possessive, we add an apostrophe and another *s: Steve Jones's recent bestseller.* We should note two possible exceptions to this rule. Some editors recommend adding just an apostrophe when a name such as *Socrates* ends in the sound "eez": *Socrates' reasons.* They also suggest using just an apostrophe after singular common nouns that end in *s: mathematics' contribution.*

Plural-Only Forms. Some nouns, even when singular in meaning, are plural in form. One such group refers to things that are in two parts— that are bifurcated, or branching: *scissors, shears, clippers, pliers, pants, trousers, slacks, shorts, glasses, spectacles.* As subjects of sentences, these nouns present no problems with **subject–verb agreement:** They take the same verb form as other plural subjects do. Interestingly, even though a pair of shorts is a single garment and a pair of pliers is a single tool, we generally use the plural pronoun in reference to them:

> I bought a new pair of shorts today; <u>they're</u> navy blue.
>
> I've lost my pliers; have you seen <u>them</u>?

A different situation arises with certain plural-in-form nouns that are some-times singular in meaning. Nouns such as *physics, mathematics,* and *linguistics,* when referring to an academic discipline or course, are treated as singular:

> Physics <u>is</u> my favorite subject.
>
> Linguistics <u>is</u> the scientific study of language.

But such nouns can also be used with plural meanings:

> The mathematics involved in the experiment <u>are</u> very theoretical.
>
> The statistics on poverty in this country <u>are</u> quite depressing.

Again, you can use your intuitive knowledge of pronouns to test these nouns:

> <u>It</u> [mathematics] <u>is</u> my favorite subject.
>
> <u>They</u> [the statistics on poverty] <u>are</u> quite depressing.

Collective Nouns. **Collective nouns** such as *family, choir, team, majority, minority*—any noun that names a group of individual members—can be treated as either singular or plural, depending on context and meaning:

> The <u>family have</u> all gone their separate ways. (<u>they</u>)

(It would sound strange to say "The family *has* gone *its* separate way.")

The whole <u>family is</u> celebrating Christmas at home this year. (<u>it</u>)

The <u>majority</u> of our city council members <u>are</u> Republicans. (<u>they</u>)

The <u>majority</u> always <u>rules</u>. (<u>it</u>)

Certain noncountable nouns take their number from the modifier that follows the headword:

> The remainder of the building <u>materials are</u> being donated to Habitat for Humanity.

> The rest of the <u>books are</u> being donated to the library.

The headwords *remainder* and *rest* are noncountable nouns in this context; their plurality clearly derives from the modifier, which determines the form of the verb. A singular noun in the modifier would change the verb:

> The remainder of the <u>wood is</u> being donated to Habitat for Humanity.

> The rest of the <u>manuscript is</u> being donated to the library.

Some of our **indefinite pronouns,** among them *some, all,* and *enough,* work in the same way.

Proper Nouns. In contrast to **common nouns,** which refer to general things, places, attributes, and so on, **proper nouns** are those with a specific referent: *Empire State Building, Grand Canyon, William Shakespeare, London, The CBS Evening News, Aunt Mildred, November, Thanksgiving.* Proper nouns name people, geographic regions and locations, buildings, events, holidays, months, and days of the week; they usually begin with capital letters. Most proper nouns are singular; exceptions occur with the names of mountain ranges (*the Rocky Mountains, the Rockies, the Andes*) and island groups (*the Falklands*), which are plural.

EXERCISE 38

Problems of subject–verb agreement sometimes occur when modifiers follow the headword of the subject noun phrase:

> *The <u>instructions</u> on the loan application <u>form was</u> very confusing.

> *This <u>collection of poems</u> by several of my favorite romantic poets <u>were</u> published in 1910.

In these incorrect examples, the writer has forgotten that the headword determines the number of the noun phrase. To figure out the correct form of the verb, you can use the pronoun-substitution test:

The instructions [they] were very confusing.
This collection [it] was published in 1910.

Now test the following sentences to see if they are grammatical:

1. The statement on the income tax form about deductions for children and other dependents were simply not readable.

2. The type of career that many graduates are hoping to pursue pay high salaries and provide long vacations.

3. Apparently the use of robots in Japanese factories have been responsible for a great deal of worker dissatisfaction.

4. The problems associated with government deregulation have been responsible for the economic plight of several major airlines in recent years.

5. The impact of computers on our lives is comparable to the impact of the industrial revolution.

6. The amount of money and time I spend on computer games is more than I can afford.

Verbs

Although traditional grammar books often describe **verbs** in ways that make them seem complicated, they are really quite simple and systematic, especially when compared with verbs in other languages. With one exception—*be*—English verbs have only five forms—the base and four inflected forms. The forms and uses of verbs are described in Chapter 1, page 10, and in Chapter 3, pages 39–45.

Adjectives

A third open class of words is that of **adjectives,** which can sometimes be recognized by their comparative and superlative inflections, a semantic feature known as **degree:**

Positive	Comparative	Superlative
big	bigger	biggest
silly	sillier	silliest
intelligent	more intelligent	most intelligent

Note that *more* and *most* are variations of the inflections *-er* and *-est*.

A number of adjectives do not fit this set. For example, we do not say "the mainest reason" or "a more principal reason." The adjectives that do not take the inflections of degree also do not fit into the "adjective test frame":

The _____ NOUN is very _____.

The adjective test frame is useful in identifying adjectives: A word that fits into both slots is an adjective—and most adjectives do fit:

The frisky kitten is very frisky.

The comical clown is very comical.

The tough assignment is very tough.

The formula illustrates the two main positions that adjectives take; however, not all adjectives take both positions:

*The principal reason is very principal.

*The afraid children are very afraid.

*The medical advice was very medical.

The test frame, then, can positively identify adjectives: Only an adjective can fit both slots. But it cannot rule them out—that is, just because a word doesn't fit, that doesn't mean it's *not* an adjective.

Adverbs

Our most recognizable **adverbs**—and the most common—are those that are formed by adding *-ly* to the adjective: *slowly, deliberately, exclusively, perfectly.* Most *-ly* adverbs are **adverbs of manner.** Some common adverbs have the same form as the adjective: *fast, far, near, hard, long, high, late.* These are sometimes called **flat adverbs.**

Like adjectives, the *-ly* adverbs and the flat adverbs have comparative and superlative forms:

Positive	Comparative	Superlative
slowly	more slowly	most slowly
fast	faster	fastest

The comparative form of *-ly* adverbs, usually formed by adding *more* rather than *-er,* is fairly common. However, the superlative degree of the *-ly* adverbs—*most suddenly, most slowly, most favorably*—is rare enough in both speech and writing to have impact when used; these forms invariably call attention to themselves and in most cases will carry the main stress:

> The committee was most favorably disposed to accept the plan.
>
> The crime was planned most ingeniously.

There are a number of adverbs, in addition to the flat adverbs, that have no endings to distinguish them as adverbs, nor are they used with *more* or *most.* Instead we recognize them by the information they provide, by their position in the sentence, and often by their movability, as we saw in Chapter 8.

Time: *now, today, nowadays, yesterday, then, already, soon*
Duration: *still*
Frequency: *often, seldom, never, sometimes, always*
Place: *here, there, everywhere, somewhere, elsewhere, upstairs*
Direction: *away*

There are also a number of words that can serve as either prepositions or adverbs: *above, around, behind, below, down, in, inside, out, outside, up.*

Derivational Affixes

Besides the inflectional endings that identify the form classes, we also have an extensive inventory of **derivational affixes,** suffixes and prefixes that provide great versatility to our lexicon by allowing us to shift words from one class to another and/or to alter their meanings. For example, the noun *beauty* becomes a verb with *-ify (beautify),* an adjective with *-ful (beautiful),* and an adverb with *-ly* added to the adjective *(beautifully).*

Some of our suffixes change the meaning rather than the class of the word: *boy/boyhood; citizen/citizenry; king/kingdom; terror/terrorism.* Prefixes, too, generally change the meaning of the word rather than the class: *un*deniable, *pro*-American, *inter*action, *intra*murals, *il*legal, *dis*enchanted. Some prefixes enable us to derive verbs from other classes: *en*chant, *en*courage, *en*able, *de*rail, *de*throne, *be*witch, *be*devil, *dis*able, *dis*member.

This remarkable ability to expand our lexicon with uncountable new forms provides yet more evidence (if we needed more) for the idea of the inherent language expertise that native speakers possess. With this system of word expansion it's easy to understand why no one has yet come up with a definitive number of words in English. And although we follow certain rules in shifting words from one class to another, there is no real system: We can take a noun like *system,* turn it into an adjective *(systematic),* then a verb *(systematize),* then a noun again *(systematization).*

There's also the adverb *systematically* in that set; and the same base, *system*, produces *systemic* and *systemically*. But we can't distinguish between those adjectives that pattern with *-ize* to form verbs (*systematize, legalize, realize, publicize*) and those that pattern with *-ify* (*simplify, amplify, electrify*) or another affix (*validate, belittle*).

EXERCISE 39

Fill in the blanks with variations of the words shown on the chart, changing or adding derivational affixes to change the word class. In some cases, you may think of more than one possibility.

	NOUN	VERB	ADJECTIVE	ADVERB
1.	grief			
2.		vary		
3.				ably
4.		defend		
5.				quickly
6.			pleasant	
7.	type			
8.		prohibit		
9.				critically
10.			valid	
11.		appreciate		
12.	danger			
13.		accept		
14.			pure	
15.		steal		

THE STRUCTURE CLASSES

The **structures classes**—determiners, auxiliaries, qualifiers, prepositions, particles, conjunctions, and pronouns—are by no means new
to you. Throughout the discussions of sentence structure, you have
been working with these word categories: with the determiners that
signal noun phrases, auxiliaries that alter the meaning of verbs, conjunctions that connect ideas, pronouns that serve in a variety of ways,
including that of determiner. In some ways, the information you will
find on the following pages will be a review of what you studied previously. However, by studying the structure classes in more detail,
you will see how together they provide the mortar that holds the
form-class bricks in place.

Determiners

You were introduced to the word *determiner* in Chapter 1, where
you saw how our most common determiners—the articles *a, an,*
and *the*—signal the noun phrase. You've also seen other word classes
that function as determiners: the demonstrative pronouns (*this/that*
car, *these/those* cars); possessive pronouns (*my, your, his, her, its, our,
their* potential); possessive nouns and noun phrases (*Joe's* book; *our
neighbor's* dog). Many of the indefinite pronouns you will read
about later in this chapter also function as determiners (*every, each,
any* person; *several, many, few, all* people). It's accurate to think
of "determiner" as the name of a function rather than a specific
word class.

Auxiliaries

When you read about verb tenses in Chapter 3, you learned about auxiliary verbs. *Be* is used in the progressive tense, *have* is used in the perfect
tense, and both *have* and *be* are used in the present-progressive tense:

Progressive:	*am, is, are, was, were* laughing
Perfect:	*has, have, had* laughed
Perfect-Progressive:	*has, have, had been* laughing

The auxiliary *be* also plays a role in forming the passive voice. It
joins with the past participle of the main verb: *am, is, are, was, were*
intrigued.

Do is another auxiliary verb, but it does not mark tense or voice.
Instead, it is used for three special purposes—to form questions,

negations, and emphatic sentences when there is no other auxiliary in the sentence:

> <u>Did</u> you finish your work?
>
> He <u>didn't</u> agree with the decision.
>
> I <u>did</u> pay my taxes!

Note that when the main verb is a form of *be, do*-support is not required.

Another important class of auxiliaries is that of the **modals**— auxiliaries that add shades of meaning to the main verb. In Chapter 3 we listed ten modal auxiliaries: *can, could, will, would, shall, should, may, might, must,* and *ought to.* To this list, we are adding these common **semi-auxiliaries:**

> have (got) to   be going to

Like the modal auxiliary *must, have to* indicates obligation:

> I have to study tonight.

The semi-auxiliary *be going to* is another way of indicating future time:

> I'm going to take four classes next semester.

Qualifiers

A **qualifier** is a word that modifies an adjective or adverb: It either amplifies or diminishes the meaning of the word it precedes.

> The air was <u>somewhat</u> cold that morning.
>
> The climber <u>very</u> cautiously set her route.

Among the most common words that qualify adjectives and adverbs are *very, quite, rather, too, still, even, much,* and *fairly.* Some adverbs of manner, the *-ly* adverbs, are themselves used as qualifiers with certain adjectives: *dangerously* close, *particularly* harmful, *absolutely* true. In the discussion of "Power Words" in Chapter 6, we saw the effect that qualifiers such as these can have on sentence rhythm.

As a rule, it's a good practice to let a single word do all the work it can. *Rushed* and *dashed* and *bolted* are stronger than *ran very fast;* leaves that *flickered* are more delicate in movement than leaves that *moved slightly.* The experienced writer, instead of describing a person as *really nice* or *very nice* or *very beautiful,* might say instead *cooperative* or *charming* or *stunning.* In most cases the difference is not a matter of knowing "big" words or unusual words. The difference is a matter of precision, of choosing words carefully. Such precision, even in small details, can make a difference in the overall effect on the reader.

One further caveat concerns the use of qualifiers with certain adjectives that have **absolute** meanings. Careful writers try to avoid *very* with *perfect* or *unique* or *round*. Although we might say *absolutely perfect* to emphasize the perfection, to say *very perfect* would probably have a negative effect on the reader. And certainly as careful users of language we should respect the meaning of *unique:* "one of a kind." *Round* and *square* have meanings in our lexicon other than their geometric absolutes, so it is possible for the shape of an object to be "nearly round" or "almost square." But qualifiers such as *very* or *quite* are best reserved for other kinds of qualities.

EXERCISE 40

As you read the following sentences, pay particular attention to the italicized words; replace them with words that are more precise.

1. Ben was so *very careful* about his wardrobe, he had his ties pressed after every wearing.

2. The guest speaker's *really strong* denunciation of our foreign policy seemed *quite out of place* at the awards banquet.

3. The foreman gives his orders in a *very abrupt* manner.

4. To me, the tropical garden is the *most intriguing* display in the conservatory. *Completely covered* with orchids and vines, the towering palm trees and *really unusual* large-leafed plants seem to belong in a fairy tale.

5. It is usually *an absolute waste of time* to argue with radicals of any persuasion; they are unlikely to be influenced by mere reason.

6. Our host's *overly enthusiastic* welcome embarrassed me: First he kissed me on both cheeks; then he bowed and kissed my hand.

7. The basketball players seemed *really tired* as they took the court for the second half.

8. Our history teacher was *extremely upset* when he discovered that almost half the class had cheated on the midterm exam.

9. The choir members were *really excited* about their summer trip to Europe.

10. The members of Congress were *really very surprised* at the extent of voter cynicism toward Washington.

....

Prepositions

Like many of the words you have studied in this chapter, **prepositions** are small words that have a large impact. To appreciate their contribution to meaning, try reading the following passage from Michael Chabon's novel *The Amazing Adventures of Kavalier and Klay* without the prepositions (shown in parentheses):

> (Atop) the thick concrete parapet (of) the eight-sixth floor, (like) a bright jagged hold punched (in) the clouds, balanced a smiling man (in) a mask and a gold-and-indigo suit. The suit clung (to) his lanky frame, dark blue (with) an iridescent glint (of) silk. He had (on) a pair (of) gold swim trunks, and (on) the front (of) his blue jersey was a thick gold appliqué, (like) the initial (on) a letterman's jacket, (in) the shape (of) a skeleton key.

You have probably discovered that without its prepositions the passage has lost not only its meaning but also its sense of rhythm.

The following are common one-word prepositions:

about	above	across	after
against	along	among	around
at	before	behind	below
beneath	beside	between	by
down	during	except	for
from	in	inside	into
of	on	over	past
since	through	to	toward
under	underneath	until	up
upon	with	within	without

Some prepositions consist of more than one word. Here is a list of common **phrasal prepositions**:

according to	because of	next to
ahead of	as for	instead of
in back of	in front of	in spite of

EXERCISE 41

Prepositions most frequently precede noun phrases, but they can precede other types of nominals as well. Locate the prepositions in the following sentences and identify the nominals that follow them (noun phrases, pronouns, gerunds, nominal clauses).

1. The canyon formed in a relatively short period of time.

2. We were interested in exploring the canyon, so we spoke to the guide about camping overnight.

3. We listened closely to what the guide told us about the trail leading into the canyon.

4. We trekked fifteen miles without really knowing where we were headed.

Particles

Particles join primarily one-syllable verbs such as *come, go, get,* and *take* to form **phrasal verbs.** The most common particles are words you've seen on the list of common one-word prepositions: *up, out, on, in, off,* and *down.* However, particles differ from prepositions: They combine with verbs to produce a new meaning.

> I <u>looked up</u> your phone number. (particle)
> I looked <u>up the narrow street.</u> (preposition)

Another distinguishing feature of some particles is their movability.

> I <u>looked</u> your number <u>up.</u>

Phrasal verbs can often be replaced by a single word, so if your rhetorical situation calls for a formal tone, consider replacing the phrasal verb with a single word.

> We have to ~~turn in~~ *submit* the report tomorrow.

For more information on this topic, review pages 130–131 in Chapter 7.

Conjunctions

In Chapter 4 you first learned about **coordinating conjunctions** (*and, but, or, nor, for, yet,* and *so*) and **subordinating conjunctions** (*when, before, if, because, although,* etc.). To writers, these words are particularly important because they indicate reasoning. They show how entities or ideas are related. The following list contains examples of conjunctions and the relationships they indicate.

Addition: *and*
Alternate: *or*
Cause or reason: *for, because, since, as long as*
Contrast: *but, yet, while, whereas*
Result: *so, so that*

You'll also want to review the transitional phrases and the conjunctions with an adverbial meaning, the conjunctive adverbs, which you studied in Chapter 4.

PRONOUNS

We looked briefly at pronouns in earlier chapters when we substituted them for noun phrases in order to demonstrate whether the subject of the sentence was singular or plural and to figure out where the subject ended and the predicate began:

Jenny's sister *[she]* graduated from nursing school.

The gymnasium *[it]* needs a new roof.

Those substitutions—*she* and *it*—are among the personal pronouns, the kind you probably recognize most readily. But there are many other classes of pronouns as well—reflexive, demonstrative, relative, indefinite, and others. In this discussion we look at all the pronouns, concentrating especially on those members of various classes that sometimes cause problems for writers.

Personal Pronouns

The easiest way to understand the system of personal pronouns is to first understand the concepts of **number, person,** and **case.** *Number* refers to the singular/plural distinction. *Person* is related to point of view, the relationship of the writer to the reader. The reference of the first person includes the writer; second person refers to the person or people addressed; third person refers to "third parties," someone or something other than the writer or the person addressed. (Notice that the form of the second person is the same regardless of number.) The choice of *case* is determined by the pronoun's function in the sentence—**subjective, objective,** or **possessive.**

Case	1st-Person Singular	1st-Person Plural	2nd-Person Singular and Plural	3rd-Person Singular	3rd-Person Plural
Subjective	I	we	you	he, she, it	they
Objective	me	us	you	him, her, it	them
Possessive	my (mine)	our (ours)	your (yours)	his, her, its (his, hers its)	their (theirs)

The Missing Pronoun. This set of personal pronouns may look complete—and, unfortunately, it does include all we have. But, in fact, it has a gap, one that is responsible for a great deal of the sexism in our language. The gap occurs in the third-person singular column, the column that already includes three pronouns representing masculine (*he*), feminine (*she*), and neuter (*it*). You'd think that those three would be up to the task of covering all contingencies, but they're not. For third-person singular we have no choice that is gender-neutral. In the past when writers needed a pronoun to refer to an unidentified person, such as "the teacher" or "a student" or just "someone," they used the masculine:

> The reporter should have left out <u>his</u> personal opinion.
>
> Someone left <u>his</u> book on the table.

But that usage is no longer accepted practice. Times and attitudes change, and we have come to recognize the power of language in shaping those attitudes. So an important step in reshaping society's view of women has been to eliminate the automatic use of *he* and *his* and *him* when someone referred to could just as easily be female.

In a paragraph we looked at in Chapter 6 in connection with sentence rhythm, the writer has made an effort to avoid sexism with the generic *salesperson,* a title that has all but replaced the masculine *salesman.* But notice the pronoun in the last sentence:

> Never invest in something you don't understand or in the dream of an artful salesperson. Be a buyer, not a sellee. . . . Don't let someone else tell you what you need—at least not if he happens to be selling it.

In speech we commonly use *they* for both singular and plural:

> Don't let someone else tell you what you need—at least not if <u>they</u> happen to be selling it.

Eventually, perhaps, the plural pronoun will take over for the singular; in the second person *(you/your/you)*, we make no distinction between singular and plural, so it's not unreasonable to do the same in the third person. But such changes come slowly. What should we do in the meantime?

One common, but not necessarily effective, way to solve the problem of the pronoun gap is with *he or she:*

> . . . at least not if <u>he or she</u> happens to be selling it.

An occasional *he or she* works in most situations like this one, but more than one in a paragraph will change the rhythm of the prose, slow the reader down, and call attention to itself when such attention is simply uncalled for.

The awkwardness of *he or she* in a passage becomes even more obvious when the possessive and objective case pronouns are also required. Avoiding sexist language by using *his or her* and *him or her* as well as *he or she* quickly renders the solution worse than the problem. Here, for example, is a passage from a 1981 issue of *Newsweek:*

> To the average American, the energy problem is mainly his monthly fuel bill and the cost of filling up his gas tank. He may also remember that in 1979, and way back in 1974, he had to wait in long lines at gasoline stations.

Because we do have a gender-neutral pronoun in the plural, often the **antecedent** noun (the noun the pronoun stands for) can be changed to plural. In the *Newsweek* article, for example, the writer could have started out by discussing "average Americans":

> To <u>average Americans,</u> the energy problem is mainly <u>their</u> monthly fuel bills and the cost of filling up <u>their</u> gas tanks.

That revision, of course, has changed the relationship of the writer to the reader: The writer is no longer addressing the reader as an individual—a change the writer may not want. Often, however, the plural is an easy and obvious solution. For example, in the following passage from a book about language, the change to plural does not affect the overall meaning or intent:

> It has been said that whenever a person speaks he is either ~~a person speaks he is~~ either mimicking or analogizing.
> —Charles Hockett

We should emphasize that these quoted examples of sexist language were written several decades ago, when the masculine pronoun was the norm. Chances are, the sentence would not have been written in this way today.

Here, then, are some of the ways in which you can make up for the pronoun gap when you write and/or revise your own sentences:

1. USE THE PLURAL:

   > Every writer should be aware of the power of language
   >   when <u>he</u> chooses <u>his</u> pronouns.
   > *Revision:* Writers should be aware of the power of lan-
   >   guage when <u>they</u> choose <u>their</u> pronouns.

2. USE *HE OR SHE* IF YOU CAN USE IT ONLY ONCE:

   > *Revision:* Every writer should be aware of the power of
   >   language when <u>he or she</u> chooses pronouns.

3. AVOID *HIS* AS A DETERMINER, EITHER BY SUBSTITUTING ANOTHER ONE OR, IN SOME CASES, DELETING THE DETERMINER:

   > The writer of the news story should have kept <u>his</u> opin-
   >   ion out of it.
   > *Revision:* The writer of the news story should have kept
   >   (<u>all</u>) opinion out of it.

4. TURN THE FULL CLAUSE INTO AN ELLIPTICAL CLAUSE OR A VERB PHRASE, THUS ELIMINATING THE PROBLEM SUBJECT:

   > *Revision:* Every writer should be aware of the power of
   >   language when <u>choosing pronouns.</u>

   This fourth method of revision is often a good possibility because the offending pronoun nearly always shows up in the second clause of a passage, often as part of the same sentence. In our example, we have turned the complete dependent clause into an elliptical clause—that is, a clause with something missing. In this case what's missing is the subject. (The elliptical clause, which may have hidden pitfalls, is discussed in Chapter 8.)

5. REWRITE THE ADVERBIAL CLAUSE AS A RELATIVE (*WHO*) CLAUSE:

   > When <u>a person</u> buys a house, he should shop carefully
   >   for the lowest interest rate.
   > *Revision:* <u>A person who</u> buys a house should shop care-
   >   fully for the lowest interest rate.

   The relative clause, with its neutral *who,* eliminates the necessity of a personal pronoun to rename *a person.*

6. CHANGE THE POINT OF VIEW:

> *Second person:* As a writer <u>you</u> should be aware of the
> power of language when you choose (<u>your</u>)
> pronouns.
> When you buy a house, <u>you</u> should. . . .
> *First person:* As writers, <u>we</u> should be aware of the power
> of language when we choose (<u>our</u>) pronouns.

See also the section called "The *Everyone/Their* Issue" on pages 255–256.

Case Errors. Among the most common pronoun errors that writers make are the errors of case. As the chart on page 246 shows, case refers to the change that pronouns undergo on the basis of their function in the sentence. The subject of the sentence, of course, takes the subjective case.

> <u>I</u> finished the report yesterday.

When a pronoun is in the object position (as a direct object or an indirect object), we use the objective case:

> My roommate helped <u>me</u> with my math assignment. (direct object)
> Marie gave <u>him</u> a gift. (indirect object)

We also use the objective case for the object of the preposition:

> I walked to town <u>with him.</u>
> I walked to town <u>with Joe and him.</u>
> Joe walked to town <u>with him and me.</u>
> Marie walked <u>between Joe and me.</u>

Pronouns in the possessive case function as determiners, or noun signalers. The alternative forms of the possessive case, shown on the chart in parentheses, are used when the headword of the noun phrase, the noun, is deleted:

> This is <u>my bicycle.</u> ⟶ This bicycle is <u>mine.</u>
> This is <u>her bicycle.</u> ⟶ This is <u>hers.</u>

We should note that nouns in the possessive case function in the same way:

> This is <u>Pete's bicycle.</u> ⟶ This is <u>Pete's.</u>

Most errors of case that writers make occur with the subjective and objective cases. And most of them probably occur as the result of **hypercorrection**—making a correction when one isn't called for:

> *There's no rivalry between <u>my brother and I.</u>
>
> *The supervisor told <u>Jenny and I</u> that we might get a raise next week.

In both cases, the noun/pronoun compound is functioning as an object, so the correct pronoun choice is *me*, not *I*. This is a common error, however, possibly made because people remember being corrected by their parents or teachers when they said such sentences as

> Me and Bill are going for a bike ride. ("No, dear. Bill and *I*.")
>
> Bill and me are going to be late. ("No, dear. Bill and *I*.")

As a consequence of those early lessons, some people simply find it hard to say "my brother and me" or "Jenny and me," no matter what function the pronoun has in the sentence. The correct version of those sentences is,

> There's no rivalry <u>between my brother and me.</u>
>
> The supervisor told <u>Jenny and me</u> that we might get a raise next week.

If we substituted pronouns for the complete noun phrases, the sentences would be written as follows:

> There's no rivalry <u>between us.</u>
>
> The supervisor told <u>us</u> that we might get a raise next week.

We wouldn't consider for a moment using *we*.

The Unwanted Apostrophe. Another common pronoun error occurs with the pronoun *it*:

> *The cat caught it's tail in the door.

Here's the rule that's been broken with the word *it's*:

> **Personal pronouns have no apostrophes in the possessive case.**

If you check the chart showing the case of the personal pronouns on page 246, you'll see that there are no apostrophes. Notice that the rule also applies to other commonly confused pairs:

> *your* (possessive)/*you're* (*you are*)
>
> *their* (possessive)/*they're* (*they are*)

Here's what you have to remember—and check for: When you add *'s* to *it*, you're actually writing "it is" or "it has"; when you add *'re* to *you* or *they*, you're writing "you are" or "they are." Unlike nouns, possessive pronouns have no apostrophe. The possessive *whose* is another word commonly confused with a contraction, in this case *who's* ("who is"). Because *it, you, they*, and *who* are such common words, and because the unwanted apostrophe is such an easy error to slip in, you should probably, during your final proofreading, make a point of double-checking all instances of *its* and *it's, whose* and *who's, your* and *you're*, and *their* and *they're*—and even *there!*

The Ambiguous Antecedent. Another error that turns up with personal pronouns is the ambiguous **antecedent**—the pronoun that has more than one possible referent:

> When Bob accidentally backed the car into the toolshed, <u>it</u> was wrecked beyond repair.

Here we can't be sure if the pronoun *it* refers to the car or to the toolshed.

> Just before they were scheduled to leave, Shelley told Ann that <u>she</u> couldn't go after all.

Here we may suspect that *she* refers to Shelley—but we can't be sure. And the careful writer wouldn't make us guess.

> Uncle Dick and Aunt Teresa took the kids to <u>their</u> favorite restaurant for lunch.

Whose favorite restaurant?

The ambiguous antecedent often gets resolved by the context; within a sentence or two the reader will very likely understand the writer's intention. But not always. And, of course, the reader shouldn't have to wait. It's the writer's responsibility to make sure antecedents are clear.

Reflexive Pronouns

Reflexive pronouns are those formed by adding *-self* or *-selves* to a form of the personal pronoun: *myself, ourselves, yourself, yourselves, himself, herself, itself, themselves.* The standard rule for using the reflexive is straightforward. We use it as an object in a clause when its antecedent is the subject:

> <u>John</u> cut <u>himself.</u>
>
> <u>I</u> glanced at <u>myself</u> in the mirror.

Jack cooked an omelet for Barbara and <u>himself.</u>

I cooked breakfast for Kelly and <u>myself.</u>

The tendency toward hypercorrection occurs with the reflexives as well as with the personal pronouns. It's quite common to hear the reflexive where the standard rule calls for *me,* the straight objective case:

*Tony cooked dinner for Carmen and <u>myself.</u>

*The boss promised Pam and <u>myself</u> a year-end bonus.

Note that the antecedent of *myself* does not appear in either sentence. Another fairly common nonstandard usage occurs when speakers use *myself* in place of *I* as part of a compound subject:

*Ted and <u>myself</u> decided to go out and celebrate.

These nonstandard ways of using the reflexive are probably related to emphasis as well as to hypercorrection. Somehow the two-syllable *myself* sounds more emphatic than either *me* or *I.*

The nonstandard use of the reflexive occurs only with the first-person pronoun, *myself,* not with *himself* or *herself.* In the case of third person, the personal pronoun and the reflexive produce different meanings:

John cooked dinner for Jenny and <u>himself</u> (John).

John cooked dinner for Jenny and <u>him</u> (someone else).

This second interpretation assumes that another person, a known "someone else," is part of the situation, otherwise, *him* refers to *John.*

Intensive Pronouns

When we use the reflexive to add emphasis to a noun, we call it the **intensive reflexive pronoun.** It can appear in a number of positions:

I <u>myself</u> prefer classical music.

I prefer classical music <u>myself.</u>

<u>Myself,</u> I prefer classical music.

Each of these versions produces a different rhythm pattern. In the first version, the main stress falls on *myself,* whereas in the second it probably falls on *classical.* In the third, added stress is given to *I.*

EXERCISE 42

Edit the following passages, paying special attention to the pronoun problems.

1. Claire has always been interested in children and plans to make that her profession when she graduates. Both Claire and myself are majoring in early childhood education.

2. The goal of animal-rights activists is not just to prevent animal cruelty, as they advocated in earlier times, but also to promote the idea that they have intrinsic value, that they have a right to live. As a result of their efforts, the Public Health Service has revised their policy regarding the treatment of laboratory animals.

3. When my sister Beth asked me to go to Salem with her to visit our grandmother, I had no idea that she was sick. We were almost there before she told me she had experienced stomach cramps since early morning. Our grandmother took one look at her, called the doctor, and drove her to the hospital, which turned out to be a good decision. It turned out to be appendicitis.

Reciprocal Pronouns

Each other and *one another* are known as the **reciprocal pronouns.** They serve either as determiners (in the possessive case) or as objects, referring to previously named nouns: *Each other* refers to two nouns; *one another* refers to three or more, a distinction that careful writers generally observe.

> David and Ann help <u>each other.</u> They even do <u>each other's</u> laundry.
>
> All the students in my peer group help <u>one another</u> with their rough drafts.

Demonstrative Pronouns

As you recall from Chapter 5, a **demonstrative pronoun** (*this, that, these,* or *those*) can be a substitute for a noun phrase (or other nominal structure) as well as a signal for one:

> <u>These old shoes and hats</u>   will be perfect for the costumes.
>
>   ↓
>
> <u>These</u>   will be perfect for the costumes.

The role of demonstrative pronouns in cohesion is discussed on pages 95 to 97.

Indefinite Pronouns

The **indefinite pronouns** include a number of words that we use as determiners:

Quantifiers: *enough, few, fewer, less, little, many, much, several, more, most*

Universals: *all, both, every, each*

Partitives: *any, either, neither, none, some*

One is also commonly used as a pronoun (as are the other cardinal numbers—two, three, etc.) along with its negative, *none*. As a pronoun, *one* (or *ones*) often replaces only the headword, rather than the entire noun phrase:

<u>The blue shoes</u> that I bought yesterday will be perfect for the trip.
<u>The blue ones</u> that I bought yesterday will be perfect for the trip.

The personal pronoun, on the other hand, would replace the entire noun phrase:

<u>They</u> will be perfect for the trip.

The universal *every* and the partitives *any, no,* and *some* can be expanded with *-body, -thing,* and *-one*:

$$
\text{some} \begin{cases} \text{body} \\ \text{thing} \\ \text{one} \end{cases}
\text{every} \begin{cases} \text{body} \\ \text{thing} \\ \text{one} \end{cases}
\text{any} \begin{cases} \text{body} \\ \text{thing} \\ \text{one} \end{cases}
\text{no} \begin{cases} \text{body} \\ \text{thing} \\ \text{one (two words)} \end{cases}
$$

These pronouns can take modifiers in the form of clauses:

<u>Anyone</u> *who wants extra credit in psych class* can volunteer for tonight's experiment.

They can also be modified by participles or participial phrases:

<u>Everyone</u> *reporting late for practice* will take fifteen laps.

And by prepositional phrases:

<u>Nothing</u> *on the front page* interests me anymore.

And, unlike most nouns, they can be modified by adjectives that follow the headword:

> I don't care for <u>anything</u> *sweet*.
>
> I think that <u>something</u> *strange* is going on here.

Notice the strong stress that you put on the adjective following the pronoun.

The *Everyone/Their* Issue. The question of number—that is, whether a word is singular or plural—often comes up in reference to the indefinite pronouns *everyone* and *everybody*. In form they are singular, so as subjects they take the *-s* form of the verb or auxiliary in the present tense:

> <u>Everyone is</u> leaving the room at once.

An illustration of the scene described by this sentence, however, would show more than one person—more than two or three, probably—leaving the room, even though the form of *everyone* is singular. In spite of this anomaly, the issue of subject–verb agreement is not a problem.

But often such a sentence calls for the possessive pronoun. And when it does, the traditional choice has been the singular masculine:

> Everyone picked up <u>his</u> books and left the room.

However, that makes no sense—even if the *everyone* refers to men only. And it certainly makes no sense if the group of people includes women. The only reasonable solution is the plural, in spite of the singular form of *everyone:*

> Everyone picked up <u>their</u> books and left the room.

Unfortunately, even though the solution may be reasonable, your teacher is likely to mark *their* an error of pronoun/antecedent agreement.

It's true that in form *everyone* is singular; this is also true of collective nouns, such as *crowd* or *group*. But these nouns call for plural pronouns when the members of the collection are seen as individuals:

> The crowd began to raise <u>their</u> voices.
>
> Everyone in the group began to raise <u>their</u> voices.

No matter how logical it may be to use the plural pronoun in reference to these indefinite pronouns, to do so contradicts the advice in most handbooks, most of which take the traditional view that *everyone* and *everybody* are singular and cannot be replaced by *they.* If you feel uneasy about using the plural because your reader—your composition teacher, perhaps, or your boss—may take the traditional view, you can always avoid the problem by substituting a different subject:

<u>All of the people</u> began to raise their voices.

<u>All of the students</u> picked up their books and left the room

English is such a versatile language that we nearly always have alternatives.

EXERCISE 43

Edit the following passages, paying particular attention to the nonstandard use of pronouns and to those with unclear referents.

1. I recall with great pleasure the good times that us children had at our annual family reunions when I was young. Our cousins and ourselves, along with some younger aunts and uncles, played volleyball and softball until dark. They were a lot of fun.

2. Aunt Yvonne and Uncle Bob always brought enough homemade ice cream for them and everyone else as well. There was great rivalry, I remember, between my brother and I over who could eat the most. Nearly everyone made a pig of himself.

3. It seemed to my cousin Terry and I that the grownups were different people at those family reunions. That may be true of family reunions everywhere.

4. Nowadays my grandfather seems to forget about them good days and concentrates on the sad ones instead. He often tells my brother and myself about his boyhood during the Great Depression. He remembers the long years of unemployment for he and his whole family with very little pleasure. That doesn't really surprise me, because they were hard times.

KEY TERMS

Absolute adjective	Case	Definite article
Abstract noun	Collective noun	Degree
Adjective	Common noun	Demonstrative
Adverb	Comparative degree	pronoun
Adverb of manner	Conjunction	Derivational affix
Ambiguity	Coordinating	Determiner
Antecedent	conjunction	Flat adverb
Auxiliary	Countable noun	Form classes

Hypercorrection
Indefinite article
Indefinite pronoun
Inflection
Intensive reflexive
   pronoun
Lexical rule
Lexicon
Mass noun
Modal auxiliary
Noncountable noun
Noun
Number

Objective case
Particle
Person
Personal pronoun
Phrasal preposition
Phrasal verb
Plural-only noun
Positive degree
Possessive case
Preposition
Pronoun
Proper noun
Qualifier

Reciprocal pronoun
Reflexive pronoun
Semi-auxiliary
Sexist language
Structure classes
Subjective case
Subject–verb
   agreement
Subordinating
   conjunction
Superlative degree
Verb

RHETORICAL REMINDERS

Word Choice

Have I selected words with clear and precise meanings?

Subject–Verb Agreement

Have I been careful to recognize the singular/plural meaning of the subject noun phrase, especially when collective nouns, plural-only forms, and indefinite pronouns are involved?

Sexist Language

Have I avoided sexism in my choice of pronouns?

Have I avoided the awkward *he/she* and *his/her?*

Case

Have I used the objective case (*me, him, her*) for pronouns in the object positions (direct object, indirect object, object of the preposition)?

Have I avoided "between _____ and I"?

Unwanted Apostrophe

Have I kept apostrophes out of possessive pronouns (*its, whose, your, their*)?

Antecedents

Have I avoided ambiguous antecedents? Does my reader understand the referent of every *he, his, him, she, they, it, this, that?*

Reflexives

Have I used the reflexive pronoun (*-self, -selves*) only in object positions and only when its referent precedes it in the clause?

Auxiliaries

Is my choice of modal auxiliary or semi-auxiliary effective?

Qualifiers

Have I used qualifiers sparingly, choosing instead precise adjectives, adverbs, or verbs whenever possible?

Conjunctions

Do the conjunctions in my paper accurately express my reasoning?

PUNCTUATION REMINDERS

Have I remembered that personal pronouns do not take an apostrophe in the possessive case?

Have I remembered that the apostrophe added to a noun turns it into the possessive case: *cat/cat's* (singular); *cats/cats'* (plural)?

PART V

Punctuation

Punctuation is a reasoned art.
—REBECCA BRITTENHAM AND HILDEGARD HOELLER

In the preceding chapters, you learned about the structure of sentences: their basic units and the options we have for expanding and combining them. An important consideration throughout the book has been the effect of those options on the reader—hence the word *rhetorical* in the title. Those rhetorical effects extend to punctuation, so in addition to the possibilities for constructing sentences, you have learned about both the required and the optional punctuation rules that apply.

As you might expect, the conventions of punctuation have changed through the centuries. Early punctuation practices, designed to assist in the oral reading of medieval manuscripts, eventually evolved into our modern system, based more on structural boundaries than on the oral reader's needs. By the nineteenth century, the system we know today was generally in place. However, even though our punctuation rules are well established, they still include a great deal of flexibility. Today we tend toward an "open" or "light" style—omitting commas, for example, where the boundaries are apparent without them.

In Chapter 13 we look more closely at the punctuation decisions that writers make and the rhetorical impact those decisions have. At the end of the chapter you will find a brief glossary of the punctuation rules described in the earlier chapters, covering commas, colons, dashes, semicolons, and parentheses, along with a few other concerns that writers must address in connection with these and other punctuation marks. This section should serve as a handy reference.

Punctuation:
Its Purposes, Its Hierarchy,
and Its Rhetorical Effects

THE PURPOSES OF PUNCTUATION MARKS

In *A Linguistic Study of American Punctuation,* Charles F. Meyer classifies the purposes of punctuation into three categories: syntactic, prosodic, and semantic. Although you may not recognize these three words, they do describe the punctuation principles you have been studying in the preceding chapters.

Syntax refers to the structure of sentences—the main subject matter of this book. When you learned about the parts of the sentence and their relationships and their expansions, you were learning about syntax.

Prosody is the study of rhythm and intonation, which you remember especially from Chapter 6.

Semantics is the study of meaning.

Syntax

Linguists generally agree that the purpose underlying most of our punctuation rules is syntactic: In other words, the structure of the sentence determines the punctuation marks it will contain. A good example of a syntactically based punctuation rule is the one you learned in connection with the sentence patterns in Chapter 2: "Do not mark boundaries of the required sentence units with punctuation." This rule is clearly based on syntax, on sentence structure. In fact, syntax overrides all considerations of rhythm. Even though the reader may have to stop for breath between sentence units, that pause is not marked by a comma. Here's an example from Chapter 1 of a fairly long sentence, one that requires an extra breath—but has no boundaries that take punctuation:

> The images and information sent back by *Voyager 2* have given space scientists here on Earth enough information about four of our distant planets to keep them busy for years to come.

The predicate contains an indirect object and a direct object with two postnoun modifiers, but not one of those boundaries calls for punctuation.

Prosody

We often revise a sentence in order to change the way that the reader will read it—to change its rhythm pattern. For example, the intonation pattern of the sentence you just read would change if the first two words were reversed:

> Often we revise a sentence . . .

With this word order the reader will probably put more stress on *often*. To guarantee that emphasis, we can follow *often* with a comma. You'll recall from the discussion of sentence rhythm in Chapter 6 that the visual signal of a comma causes the reader to give added length and stress to the preceding word.

> Often, we revise a sentence . . .

This, then, is an example where the purpose of the punctuation mark can be attributed to prosody.

In Chapter 11 we saw another example of prosody in the discussion of the coordinate series, when we compared the rhythm patterns of two punctuation styles:

1. You have your own style of writing, just as you have your own style of walking and whistling and wearing your hair.
2. You have your own style of writing, just as you have your own style of walking, whistling, wearing your hair.

It is the rhythm of (2) that changes the message: It has an open-ended quality, as if to suggest, "I could go on and on with the list." Again, the purpose of the punctuation is to produce that rhythm. In this case, however, we would have to say that semantics is also involved: The punctuation affects both the rhythm and the meaning.

Semantics

One situation in which semantics, or meaning, determines the need for punctuation is that of the nonrestrictive phrase or clause, as we saw in the discussion of noun modifiers in Chapter 9. Syntax, of course, determines the boundaries of that modifier, but semantic considerations dictate the presence or absence of the commas: Does the modifier define the noun or simply comment on it?

This pair of sentences illustrates the distinction:

1. The man sitting by the window is talking to himself.
2. My mother, sitting by the window, is talking to herself.

We can assume in (1) that the scene includes at least one other man and that the purpose of the participial phrase is to identify the referent of the subject noun phrase, *the man*. That kind of identification is unnecessary in (2), where the subject noun phrase, *my mother,* has only one possible referent—no matter how many other women are present. Here the participial phrase merely comments.

The purpose of the punctuation is perhaps even more obviously a semantic one for the writer who has to decide between the following:

1. My sister Mary is coming for a visit.
2. My sister, Mary, is coming for a visit.

The sentence without commas implies that the writer has more than one sister. Clearly, it's the meaning that dictates the use of the comma.

The following pair also makes clear that the purpose of punctuation is sometimes semantic:

1. Call the boss Henry.
2. Call the boss, Henry.

These two are different sentence patterns: In (1) *Henry* is an object complement; in (2) *Henry* is a noun of direct address, known as a **vocative.**

Meyer cites the following pair of sentences to illustrate another situation where the comma changes the meaning:

1. Earlier negotiations were planned.
2. Earlier, negotiations were planned.

Here the punctuation has actually changed the class of the word *earlier.* In (1) it is an adjective, a modifier of the noun; in (2) it is an adverb, modifying the whole sentence.

In both of these last two examples, where the comma changes the meaning, it also alters the structure, the syntax, of the sentence. And it changes the rhythm. So these are probably good examples to illustrate the combination of all three punctuation purposes: syntactic, prosodic, and semantic.

THE HIERARCHY OF PUNCTUATION

If you were asked to place the parts of the sentence into a hierarchy, starting with "word," the result would look like this:

word

phrase

clause

sentence

The hierarchy of punctuation works in much the same way, usually in reverse order, with "sentence" at the top.

In the study of punctuation cited earlier, Meyer describes the hierarchy, the levels of punctuation, according to the kinds of boundaries that a particular punctuation mark encloses. For example, occupying the top level are the period, the question mark, and the exclamation point, all of which define sentence boundaries—and only sentence boundaries.

At the next level are the colon, the dash, and parentheses, all of which can define not only the boundaries of independent clauses, but also the boundaries of words, phrases, and dependent clauses.

The semicolon occupies the next level. It also defines clause boundaries, but in a much more limited way than the other three; and it has only one other role—to separate items in the coordinate series.

At the bottom level of the hierarchy is the comma, which can define the boundaries of words, phrases, and dependent clauses, but not the boundaries of independent clauses (unless a coordinating conjunction precedes it).

Here then is the hierarchy of punctuation marks:

period, question mark, exclamation point

colon, dash, parentheses

semicolon

comma

The hierarchy is obviously not a measure of importance or of frequency. In fact, the comma, although it occupies the lowest level, is our most frequent punctuation mark; and the exclamation point, one of three marks at the highest level, is the least frequent. The purpose of this scheme, rather, is to recognize the level of the functions that these marks can perform. For example, in Chapter 10 we looked at the following sentence in connection with appositives:

> Three committees—program, finance, and local arrangements—
> were set up to plan the convention.

The word boundaries here, marked by commas, are subordinate to those of the phrase boundaries; in order to distinguish the two levels, then, we use two different punctuation marks. The dashes mark the higher, or superordinate, level. To use commas for both levels of punctuation would make the sentence difficult to read. In the following version of the sentence, where the word boundaries are taken care of by conjunctions rather than commas, we have used commas for the phrase boundaries:

> Three committees, program and finance and local arrangements,
> were set up to plan the convention.

However, we could have retained the dashes in this revision, even though the phrase has no internal commas. Dashes would make the series stand out more strongly.

Because commas play so many roles in the sentence—providing boundaries for words and phrases and clauses—a sentence, especially a long one, can sometimes become heavy with commas:

> During the second two-year stretch of a term in office, the president may have to be on defensive, even with the norminating party, and, when, as frequently happens, this party loses a number of Senate and House seats in the midterm election, that second stretch can become even more defensive.

This sentence contains many levels of punctuation, with its coordinate independent clauses. The first clause contains opening and closing adverbial phrases, both of which are set off by commas. The other independent clause includes a dependent *as* clause embedded in a dependent *when* clause. Yet the only internal punctuation mark used for all of these levels is the comma.

One way to improve the sentence, to make it clearer for the reader, is to consider other punctuation marks that perform at some of these levels. One obvious boundary where we can use different punctuation is at the clause level—that is, to mark the two independent clauses—in place of the comma following *party.* We know that colons, dashes, and semicolons can all mark the boundary of an independent clause. In this case the best choice is the semicolon, because of its "and" meaning. (You'll recall that the colon generally connects two independent clauses with a "namely" or "here it comes" meaning—rather than "and.") Another choice is to begin a new sentence here. The semicolon, however, makes clear the close connection of the two independent clauses.

Next we should look at the comma following *and:* What is its function? It works with a partner, the comma after *election,* to set off the dependent *when-* clause. Is there any other mark that can do that job? In this position, the answer is probably "no." (On some occasions, dashes or parentheses can enclose dependent clauses, as we shall see later.) But now that we've substituted a semicolon, it is possible to eliminate *and.* After all, the reason for the *and* was the comma, which we've deleted. (You'll recall the rule about connecting two independent clauses with a comma: It requires a conjunction.)

Already our sentence looks better—and reads much more easily:

> During the second two-year stretch of a term in office, the president may have to be on the defensive, even with the nominating party; when, as frequently happens, his party loses a number of Senate and House seats in the midterm election, that second stretch can become even more defensive.

We're also using a comma here to set off the opening prepositional phrase. There's nothing else that can do that job, so that one has to stay. And we're using commas to set off the *as* clause within the *when* clause. Have we any other choice? Well, yes. We could mark that boundary with dashes—if we think it deserves the extra attention that dashes provide:

> During the second two-year stretch of a term in office, the president may have to be on the defensive, even with the nominating party; when—as frequently happens—this party loses a number of Senate and House seats in the midterm election, that second stretch can become even more defensive.

You may have noticed another place where a dash would fit: in the first clause after *defensive,* to set off the adverbial *even* phrase—in this case, only one dash, not a pair. But we probably don't want dashes in both places: They lose their special quality when they're used too often. And twice in one sentence is probably too often. We'll want to try it out in that earlier spot, just to see the difference. But chances are we'll leave the dashes where we have them now, where they replace two commas.

Now compare the two versions of that sentence—the original and the last revision. They're both punctuated "correctly." But certainly the difference makes clear how important it is for the writer to understand the various boundaries that require punctuation, to know how the tools of punctuation work.

EXERCISE 44

Revise the following passages, turning some of the sentences into modifiers. Experiment with commas, colons, and dashes.

1. The cost of repairs to the nation's public transportation facilities is an expenditure that cannot be delayed much longer if the system is to survive. Roads, bridges, and railroads are all in need of repair.

2. To many people, the mushroom is a lowly fungus. It has little food value. To other people, it is a gourmet's delight.

3. The paper nautilus octopus is a rare marine animal. It normally lives in the coastal waters of Japan. It was found recently in the squid nets off Santa Catalina in California.

4. The ivory-billed woodpecker is one of North America's rarest birds. It is North America's largest woodpecker. There have been documented sightings of this woodpecker in recent years.

5. Potatoes have the reputation of being fattening. A medium potato has only 100 calories. It's the butter and gravy that make the potato fattening. Potatoes are highly nutritious. They contain vitamin C and a number of trace minerals. They are low in sodium, high in potassium, and thus the ideal food for preventing high blood pressure. The potato is even high in vegetable protein. All in all, the lowly potato is a nutrient bargain. (Information adapted from Jane Brody's *Good Food Book*.)

THE RHETORICAL EFFECTS OF PUNCTUATION

The subtitle of this book is *Grammatical Choices, Rhetorical Effects*. Those grammatical choices, of course, include punctuation choices, and such choices also have rhetorical effects. In Chapter 4 you studied a variety of ways to combine the clauses into a compound sentence with the comma, the semicolon, and the colon. These five variations offer as many choices as you will ever need in this situation for effecting appropriate responses in your reader:

1. I loved the book, but I hated the movie.
2. I loved the book; I hated the movie.

3. I loved the book; and I'm amazed the movie was so bad.
4. I loved the book; however, I hated the movie.
5. I loved the book: It made me want to try to write my own memoir.

The first one we might think of as the basic compound sentence rule, with fairly equal emphasis on the two clauses. In (2) and (3), the greater pause that the semicolon provides puts more emphasis on the second clause. The addition of *however* in (4) adds a note of deliberation, a degree of thoughtfulness in coming to a decision about the movie. The colon in (5) commands special attention: The reader expects to learn why I loved the book.

How about using just the comma—in other words, a comma splice? The sentences are certainly short and closely connected:

I loved the book, I hated the movie.

Yes, that choice could work. (After all, it's not always an error—at least, not when famous writers use it.) The comma splice gives both clauses a kind of flatness—especially the second one. As in the version with the bare semicolon, the reader will sense that same "no argument" tone. However—and this "however" is important—that comma splice will work best if you're one of those famous writers. Then the reader will recognize your choice as deliberate, not as an error: The reader will know that you know the rule. But in an essay for your English class, the teacher will probably mark the comma splice as an error and ask you to review the rule. On the job, your supervisor will probably fix the splice before handing your report on to the next level—and be on the lookout in your next report. And a prospective employer who spots a comma splice in your letter of application might see it as an error—and remain prospective.

Another commonly marked punctuation error is the omitted comma following an introductory element. This situation is covered in several of the highlighted rules you read in previous chapters: Where that introductory element is a verb phrase or contains a verb phrase and where the introductory element is an adverbial clause, the comma is required. Here are some examples:

To understand the punctuation of compound sentences, you have to recognize independent clauses.

Before studying the punctuation of compound sentences, you must learn to recognize independent clauses.

If you can recognize independent clauses, you will find it easy to punctuate compound sentences.

Writers rarely deviate from this punctuation. However, when that opening structure is a prepositional phrase, you have a choice. If you want the reader to pause, to put strong stress on the opening element, particularly on its last word, then go ahead and use the comma:

> From the doorway, I can see the last of my students walking
> up the dirt road into the school grounds.
>
> —Frank Bures, "Test Day"

You might recall that the comma is recommended for the opening prepositional phrase if it exceeds five or six words. That recommendation is related to readability. If the comma would help the reader, you'll want to include it, no matter how many words in the opener.

The highlighted boxes throughout the book are reserved for those rules that constitute agreed-upon conventions. They are rules that you should know thoroughly. And while it's true that writers do deviate from them on occasion, you will want to consider the effect on your reader before doing so. Chances are, the reader will have more confidence in your ideas when you demonstrate your expertise of the standard punctuation conventions—even those situations where deviations from the standard may be common.

Not all of the punctuation rules in this book are highlighted. For example, there is no hard and fast rule about the serial comma (page 57). And certainly the use of conjunctions in the series rather than commas will produce quite different rhetorical effects. Other discussions that emphasize variation describe the choices we have with dashes and colons for special emphasis. With these two punctuation marks, you achieve different levels of formality. And using them well can affect the reader's judgment of your ability as a writer—and very likely the reader's judgment of your ideas.

If you had the notion, before studying *Rhetorical Grammar,* that punctuation is nothing more than a final, added-on step in the writing process, we hope you have learned otherwise. Many of the punctuation choices you make are determined by the rhetorical situation; those choices are an integral part of the composing and revision stages in all of your writing tasks.

Remember, punctuation can do in writing what your voice does in speech—not as well in many cases, but even better in some. Punctuation helps the reader hear your voice and understand your message.

FOR GROUP DISCUSSION

1. One of Robert Frost's most famous poems is "Stopping by Woods on a Snowy Evening." In some printed versions the last stanza begins like this:

> The woods are lovely, dark, and deep,
> But I have promises to keep

In others, the punctuation of the first line follows the poet's original:

> The woods are lovely, dark and deep,

Given what you know about the punctuation of the series and of the appositive, do you think that these two versions mean the same thing? If they do, why would anyone object to that extra comma?

2. In the following sentence from *The New York Times,* written by John Tierney, there are two series of noun phrases, neither of which includes the serial comma, the comma before *and:*

> Individuals are acquiring more control over their lives, their minds and their bodies, even their genes, thanks to the transformations in medicine, communications, transportation and industry.

Is it possible that the group of three noun phrases—*their lives, their minds, their bodies*—is not intended to be a group, a series? What other function might "their minds and their bodies" have? Show how we might punctuate it without ambiguity in two different ways, depending on its meaning.

EXERCISE 45

The following paragraphs are reproduced exactly as they were published—with one exception: *All internal punctuation has been removed; only the sentence-end marks have been retained.* Your job is to put the punctuation marks back into the sentences. (Don't forget hyphens and apostrophes!) As you know, punctuation rules are not carved in stone; consequently, in some places your version may differ from the original—and still be correct. You can check your version against that of the author in the Answers to the Exercises section.

> Management is still taught in most business schools as a bundle of techniques such as budgeting and personnel relations. To be sure management like any other work has its own tools and its own techniques. But just as the essence of medicine is not urinalysis important though that is the essence of management is not techniques and procedures. The essence of management is to make knowledge productive. Management in other words is a social function. And in its practice management is truly a liberal art.

The old communities family village parish and so on have all but disappeared in the knowledge society. Their place has largely been taken by the new unit of social integration the organization. Where community was fate organization is voluntary membership. Where community claimed the entire person organization is a means to a person's ends a tool. For 200 years a hot debate has been raging especially in the West are communities organic or are they simply extensions of the people of which they are made? Nobody would claim that the new organization is organic. It is clearly an artifact a creation of man a social technology.

—Peter F. Drucker (*The Atlantic Monthly*)

KEY TERMS

Colon	Prosody	Semantics
Comma	Punctuation	Semicolon
Dash	Punctuation	Syntax
Exclamation point	hierarchy	Vocative
Parentheses	Question mark	

Glossary of Punctuation

Apostrophe

1. Possessive Case

A. For Singular Nouns
To show the possessive case, add *'s* to singular nouns, both common and proper:

Bob's friend	the ocean's blue color

The rule also applies to indefinite pronouns:

someone's book	everyone's vote

Note. Remember that possessive pronouns do not have apostrophes. Some pronouns are easily confused with contractions:

its (possessive)	it's (it is)
your (possessive)	you're (you are)
their (possessive)	they're (they are)
whose (possessive)	who's (who is)

When a singular noun ends in *s,* the rule gets a bit fuzzy. Generally, we add an apostrophe and another *s: Brooks's poetry.* However, there are two possible exceptions to this rule. Some editors recommend adding just an apostrophe when a name such as *Achilles* ends in the sound "eez": *Achilles' heel.* They also suggest using just an apostrophe after some singular common nouns that end in *s: physics' offering.*

B. For Plural Nouns
To make a regular plural noun possessive, add only the apostrophe:

the cats' tails	the students' complaints

For irregular plurals (those formed without adding *s*), add *'s:*

the women's movement	children's books

2. Plurals of Initials and Words Other Than Nouns
In making initials and non-nouns plural, when the addition of *s* alone would be misleading, include an apostrophe:

two B's (sometimes two Bs)	p's and q's	yes's and no's

3. **Contractions**

In writing contractions, use an apostrophe to replace the missing syllable or letter(s):

don't = do not   he'll = he will   Pat's = Pat is, Pat has
it's = it is, it has   can't = cannot

Brackets

1. **Within Parentheses**

Use brackets for parenthetical material that is already within parentheses:

Mount Washington is so dangerous because of its location amid three storm routes (reported by *National Geographic* staff writer Neil Shea in "Backyard Arctic" [February 2009]).

2. **In Quoted Material**

Use brackets for interpolations or explanations within quoted material—to show that it is not part of the quotation:

"Everyone close to the king surmised that she [Mrs. Simpson] would be nothing but trouble for the realm."

Colon

1. **Appositives**

Use the colon to introduce an appositive or a list of appositives:

The board appointed three committees to plan the convention: finance, program, and local arrangements.

Often such a list is introduced by "as follows" or "the following":

The three committees are as follows: finance, program, and local arrangements.
The board appointed the following committees: finance, program, and local arrangements.

Remember that a complete sentence precedes the colon; what follows the colon is an appositive. *Do not* put a colon between a linking verb and the subject complement:

*The committees that were appointed are: finance, program, and local arrangements.

2. **Coordination of Independent Clauses**

Use a colon to join the two independent clauses of a compound sentence, where the second completes the idea, or the promise, of the first. The connection often means "namely" or "that is":

Only one obstacle lay between us and success: We had to find the money.

Note: The convention of capitalizing the first word of a complete sentence following the colon is on the fence: Some publishers always capitalize; others capitalize only when what follows is a direct quotation; others capitalize questions and direct quotations. Whichever method you follow, as with any optional convention, be sure to follow it consistently.

Comma

1. **Compound Sentences**

   Use a comma along with a coordinating conjunction between the independent clauses in a compound sentence:

   > I didn't believe a word Phil said, and I told him so.

   Remember that the comma alone produces a comma splice.

2. **Series**

   Use commas when listing a series of three or more sentence elements:

   > We gossiped, laughed, and sang the old songs at our class reunion.
   > We hunted in the basement, in the attic, and through all the storage rooms, to no avail.

   The serial comma, the one before *and,* is optional; however, usage—either with or without it—must be consistent.

3. **Introductory Dependent Clauses**

   Use a comma to set off an introductory dependent clause:

   > When the riot started, the police fired tear gas into the crowd.

4. **Sentence–Ending Clauses**

   Use a comma to set off a dependent adverbial clause following the main clause if the adverbial clause has no effect on the outcome of the main clause:

   > Some people refused to leave, even though the hurricane winds had started.

   Note that in the following sentences the idea in the main clause will not be realized without the adverbial clause; therefore, we do not use a comma:

   > I'll pack up and leave if you tell me to.
   > We left the area because we were afraid to stay.

   In general, *if* and *because* clauses are not set off; those introduced by *although* and *even though* are.

   You should also be aware that the rules regarding adverbial clauses are among the least standardized of our punctuation conventions.

5. **Introductory Verb Phrases**

   Use a comma to set off any introductory phrase that contains a verb:

   > After studying all weekend, I felt absolutely prepared for the midterm exam.
   > Having worked at McDonald's for the past four summers, Maxie felt confident when he applied for the job of assistant manager.
   > To get in shape for ski season, my roommate has begun working out on the NordicTrack.

   Note: In most cases the subject of the sentence must also be the subject of the verb in that introductory phrase; otherwise, the verb phrase dangles. Exceptions occur with set phrases:

   > Speaking of the weather, let's have a picnic.
   > To tell the truth, I have never read *Silas Marner.*

6. **Introductory Prepositional Phrases**

Use a comma to set off adverbial prepositional phrases of approximately six or more words:

> Toward the end of the semester, everyone in my dorm starts to study seriously.

It is perfectly acceptable to set off shorter prepositional phrases, especially if you think the reader should pause. For example, information of specific dates is sometimes set off:

> In 1990, the official dismantling of the Berlin Wall began.

In making the decision about such commas, consider the punctuation in the rest of the sentence: Don't overload the sentence with commas.

Set off any prepositional phrase that might cause a misreading:

> During the summer, vacation plans are our main topic of conversation.

See the next section for prepositional phrases that are parenthetical.

7. **Other Sentence Modifiers**

Set off words and phrases that modify the whole sentence, serve as transitions, or have a parenthetical meaning—at both the beginning and the end of the sentence:

A. Adverbs

> Luckily, we escaped without a scratch.
> We escaped without a scratch, luckily.
> Meanwhile, there was nothing to do but wait.

B. *Yes* and *no:*

> Yes, he's the culprit.   No, I can't go out tonight.

C. Transitional prepositional phrases

> In fact, there was nothing I could do about her problem.
> In the meantime, I listened to her sad tale.

These parenthetical words and phrases often provide a transitional tie to the previous sentence, which the comma emphasizes. They are also used to slow the reader down or to shift the point of sentence stress.

D. Absolute phrases

> Money in our pockets, we headed to town.
> Ginny relaxed before the fire, her feet propped on the footstool.

8. **Nonrestrictive Modifiers**

Use commas to set off commenting (nonrestrictive) modifiers in the noun phrase. Remember that an adjectival is nonrestrictive when the referent of the noun it modifies is already clear to the reader or if the noun has only one possible referent:

> My oldest brother, a history major, spends every night in the library.

9. **Coordinate Adjectives**

Use commas in the noun phrase between coordinate adjectives in preheadword position. Coordinate refers to adjectives of the same class—for example, subjective qualities:

> a tender, delightful story   an easy, winning smile

If the adjectives are of different classes, no comma is necessary.

a tall young man   a huge red ball

A good rule of thumb for making a decision about commas between these prenoun modifiers is this: If you could insert *and* or *but*, use a comma:

A tender and delightful love story

Notice that the two phrases without commas contain adjectives from different classes (height, age, size, color)—so they will not be separated:

*a tall and young man   *a huge and red ball

10. **Nouns of Direct Address (Vocatives)**
Use a comma to set off vocatives in both opening and closing position:

Students, your time is up.   Put your pencils down, everyone.

11. **Direct Quotations**
Use commas to set off direct quotations after verbs such as *say* and *reply:*

The waiter said, "Good evening. My name is Pierre."
Harold replied, "I'm Harold, and this is Joyce."

Note: This is actually an exception to the punctuation rule you learned in Chapter 2: "Do not mark the boundaries of the basic sentence units with commas." When the direct object is a direct quotation, we do mark the boundary.

Direct quotations can also be introduced by colons:
Harold replied: "I'm Harold, and this is Joyce."

12. **State and Year**
Use commas to set off the name of a state when it follows the name of a city:

I was surprised to learn that Cheyenne, Wyoming, isn't a larger city.

Also set off the year in a complete date:

Born on August 13, 1899, Alfred Hitchcock was the youngest of three children.

Dash

1. **Interruptions Within a Sentence**
Use a dash (or pair of dashes) to set off any interrupting structure within the sentence or at the end:

Tim quit his job—a brave decision, in my opinion—to look for something new.
Tim decided to quit his job and look for another—a brave decision.

When the interrupter is a complete sentence, it is punctuated as a phrase would be:

Tim quit his job—he was always a rash young man—to follow Horace Greeley's advice and go West.

2. **Appositives**
Use dashes to call attention to an appositive:

The microorganisms that seem to have it in for us in the worst way—the ones that really appear to wish us ill—turn out on close examination to be rather more like bystanders, strays, strangers in from the cold.

—Lewis Thomas

Use a pair of dashes to set off a list of appositives that are themselves separated by commas:

> All the committees—finance, program, and local arrangements—went to work with real enthusiasm.

The list of appositives set off by a dash can also come at the beginning of the sentence when the subject is a pronoun referring to the list:

> The faculty, the students, the staff—all were opposed to the provost's decision to reinstate the old dormitory regulations.

Namely and *that is,* both of which are signalers of appositives, can be preceded by either a dash or a comma; the dash gives the appositive more emphasis:

> Some mammals have no hair—namely, the whales.
> The provost's decision brought out over 1,500 student protesters, that is, a third of the student body.

Ellipsis Points

1. Three periods, each preceded and followed by a space, are used to indicate the omission of one or more words within a quoted sentence. An omission at the end of a sentence is indicated by a period (preceded by no space) followed by three spaced periods. Here is an original sentence and the cut versions that illustrate these two styles:

> A group of the West Oxfordshire local squires and the wealthier farmers, just like their opposite numbers in countless other towns and villages up and down the country, had decided to have the local fields apportioned privately, and farmed efficiently. A surveyor was needed, and Webb was brought over from Stow-on-the-Wold, ten miles away.
> —Simon Winchester (*The Map That Changed the World*)

> A group of the West Oxfordshire local squires and the wealthier farmers . . . had decided to have the local fields apportioned privately, and farmed efficiently. A surveyor was needed. . . .

2. Four periods are also used for the omission of a complete sentence or more, even a complete paragraph. In poetry the omission of a line is indicated by a complete line of periods.

Exclamation Point

1. **Exclamatory Sentence**
   The exclamation point is the terminal punctuation for the exclamatory sentence, a transformation that changes the emphasis of a declarative sentence, usually with a *what* or *how*:

We have a hard-working committee.	*What a hard-working committee we have!*
It's a gorgeous day.	*What a gorgeous day it is!*

   The exclamation point is actually optional—and in some cases would be inappropriate:

How calm the ocean is today.	What a sweet child you have.

2. **Emphasis**

The exclamation point is used in sentences that call for added emotions; however, it should be used sparingly. It is rarely used in formal prose.

> "Get out!" he shouted. "I never want to see you again!"
>
> The history exam took me by surprise: I had studied the wrong chapters!

Hyphen

1. **Compound Words or Phrases**

The hyphen expresses a compound word or phrase in prenoun position as a unit:

a two-inch board	a silver-plated teapot
a well-designed running shoe	an out-of-work carpenter

Note that when they are not in prenoun position, the hyphens are not needed in most cases:

The board is two inches wide.	The shoe was well designed.

When the modifier in prenoun position is an *-ly* adverb, the hyphen is not used:

a nicely designed running shoe	a clearly phrased message

Parentheses

1. **Interruptions**

Parentheses, in many cases, function just as dashes and commas do—to set off explanatory information or, in some cases, the writer's digressions:

> I stopped her and put a five-sou piece (a little more than a farthing) into her hand.
>
> —George Orwell

Unlike dashes, which call attention to a passage, the parentheses generally add the information as an aside: They say, "By the way," whereas the dash says, "Hey, listen to this!"

2. **Technical Information**

Parentheses are also used for including technical information within a text:

> For years I never missed an issue of *Astounding* (now published as *Analog*).

3. **Punctuation Notes**

A complete sentence added parenthetically within another sentence has neither an opening capital letter nor end punctuation:

> The long winters in North Dakota (newcomers quickly learn that March is a winter month) make spring a time of great joy.

However, when a complete sentence is enclosed in parentheses but it is not embedded in another sentence, the terminal punctuation is placed within the parentheses:

> I look forward to every month of the year. (February, I will admit, is short on saving graces, but at least it's short.)

Period

1. Sentence End

The period marks the end of a declarative or imperative sentence:

It's raining. Close the window.

2. Abbreviations

Abbreviations with internal periods have no space after the internal period.

U.S.   B.A.   a.m.

Initials of personal names, however, retain the space:

J. F. Kennedy   H. L. Mencken

The period is omitted after an abbreviation at the end of a sentence that has a period of its own:

My publisher is part of Pearson Education, Inc.

The abbreviating period is retained before other end punctuation:

Did you remember to bring the pillows, blankets, towels, etc.?

Question Marks

1. End of Question

Use the question mark as terminal punctuation in all direct questions:

Do you have anything to add?   He said what?

However, polite requests in the form of questions are often punctuated with the period:

Would you mind opening the window.

2. Quotations

In punctuating quoted questions, include the question mark within the quotation marks:

John asked, "Do you have anything to add?"

When a quoted statement is embedded at the end of a question, the question mark is outside the quotation marks:

Who said, "Give me liberty or give me death"?

Note that the period is omitted from the quoted sentence.

When a quoted question is embedded in another question, only one question mark is used—and that one is inside the quotation marks:

Did he ask you straight out, "Are you a shoplifter?"

Quotation Marks

1. For Direct Quotations

Use double quotation marks to indicate another person's exact words, both spoken and written:

In 1943 Churchill told Stalin, "In war-time, truth is so precious that she should always be attended by a bodyguard of lies."

Notice that the quotation marks are outside the period. This system applies even when the quotation marks enclose a single word, such as a title:

My father's favorite poem is Rudyard Kipling's "If."

However, quotation marks are placed inside semicolons and colons:

She said, "Come to the party"; I had to turn her down.

2. Within Direct Quotations

Use single quotation marks when the quoted material is within a quoted passage:

Describing the degeneracy of the nation in a letter to Joshua F. Speed, Lincoln wrote that "as a nation we began by declaring that 'all men are created equal.' We now practically read it 'all men are created equal except Negroes.'"

Notice that both the single and the double quotation marks are outside the period.

For quotation marks with questions, see the preceding section under "Question Marks."

Semicolon

1. As a Conjunction

Use a semicolon to connect independent clauses in a compound sentence. You can think of the semicolon as having the connective force of the comma-plus-conjunction:

The use of the semicolon indicates a close relationship between clauses; it gives the sentence a tight, separate-but-equal bond.

2. In the Separation of a Series

Use semicolons to separate a series of structures that have internal punctuation:

In this chapter we looked at three purposes underlying our punctuation system: syntactic, related to structure; prosodic, related to sentence rhythm; and semantic, related to meaning.

Glossary of Terms

For further explanation of the terms listed here, check the index for page references.

Absolute adjective. An adjective with a meaning that is generally not capable of being intensified or compared, such as *unique* or *perfect* or *square*. Careful writers avoid such usages as *very perfect* or *more unique*.

Absolute phrase. A noun phrase that includes a postnoun modifier and is related to the sentence as a whole, providing a detail or point of focus: "She sat quietly, *her hands folded in her lap*."

Abstract noun. A noun that refers to a quality, such as peace or happiness, rather than a material, concrete object.

Active voice. A feature of transitive verb sentences in which the subject is generally the agent and the direct object is the goal or objective of the action. *Voice* refers to the relationship of the subject to the verb. See also *Passive voice*.

Adjectival. Any structure, no matter what its form, that functions as a modifier of a noun—that is, that functions as an adjective normally functions. See Chapter 9.

Adjectival clause. *See* Relative clause.

Adjective. One of the four form classes, whose members act as modifiers of nouns; most adjectives can be inflected for comparative and superlative degree (*big, bigger, biggest*); they can be qualified or intensified (*rather big, very big*); they have characteristic derivational affixes such as *-ous (famous)*, *-ish (childish)*, *-ful (graceful)*, and *-ary (complementary)*.

Adjective phrase. An adjective that includes a modifier: *very nice, afraid to fly*.

Adverb. One of the four form classes, whose members act as modifiers of verbs, contributing information of time, place, reason, manner, and the like. Like adjectives, certain adverbs can be qualified (*very quickly, rather fast*); some can be inflected for comparative and superlative degree (*more quickly, fastest*); they have characteristic derivational endings such as *-ly (quickly)*, *-wise (lengthwise)*, *-ward (backward)*.

Adverbial. Any structure, no matter what its form, that functions as a modifier of a verb—that is, that functions as an adverb normally functions. See Chapter 8.

Adverbial of emphasis. An adverbial, generally a single word, that shifts emphasis to a particular structure: for example *hardly, always, rarely, never*.

Agency. The relationship of the subject and verb. See also *Agent*.

Agent. The initiator of the action in the sentence—the "doer" or "perpetrator" of the action. Usually the agent is the subject in an active sentence: "*John* groomed the dog"; "*The committee* elected Pam." In a passive sentence the agent, if mentioned, will be the object of a preposition: "Pam was elected by *the committee*."

Agreement. (1) Subject–verb. A third-person singular subject in the present tense takes the *-s* form of the verb: "*The dog barks* all night"; "He *bothers* the neighbors." A plural takes the base form: "*The dogs bark*"; "*They bother* the neighbors." (2) Pronoun–antecedent. The number of the pronoun (whether singular or plural) agrees with the number of its antecedent. "*The boys* did *their* chores"; "The *man who* works for us is on vacation." (Note that both *man* and *who* take the *-s* form of their verbs.)

Ambiguity. A condition in which a structure has more than one possible meaning. The source may be lexical ("She is *blue*") or structural ("*Visiting relatives* can be boring") or both ("The detective looked *hard*").

Anaphora. A figure of speech describing repetition at the beginning of successive sentences: "*Mad* world! *Mad* kings! *Mad* composition!" [Shakespeare]

Anastrophe. A figure of speech describing a reversal of the normal order of a sentence: "*The rest of the story you know.*"

Antecedent. The noun or nominal that a pronoun stands for.

Antithesis. The juxtaposition of contrasting ideas: "I come to bury Caesar, not to praise him."

Appositive. A structure, usually a noun phrase, that renames a nominal structure, that shares a nominal slot: "My neighbor, *a butcher at Weis Market,* recently lost his job."

Article. One of the determiner classes, including the indefinite *a,* or *an,* which signals only countable nouns, and the definite *the,* which can signal all classes of nouns.

Asyndeton. A figure of speech describing the omission of a conjunction: "*I came, I saw, I conquered.*"

Attributor. A metadiscourse signal that refers to the source of quoted information: *according to, cited in.*

Auxiliary verb. One of the structure-class words, a marker of verbs. Auxiliaries include forms of *have* and *be,* as well as the modals, such as *will, shall,* and *must.* See also Do-*support.*

Backgrounding. The process of placing known information, or perhaps less important information, in a subordinate role in the sentence rather than in a position of main focus. See also *Foregrounding.*

Be patterns. Sentence Patterns 1 (Subject + *Be* + Adverbial) and 2 (Subject + *Be* + Subject Complement).

Broad reference. A pronoun that refers to a complete sentence rather than to a specific noun or nominal. The broad-reference clause is introduced by *which.* "Judd told jokes all evening, *which drove us crazy.*" The demonstrative pronouns *this* and *that* and the personal pronoun *it* are also sometimes used with broad reference: "Judd told jokes again last night; *that* really drives me crazy." Those sentences with demonstratives can be improved if the pronoun is turned into a determiner: "*That silly behavior of his* drives me crazy."

Case. A feature of nouns and certain pronouns that denotes their function in the sentence. Pronouns have three case distinctions: subjective (*I, they, who,* etc.), possessive (*my, their, whose,* etc.), and objective (*me, them, whom,* etc.). Nouns have only one case inflection, the possessive *(John's, the cat's)*. The case of nouns other than the possessive is sometimes referred to as common case.

Clause. A structure with a subject and a predicate. The sentence patterns are clause patterns.

Cleft sentence. A sentence variation using an *it* clause or *what* clause to shift the sentence focus: "Lightning caused the fire" $\longrightarrow$ "It was lightning that caused the fire"; "What caused the fire was lightning."

Cliché. A worn-out word or phrase: "hard as nails"; "cute as a bug's ear."

Climax. The arrangement of a series of words, phrases, or clauses in order of importance, scope, or length.

Code gloss. A metadiscourse signal used to clarify the meaning of a word or phrase, often a parenthetical comment.

Cohesion. The connections between sentences. Cohesive ties are furnished by pronouns that have antecedents in previous sentences, by conjunctions and conjunctive adverb, by known information, and by knowledge shared by the reader.

Collective noun. A noun that refers to a collection of individuals: *group, team, family.* Collective nouns can be replaced by either singular or plural pronouns, depending on the meaning.

Comma splice. The connection of two independent clauses in a compound sentence with a comma alone. Conventional punctuation requires a conjunction with the comma.

Command. See *Imperative sentence.*

Common noun. A noun with general, rather than unique, reference (in contrast to proper nouns). Common nouns may be countable *(house, book)* or noncountable *(water, oil)*; they may be concrete *(house, water)* or abstract *(justice, indifference)*.

Comparative degree. See *Degree.*

Complement. A structure that "completes" the sentence. The term includes those slots in the predicate that complete the verb: direct object, indirect object, subject complement, and object complement. Certain adjectives also have complements—clauses and phrases that pattern with them: "I was *certain that he would come*"; "I was *afraid to go.*"

Complementizer. A word that enables the writer or speaker to embed one sentence in another: "He loves me" $\longrightarrow$ "I know *that* he loves me."

Complex sentence. A sentence that includes a dependent clause.

Compound-complex sentence. A sentence with two or more independent clauses and at least one dependent clause.

Compound sentence. A sentence with two or more independent clauses.

Conditional mood. The attitude of probability designated by the modal auxiliaries *could, may, might, would,* and *should.*

Conjunction. One of the structure classes, which includes connectors that coordinate structures of many forms (e.g., *and, or*), subordinate sentences (e.g., *if, because, when*), and coordinate sentences with an adverbial emphasis (e.g., *however, therefore*).

Conjunctive adverb. A conjunction that connects two independent clauses with an adverbial emphasis, such as *however, therefore, moreover,* and *nevertheless.*

Connotation. The idea or feeling that a word evokes. See also *Denotation*.

Contraction. A combination of two words written or spoken as one, in which letters or sounds are omitted. In writing, the omission is marked by an apostrophe: *isn't, they're*.

Coordinating conjunction. A conjunction that connects two or more sentences or structures within a sentence as equals: *and, but, or, nor, for*, and *yet*.

Coordination. A way of expanding sentences in which two or more structures of the same form function as a unit. All the sentence parts as well as the sentence itself, can be coordinated.

Correlative conjunction. A two-part conjunction that expresses a relationship between the coordinated structures: *either–or, neither–nor, both–and, not only–but also*.

Countable noun. A noun whose referent can be identified as a separate entity; the countable noun can be signaled by the indefinite article, *a*, and by numbers: *a house; an experience; two eggs; three problems*. See also *Noncountable noun*.

Dangling modifier. A verb phrase placed so that it has no clear relationship to its subject, which is the word it should modify. The dangling participle occurs when the sentence subject is not also the subject of the sentence-opening or-closing participle: "*Wearing her new outfit,* everyone looked admiringly at Mary." Revised: "Wearing her new outfit, Mary was the center of attention." Sentences with dangling gerunds, infinitives, or elliptical clauses also require revision.

Declarative sentence. A sentence in the form of a statement (in contrast to a command, a question, or an exclamation).

Definite article. The determiner *the,* which generally marks a specific or previously mentioned noun: "*the* man on *the* corner"; "*the* blue coat I want for Christmas."

Degree. The variations in adjectives and some adverbs that indicate the simple quality of a noun, or positive degree ("Bill is a *big* boy"); its comparison to another, the comparative degree ("Bill is *bigger* than Tom"); or its comparison to two or more, the superlative degree ("Bill is the *biggest* person in the whole class"). In most adjectives of two or more syllables, the comparative and superlative degrees are marked by *more* and *most,* respectively.

Demonstrative pronoun. The pronouns *this* (plural *these*) and *that* (plural *those*), which function as nominal substitutes and as determiners. They include the feature of proximity: near *(this, these)* and distant *(that, those)*.

Denotation. The primary or dictionary definition of a word. See also *Connotation*.

Dependent clause. A clause that functions as an adverbial, adjectival, or nominal (in contrast to an independent clause).

Derivational affix. A suffix or prefix that is added to a form-class word, either to change its class *(fame–famous; act–action)* or to change its meaning *(legal–illegal; boy–boyhood)*.

Determiner. One of the structure-class words, a signaler of nouns. Determiners include articles *(a, the)*, possessive nouns and pronouns (e.g., *Chuck's, his, my*), demonstrative pronouns *(this, that, these, those)*, indefinite pronouns (e.g., *many, each, every*), and numbers.

Diction. The selection of words, usually referred to in connection with the correct choice of words in terms of their meaning and the appropriate choice in terms of the audience and purpose.

Direct address. A noun or noun phrase addressing a person or group: "*Ladies and gentlemen,* may I have your attention"; "Tell me, *dear,* what you're thinking." Also called a vocative.

Direct object. A nominal in the predicate of the transitive sentence patterns. The direct object names the objective or goal or the receiver of the verb's action: "We ate *the peanuts*"; "The boy hit *the ball*"; "I enjoy *playing chess.*"

Do-support. The addition of the auxiliary *do* to a verb string that has no other auxiliary. The question, the negative, and the emphatic transformations all require an auxiliary. *Do* also substitutes for a repeated verb phrase in compound sentences: "Bryan liked the movie, and I *did* too."

Ellipsis. See *Elliptical clause.*

Elliptical clause. A clause in which a part has been left out but is "understood": "Chester is older *than I (am old)*"; "Bev can jog farther *than Otis (can jog)*"; "*When (you are) planning your essay,* be sure to consider the audience." Ellipsis can be an effective stylistic device.

End focus. The common rhythm pattern in which the prominent peak of stress falls on or near the final sentence unit.

Existential *there*. The use of *there* to signal the existence of something, often the signal of new information: "*There* is a community garden near the playground."

Expletive. A word that enables the writer or speaker to shift the stress in a sentence. "A fly is in my soup" ⟶ "*There* is a fly in my soup."

Figurative language. Language that expresses meaning in nonliteral terms, characterized by figures of speech, such as metaphors, similes, analogies, and personification.

Figure of speech. Stylistic variations, also called figurative language, including comparisons (metaphor, similes, analogy, personification) that help the reader understand the writer's message, along with structural variations, including repetition, parallelism, and antithesis.

Flat adverb. A class of adverb that is the same in form as its corresponding adjective: *fast, high, early, late, hard, long,* and so on.

Foregrounding. The placement of important information in the position of prominent focus. See also *Backgrounding.*

Form classes. The large, open classes of words that provide the lexical content of the language: nouns, verbs, adjectives, and adverbs. Each has characteristic derivational and inflectional affixes that distinguish its forms.

Fragment. A phrase or clause that is punctuated as a full sentence. Some are simply punctuation errors; others are used deliberately for special effects.

Free modifier. A modifying phrase or clause that opens or closes the sentence, generally expanding on the main idea. Participial phrases, absolute phrases, and resumptive modifiers are among common free modifiers.

Fused sentence. A compound sentence without appropriate connectors or punctuation between independent clauses. Also called a *run-on sentence.*

Gerund. An *-ing* verb functioning as a nominal: "I enjoy *jogging*"; "*Running* is good exercise"; "After *getting* my pilot's license, I hope to fly to Lake Tahoe."

Headword. The key noun in the noun phrase: "the little *boy* across the street"; the verb that heads the verb phrase: *plays,* was *written,* has been *playing.*

Hedge. One of the metadiscourse signals in which the writer expresses uncertainty or a qualification: *may, perhaps, under certain circumstances.*

Helping verb. See *Auxiliary verb.*

Hypercorrection. Making a correction when one isn't necessary. The tendency to hyper-correct usually stems from the misapplication of rules learned in childhood.

Idiom. A combination of words whose meaning cannot be predicted from the meaning of the individual words. Many phrasal verbs are idioms: *look up* [a word]; *put up with; back down; give in.*

Imperative sentence. The sentence in the form of a command. The imperative sentence includes the base form of the verb and usually an understood subject *(you)*: "*Eat* your spinach"; "*Finish* your report as soon as possible"; "You *go* on without me."

Indefinite article. The determiner *a,* or *an,* which marks an unspecified countable noun. See also *Definite article.*

Indefinite pronoun. A large category that includes quantifiers (e.g., *enough, several, many, much*), universals *(all, both, every, each),* and partitives (e.g., *any, anyone, anybody, either, neither, no, nobody, some, someone*). Many of the indefinite pronouns can function as determiners.

Independent clause. A sequence of words that includes a subject and a predicate and can stand alone. A sentence must have at least one independent clause.

Indirect object. The nominal following verbs like *give.* The indirect object is the recipient; the direct object is the thing given: "We gave *our friends* a ride home."

Infinitive. The base form of the verb (present tense), usually expressed with *to,* which is called "the infinitive marker." The infinitive can function adverbially ("I stayed up all night *to study* for the exam"); adjectivally ("That is no way *to study*"); and nominally ("*To stay up* all night is foolish"). The only verb with an infinitive form separate from the present tense is *be.*

Infinitive phrase. A verb phrase headed by the infinitive; it can function as an adjectival, adverbial, or nominal.

Inflections. Suffixes that are added to the form classes (nouns, verbs, adjectives, and adverbs) to change their grammatical role in some way. Nouns have two inflectional suffixes (*-s* plural and *'s* possessive); verbs have four (*-s, -ing, -ed,* and *-en*); adjectives and some adverbs have two (*-er* and *-est*). Pronouns also have inflectional endings.

Intensive reflexive pronoun. The function of the reflexive pronoun when it serves as an appositive to emphasize a noun or pronoun: "I *myself* prefer chocolate." See also *Reflexive pronoun.*

Intonation. The rhythmic pattern of a spoken sentence, affected by its stress and pitch and pauses.

Intransitive verb. A verb that requires no complement to be complete: "Everyone *applauded.*"

Irregular verb. Any verb in which the *-ed* and *-en* forms are not that of a regular verb; in other words, a verb in which the *-ed* and *-en* forms are not simply the addition of *-d, -ed,* or *-t* to the base form.

Isocolon. A figure of speech describing the repetition of grammatical forms: "government *of the people, by the people, and for the people.*"

It-cleft. See *Cleft sentence.*

Known–new contract. The common feature of sentences in which old, or known, information (information that is repeated from an earlier sentence or paragraph to provide cohesion, often in the form of a pronoun or related word) will appear in the subject position, with the new information in the predicate.

Lexical cohesion. The continuity of text created by the use of related words, including pronouns, and the repetition of key words. Parallel structures are important components of lexical cohesion.

Lexical rule. The rules built into our lexicon, features of words that govern their ability to combine with other words; for example, only countable nouns can be signaled by the indefinite article, *a,* or by numbers.

Lexicon. The store of words—the internalized dictionary—that every speaker of the language has.

Linking *be*. The use of the verb *be* to link the subject to an adverbial (Pattern 1) or to link the subject to a subject complement (Pattern 2).

Linking verb. A verb that requires a subjective complement to be complete. *Be* is commonly used as a linking verb: "She *is* a freshman"; "She *seems* nice."

Main clause. See *Independent clause.*

Manner adverb. An adverb that answers the question of "how" or "in what manner" about the verb. Most manner adverbs are derived from adjectives with the addition of *-ly: quickly, merrily, candidly.*

Mass noun. See *Noncountable noun.*

Metadiscourse. Certain signals, such as connectors and hedges, that communicate and clarify the writer's attitude or help the reader understand the direction and purpose of the passage: *for example, in the first place, next.*

Metaphor. The nonliteral use of a word that allows the speaker or writer to attribute qualities of one thing to another for purposes of explanation or persuasion: the *war* on drugs, the *engine* of government, *sunset* legislation, *food* for thought.

Modal auxiliary. The auxiliaries *may/might, can/could, will/would, shall/should, must,* and *ought to.* The modals affect what is known as the mood of the verb, conveying probability, possibility, obligation, and the like. Other modal-like verbs include *have (got) to* and *be + going to.*

Nominal. Any structure that functions as a noun phrase normally functions—as subject, direct object, indirect object, object complement, subject complement, object of preposition, appositive.

Nominal clause. A dependent clause that functions as a noun phrase normally functions. See Chapter 10.

Nominalization. The process of producing a noun by adding derivational affixes to another word class: *legalize–legalization; regulate–regulation; friendly–friendliness.* Often the sentence will be more effective when the verb is allowed to function as a verb rather than being turned into a noun.

Nominalized verb. See *Nominalization.*

Noncountable noun. A noun referring to what might be called an undifferentiated mass—such as *wood, water, sugar, glass*—or an abstraction—*justice, love, indifference.* Whether or not you can use the indefinite article, *a,* is probably the best test of countability: If you can, the noun is countable.

Nonrestrictive modifier. A modifier in the noun phrase that comments about the noun rather than defines it. Nonrestrictive modifiers following the noun are set off by commas. See also *Restrictive modifier.*

Noun. One of the four form classes, whose members fill the headword slot in the noun phrase. Most nouns can be inflected for plural and possessive *(boy, boys, boy's, boys')*. Nouns have characteristic derivational endings, such as *-ion (action, compensation)*, *-ment (contentment)*, and *-ness (happiness)*.

Noun phrase. The noun headword with all of its attendant pre- and postnoun modifiers. See Chapter 9.

Number. A feature of nouns and pronouns, referring to singular and plural.

Object complement. The unit following the direct object in Pattern 7 sentences, filled by an adjectival or a nominal. The object complement has two functions: (1) It completes the idea of the verb; and (2) it modifies (if an adjectival) or renames (if a nominal) the direct object: "I found the play *exciting*"; "We consider Pete *a good friend.*"

Object of preposition. The nominal position—usually filled by a noun phrase—that follows the preposition to form a prepositional phrase.

Objective case. The role in the sentence of a noun phrase or pronoun when it functions as an object—direct object, indirect object, object complement, or object of a preposition. Although nouns do not have a special form for objective case, many of the pronouns do: Personal pronouns and the relative pronoun *who* have separate forms when they function as objects: *me, you, him, her, it, us, them, whom.*

Parallelism. See *Parallel structure.*

Parallel structure. A coordinate structure in which all the coordinate parts are of the same grammatical form: "I'll take either *a bus* or *a taxi*" (parallel noun phrases).

Participial phrase. A verb phrase containing a present or past participle and functioning as an adjectival, the modifier of a noun: "*the students organizing the march.*"

Participle. The **present participle** is the *-ing* form of the verb used in the progressive tense *(writing)*. The **past participle** *(written)* is the form of the verb used with the auxiliary *have* to form the perfect tenses in the active voice and with *be* to form the passive voice. The term *participle* refers both to these forms of the verb and to their function as adjectivals: *laughing* children; stories *written* by J. K. Rowling.

Particle. Words such as *in* and *out* that join verbs to create phrasal verbs. See *Phrasal verb.*

Passive voice. A feature of transitive sentences in which the direct object (the objective or goal) is shifted to the subject position. The auxiliary *be* is used with the past participle form of the verb. The term *passive* refers to the relationship between the subject and the verb: "Ed wrote the editorial" $\longrightarrow$ "The editorial was written by Ed." See also *Active voice.*

Past participle. See *Participle.*

Past tense. The form of the verb usually denoting a specific past action. Regular verbs take an *-ed* ending *(talked, raced)* irregular verbs vary in spelling *(went, wrote)*.

Person. A feature of personal pronouns relating to point of view, the relationship of the writer or speaker to the reader or listener: It can refer to writer or speaker (first person), the person addressed (second person), and the person or thing spoken about (third person).

Personal pronoun. A pronoun referring to a specific person or thing: In the subjective case the personal pronouns are *I, you, he, she, we, you, they,* and *it.* The personal pronouns have different forms for objective and possessive case.

Personal voice. The unique identity created through choosing words and arranging them on the page, usually indicating familiarity with the topic and with the language used to discuss the topic.

Phrasal preposition. A preposition consisting of two or three words: *according to, in front of.*

Phrasal verb. A verb combined with a particle, producing a meaning that cannot be predicted from the meaning of the separate parts: *look up, look up to, put up with, make up.*

Phrase. A word or combination of words that constitutes a unit of the sentence.

Plural-only noun. A noun that has no singular form: *shorts, trousers, slacks, scissors, clothes.*

Point of view. The relationship of the writer to the reader, as shown by the use of pronouns: first, second, and/or third person.

Polysyndeton. A figure of speech describing the addition of conjunctions in a series: "I invited Harold *and* Joyce *and* Marv *and* Jean."

Positive degree. See *Degree.*

Possessive case. The inflected form of nouns *(John's, the dog's)* and pronouns *(my, his, your, her, their, whose,* etc.*),* usually indicating possession or ownership.

Power words. Words that have the power to make a difference in the emphasis and rhythm of a sentence, often affecting reader expectation as well.

Predicate. One of the two principal parts of the sentence, the comment made about the subject. The predicate includes the verb, together with its complements and modifiers.

Preposition. A structure-class word found in pre-position to—that is, preceding—a nominal. Prepositions can be classed according to their form as simple, or single-word *(above, at, in, with, of,* etc.*),* or phrasal *(according to, along with, instead of,* etc.*).*

Prepositional phrase. The combination of a preposition and its object. In form, the object of the preposition is usually a noun phrase ("After *my nap,* I'll clean the house"), but it can also be a verb phrase, a gerund ("After *cleaning the house,* I'll take a nap").

Present participle. The *-ing* form of the verb.

Present tense. The base form and the *-s* form of the verb: *help, helps.* The present tense denotes a present point in time ("I *understand* your position"), a habitual action ("I *jog* five miles a day"), or the "timeless" present ("Shakespeare *helps* us understand ourselves").

Pronoun. A word that substitutes for a nominal. See also *Case.*

Proper noun. A noun with individual reference to a person, a geographic region or location, building, holiday, historical event, work of art or literature, and other such names. Proper nouns are capitalized.

Prosody. The study of the rhythm and intonation of language, which are determined by pitch, stress (loudness), and juncture (pauses).

Qualifier. A structure-class word that qualifies or intensifies an adjective or adverb: "We worked *rather* slowly"; "We worked *very* hard."

Reader expectation. An awareness by the writer of what the reader is expecting to read.

Reciprocal pronoun. The pronouns *each other* and *one another,* which refer to previously named nouns.

Redundancy. Unnecessary repetition.

Referent. The thing (or person, event, concept, action, etc.)—in other words, the reality—that a word stands for.

Reflexive pronoun. A pronoun formed by adding *-self* or *-selves* to a form of the personal pronoun, used as an object in the sentence to refer to a previously named noun or pronoun.

Regular verb. A verb in which the *-ed* form (the past tense) and the *-en* form (the past participle) are formed by adding *-ed* (or, in some cases, *-d* or *-t*) to the base. These two forms of a regular verb are always identical: "I *walked* home"; "I have *walked* home every day this week."

Relative adverb. The adverbs *where, when,* and *why,* which introduce adjectival (relative) clauses: "The town *where* I was born has only one traffic light."

Relative clause. A clause introduced by a relative pronoun *(who, which, that)* or a relative adverb *(when, where, why)* that modifies a noun: "The car *that Joe bought* is a lemon." See Chapter 9.

Relative pronoun. The pronouns *who (whose, whom), which,* and *that* in their role as introducers of relative (adjectival) clauses.

Repetition. A technique for strengthening the continuity of text with key words. Repetition is especially important in parallel structures.

Restrictive modifier. A modifier in the noun phrase whose function is to restrict, or define, the meaning of the noun. A modifier is restrictive when it is needed to identify the referent of the headword. The restrictive modifier is not set off by commas. See also *Nonrestrictive modifier.*

Resumptive modifier. A modifier at the end of the sentence that repeats and elaborates on a word from the main clause: "The IRS often intimidates people without cause, *intimidates and harasses them.*"

Rhythm. The intonation contour of valleys and peaks in the spoken language, characterized by variations in stress, pitch, and juncture (pauses).

Run-on sentence. See *Fused sentence.*

Second person. See *Person.*

Semantics. The study of the meaning of words and sentences.

Sentence. A word or group of words based on one or more subject–predicate, or clause, patterns. The written sentence begins with a capital letter and ends with terminal punctuation—a period, a question mark, or an exclamation point.

Sentence fragment. See *Fragment.*

Sentence patterns. The simple skeletal sentences, made up of two or three or four required elements, that underlie our sentences, even the most complex among them. The seven patterns listed in Chapter 2 account for almost all the possible sentences of English.

Serial comma. The comma that is used before the conjunction in a series: "On our fishing trip to Alaska, we caught salmon, halibut, *and* the elusive Arctic grayling." Some publications, as a matter of policy, omit the serial comma.

Series. Three or more words, phrases, or clauses joined together.

Sexist language. The use of the masculine pronoun in a general sense, to include the feminine; and the word *man* is used to mean "human being" or "people": "All *men* are created equal."

Showing. The demonstration of emotion or evaluation in writing by providing sensory details and action: "*The runner grinned as she crossed the finish line*" (instead of "*The runner was happy to win the race*").

Simile. A comparison that uses *like* or *as:* "My love is *like a red, red rose*" (Robert Burns).

Stress. See *Prosody.*

Structure classes. The small, closed classes of words that explain the grammatical or structural relationships of the form classes. The major ones are determiners, auxiliaries, qualifiers, prepositions, and conjunctions.

Style. A writer's manner of expression, influenced by word choice, sentence length and complexity, figurative language, tone, and other sentence features.

Subject. The opening position in the sentence patterns, usually a noun phrase or other nominal structure, that functions as the topic of the sentence.

Subject complement. The nominal or adjectival that follows a linking verb, renaming or describing the subject ("Pam is *the president*"). In the passive voice the transitive sentence with an object complement (Pattern 7) will have a subject complement: "We elected Pam president" ⟶ "Pam was elected *president.*"

Subject–verb agreement. See *Agreement.*

Subjective case. The role in the sentence of a noun phrase or a pronoun when it functions as the subject of the sentence. Personal pronouns have distinctive inflected forms for subjective case: *I, he, she, they,* and so on. And in the subject complement slot, a pronoun will be in the subjective case. The relative pronoun *who* is also subjective-case— *whose* (possessive), *whom* (objective).

Subjunctive mood. An expression of the verb in which the base form, rather than the inflected form, is used (1) in certain *that* clauses conveying strong suggestions or resolutions or commands ("We suggest that Mary *go* with us"; "I move that the meeting *be* adjourned"; "I demand that you *let* us in") and (2) in the expression of wishes or conditions contrary to fact ("If I *were* you, I'd be careful"; "I wish it *were* summer"). The subjunctive of the verb *be* is expressed by *were,* or *be,* even for subjects that normally take *is* or *was.*

Subordinate clause. See *Dependent clause.*

Subordinating conjunction. A conjunction that introduces a dependent clause and expresses the relationship of the clause to the main clause. Among the most common are *after, although, as, as long as, as soon as, because, before, even though, if, provided that, since, so that, though, till, until, when, whenever, whereas, while.*

Subordination. The placement of information in a dependent clause that functions adverbially or adjectivally.

Summative modifier. A modifier—usually a noun phrase—at the end of the sentence that sums up the idea of the main clause: The teacher canceled class on the Friday before spring break, *a decision that was greeted with unanimous enthusiasm.*

Superlative degree. See *Degree.*

Syntax. The way in which the words of the language are put together to form the structural units, the phrases and clauses, of the sentence.

Telling. Description that lacks the kind of sensory details, action, and dialog that would allow readers to evaluate and/or picture the scene. See *Showing*.

Tense. A grammatical feature of verbs and auxiliaries relating to time. Tense is designated by an inflectional change *(walked)*, by an auxiliary *(will walk)*, or both *(am walking, have walked)*.

***There*-transformation.** A variation of a basic sentence in which the expletive *there* is added at the beginning and the subject is shifted to a position following *be*: "A fly is in my soup" ⟶ *"There is a fly in my soup."*

Third person. See *Person*.

Time frame. The part of the verb-tense label indicating time: *present, past,* or *future*.

Tone. The writer's attitude toward the reader and the text: serious, formal, tongue-in-cheek, sarcastic, casual, and so on.

Transitional phrase. A prepositional phrase used to relate ideas in adjacent sentences.

Transitive verb. The verbs of Patterns 5, 6, and 7, which require at least one complement, the direct object, to be complete. With only a few exceptions, transitive verbs are those that can be transformed into the passive voice.

Triplet. A three-item series: "Residents of the park include *elk, bison, and grizzly bears.*"

Verb. One of the four form classes, traditionally thought of as the action word in the sentence. Every verb, without exception, has an *-s* and an *-ing* form (present participle); every verb also has a past-tense form and a past-participle form, although in the case of some irregular verbs these forms are not readily apparent. And every verb, without exception, can be marked by auxiliaries. Many verbs also have characteristic derivational forms, such as *-ify (typify), -ize (criticize), and -ate (activate)*. See Chapter 3.

Verb phrase. A verb together with its complements and modifiers; the predicate of the sentence is a verb phrase.

Vocative. See *Direct address*.

Voice. The relationship of the subject to the verb. See also *Active voice* and *Passive voice*.

***What*-cleft.** See *Cleft sentence*.

Writer's Voice. The identity the writer creates through word choice and word arrangement.

Bibliography

In the following books and articles, you can find further information about some of the topics you have studied here.

Cohesion
Fahnestock, Jeanne. "Semantic and Lexical Coherence." *College Composition and Communication* 34:4 (1983): 400–416.
Halliday, M. A. K. and Ruqaiya Hasan, *Cohesion in English*. London: Longman, 1976.
Vande Kopple, William J. "Functional Sentence Perspective, Composition, and Reading." *College Composition and Communication* 33:1 (1982): 50–63.

Comprehensive Grammar
Huddleston, Rodney, and Geoffrey K. Pullum. *The Cambridge Grammar of the English Language*. Cambridge: Cambridge UP, 2002.
Quirk, Randolph, Sidney Greenbaum, Geoffrey Leech, and Jan Svartvik. *A Comprehensive Grammar of the English Language*. New York: Longman, 1985.

Figures of Speech
Corbett, Edward P. J. *Classical Rhetoric for the Modern Student,* 2nd ed. New York: Oxford, 1971.
Quinn, Arthur. *Figures of Speech: 60 Ways to Turn a Phrase*. Davis, CA: Hermagoras Press, 1993.

Grammar and Writing Instruction
English Journal (three grammar issues). May 2006, January 2003, November 1996.
Hunter, Susan, and Ray Wallace, eds. *The Place of Grammar in Writing Instruction: Past, Present, Future*. Portsmouth, NH: Boynton/Cook, 1995.
Noguchi, Rei. *Grammar and the Teaching of Writing: Limits and Possibilities*. Urbana, Il: National Council of Teachers of English, 1991.
Weaver, Constance. *Grammar to Enhance Writing*. Portsmouth, NH: Heinemann, 2008.

Grammar Research
Noguchi (cited under "Grammar and Writing Instruction")
Pinker, Steven. *The Language Instinct: How the Mind Creates Language*. New York: HarperCollins, 1994.

Grammar Rules

Haussamen, Brock. *Revising the Rules: Traditional Grammar and Modern Linguistics,* 2nd ed. Dubuque, IA: Kendall/Hunt, 1997.

Schuster, Edgar H. *Breaking the Rules: Liberating Writers Through Innovative Grammar Instruction.* Portsmouth, NH: Heinemann, 2003.

Grammar Theory

Dillon, George L. *Constructing Texts.* Bloomington, IN: IUP, 1981.

Language Development

Gleason, Jean Berko, *The Development of Language,* 4th ed. Boston: Allyn and Bacon, 1997.

Nippold, Marilyn. *Later Language Development: School-Age Children, Adolescents, and Young Adults.* Austin: PRO-ED, 2007.

Pinker (cited under "Grammar Research")

Metadiscourse

Cheng, Xiaoguang, and Margaret S. Steffensen, "Metadiscourse: A Technique for Improving Student Writing." *Research in the Teaching of English* 30 (1996): 149–181.

Crismore, Avon. *Talking to Readers: Metadiscourse as Rhetorical Act.* New York: Peter Lang, 1989.

Hyland, Ken. *Metadiscourse.* London: Continuum, 2005.

Vande Kopple, William J. "Some Exploratory Discourse on Metadiscourse," *College Composition and Communication* 36:1 (1985): 82–93.

Modern Grammar

Hancock, Craig. *Meaning-Centered Grammar: An Introductory Text.* London: Equinox, 2005.

Kolln, Martha, and Robert Funk. *Understanding English Grammar,* 8th ed. New York: Longman, 2009.

Punctuation

Christensen, Francis. *Notes Toward a New Rhetoric: Six Essays for Teachers.* New York: Harper and Row, 1967.

Lunsford, Andrea A., and Karen J. Lunsford. "'Mistakes Are a Fact of Life': A National Comparative Study". *CCC* 59:4 (2008): 781–806.

Meyer, Charles F. *A Linguistic Study of American Punctuation.* New York: Peter Lang, 1987.

Style

Corbett (cited under "Figures of Speech")

Grant-Davie, Keith. "Functional Redundancy and Ellipsis as Strategies in Reading and Writing," *Journal of Advanced Composition* 15:3 (1995): 455–469.

Answers to the Exercises

Chapter 1

Exercise 1, page 9

1. The(d) students(H)   their(d) long trip(H)
3. Mickey's(d) roommate(H)   the(d) library(H)   rainy weekends(H)
5. This(d) new lasagna recipe(H)   an(d) enormous crowd(H)

Exercise 2, page 13

1. Our county commissioners (They)
3. The mayor (She)
5. The merchants in town (They)

Exercise 3, page 17

1. Adverbial
3. Adjectival, Adverbial
5. Adverbial

Chapter 2

Exercise 4, page 23

1. The bus from Flagstaff / arrived / at two o'clock (P 4)
3. The . . . grill / smells / wonderful (P 3)
5. AD / is / a . . . nature (P 2)
7. Our . . . meeting / is / in the library (P 1)

Exercise 5, page 29

A1. Many people / now / consider (trans) / the penny / a nuisance coin
A3. During World War II / the government / required (trans) / large amounts of copper / for war production
A5. The Philadelphia Mint / unwittingly / produced (trans) / twelve copper pennies / that year / in addition to the new model
A7. Those twelve 1943 copper pennies / soon / became (linking) / valuable collectors' items

Here are some possible revisions of the sentences in the first part:

B1. Now many people consider . . .
B3. The government required large amounts of copper for war production during World War II.

B5. Unwittingly, the Philadelphia Mint . . .

B7. Soon those twelve 1943 copper pennies . . .

Exercise 6, page 32

1. In 1747 / a physician in the British Navy / conducted / an experiment / to discover a cure for scurvy. (P 5)

3. Dr. James Lind / fed / six groups of scurvy victims / six different remedies. (P 6)

5. Although . . . findings, / it / finally / ordered / a daily dose of fresh lemon juice / for every British seaman. (P 6)

7. The British / called / lemons / "limes" / in the eighteenth century. (P 7).

Chapter 3

Exercise 7, page 46

Active to Passive:

1. The lead article in today's *Collegian* was written by my roommate.

3. An elaborate celebration has been organized by our homecoming committee.

5. A new tax-collection system is being proposed by the county commissioners this year.

Passive to Active:

1. A committee chose this year's cheerleading squad last spring.

3. We will hold the election of the class officers on Tuesday.

5. The police are keeping the suspect in solitary confinement.

Either:

1. We elected Barack Obama president in 2008. (Passive to Active)

3. Migration has affected the cities in the Northeast in recent years. (P to A)

5. A new vacation schedule is being tried out this year by our company. (A to P)

Exercise 8, page 49

Answers will vary.

Exercise 9, page 52

Answers will vary.

Chapter 4

Exercise 10, page 61

Answers may vary.

1. Both tea and coffee contain caffeine.

3. Some people drink either coffee or tea, but not both.

5. Japanese blue-collar workers not only work more hours per day than American workers but also typically do so with more dedication and energy.

7. In the U.S. neither blue-collar workers nor students spend as much time at their respective jobs as do their Japanese counterparts.

Exercise 11, page 63

1. go

3. go

5. finds

Exercise 12, page 74

1. The Smithsonian Institution comprises nineteen museums, nine research centers, and the National Zoo.

3. No extra punctuation necessary.

5. The museum . . . in 1976; however, its collection . . . Airport.

7. Together . . . air- and spacecraft; they also sponsor vital research into aviation and related technologies.
9. Approximately . . . museums, but the museums . . . as docents.

Exercise 13, page 76
Answers will vary.

Exercise 14, page 79
Here are some of the problems:
1. Unparallel verb phrases: *to lift* and *swimming*
3. Unparallel verb phrases: *enjoy flying* and *want to take*
5. Unparallel complements: *introduced* + *noun phrase* and *said* + *nominal clause*
7. Unparallel complements: *either* + *noun phrase* and *or* + *independent clause*

Chapter 5
Exercise 15, page 93
1. At the edge of the Mississippi River in St. Louis stands the Gateway Arch, the world's tallest monument. The stainless steel structure, designed by Eero Saarinen, commemorates the Westward Movement.
3. [No change in the first sentence.] It's not unusual for the temperature to reach 110° in Bakersfield, often the hottest spot in the valley. [Note that *summer* in the first sentence makes *June through September* redundant.]
5. Directed by the U.S. Marshal Service, the federal witness-protection service began in 1968. This program has relocated and created new identities for over four thousand people in extreme danger because they have testified against criminals.

Exercise 16, page 97
1. Many women . . . political status. This effort . . . .
3. Some married women . . . property, but this right . . . .
5. In 1920 the Constitution . . . vote. That amendment . . . .

Chapter 6
Exercise 17, page 109
There are, of course, no right and wrong answers for the question of main stress. The answers here are based on our readings of the passages—words that are likely candidates for strong stress:
1. Sentence 1. <u>understand</u> and <u>salesperson;</u> 2. <u>buyer, sellee;</u> 3. <u>want, vacuum, buy;</u> 4. <u>else, selling</u>
3. Sentence 1. <u>hazards</u> and <u>easy;</u> 2. <u>literature</u> and <u>body</u> and <u>one</u> conclusion and <u>contradicts;</u> 3. <u>out</u> and <u>steady.</u>

Exercise 18, page 113
Answers will vary. Here are some possibilities:
1. It was in 1912 that the *Titanic* hit . . .
3. There were hundreds of angry parents protesting the senator's position . . .
5. There have been countless travelers who have lost . . .

Chapter 7
Exercise 19, page 125
Remember! You won't be using the word *snafu!*

Exercise 20, page 131
A. Here are some possibilities for the first five in the list: turn down/reject; bring about/cause; bring on/induce; put up with/tolerate; stand for/represent, tolerate

B. (1) suggest, offer, propose; (3) replacing with, transforming into; (5) establishes, creates, produces; (7) consider; (9) replaces/represents

Exercise 21, page 133

1. Investors on Wall Street are concerned because the Japanese are buying so many American companies and so much real estate.
3. In his biography of Lyndon Johnson, Robert Caro provides a detailed account of the Senate election of 1948.
5. The overuse of salt in the typical American diet obscures the natural taste of many foods. Nutritionists maintain that if people reduced their dependence on salt they would find their food tastier and more enjoyable.

Exercise 22, page 142
Answers will vary.

Chapter 8

Exercise 23, page 154
Answers will vary.

Exercise 24, page 159
Answers will vary

Exercise 25, page 162
(*Note:* You may have come up with even tighter versions using other kinds of modifiers.)

1. Even though the famous Gateway Arch is in St. Louis, it is Kansas City that claims the title "Gateway to the West."
3. Thomas Jefferson acquired the Ozark Mountains for the United States when he negotiated the Louisiana Purchase with Napoleon in 1803.
5. When the neighbors added a pit bull to their pet population, now numbering three unfriendly four-legged creatures, we decided to fence in our backyard.
7. Fad diets that severely restrict the intake of carbohydrates are not only ineffective but also often dangerous, because carbohydrates are the body's prime source of energy.

Exercise 26, page 164

1. *To save money* (infinitive/reason); *often* (adverb/frequency); *at my desk* (prep phr/place)
3. *After . . . navy* (clause/time); *from the navy* (prep phr/place)
5. *As soon as the guests left* (clause/time); *in a heap* (prep phr/manner); *on the couch* (prep phr/place)
7. *When October came* (clause/time)
9. *slowly* (adverb/manner); *northward* (adverb/direction)
11. *home* (noun/place); *last night* (noun phr/time); *because of the snowstorm* (prep phr/reason)

Chapter 9

Exercise 27, page 172

1. The administration's recent clean-air proposals have been criticized as inadequate not only by . . . .
3. The stock market reached an all-time high last week and will probably keep going up.
5. A big yellow delivery truck is blocking the driveway, and its driver . . . .
7. I found an expensive-looking copper-colored bracelet . . . .
9. I have back-to-back exams on Wednesday.

Exercise 28, page 179

1. Having endured rain all week, we weren't surprised by the miserable weather on Saturday. [or "we weren't surprised when the weather turned miserable on Saturday."]
3. We were not at all surprised when the Republican county commissioner, known for her conservative views . . . , announced her candidacy . . . .
5. After I spent nearly all day in the kitchen, everyone agreed . . . .
7. Obviously intimidated by a long history of defeats in Morgantown, our basketball team just can't seem to beat the Virginia Mountaineers on their home court.

Exercise 29, page 183

1. My roommate's announcement that she is planning to withdraw from school came as a complete surprise.
or
When my roommate told me she is planning to withdraw from school, I was completely surprised.
3. Converting the central card catalog in the college library to a computer system took over four years.
5. Harriett was rather unhappy when Wendell didn't want to stay for the second half of the game.
7. When the president characterized the last two years as a period of "unprecedented prosperity" in his State of the Union message, one economist immediately labeled his statement "sheer hype and hyperbole."

Exercise 30, page 187

1. Sentence 2: . . . contract, expiring . . .
3. . . . husband, sitting . . . platform, both . . . . Then the mayor, turning . . . senator, shocked . . . .

Exercise 31, page 187

1. Citizens in many parts of the country, mobilizing against crime and drugs, are driving drug dealers out of their neighborhoods. [or . . . are mobilizing to drive drug dealers out of their neighborhoods.]
3. The computer has revolutionized the storage and retrieval of fingerprints, which have been used for criminal identification since 1891, when a police officer in Argentina introduced the method.
5. In 1997 an earthquake that struck the Assisi region of Italy destroyed many priceless fourteenth-century mosaics decorating the walls and ceiling of the Basilica of St. Francis. [or . . . an earthquake struck the Assisi region of Italy, destroying many priceless mosaics from the fourteenth century, which decorated the walls . . . .]
7. The amount of carbon dioxide in the air affects the rate of colon cancer because carbon dioxide absorbs ultraviolet light, which fuels the body's production of vitamin D.
9. We cannot build up our immunity to flu viruses because they mutate constantly, producing new varieties that spread from person to person and from place to place.

Exercise 32, page 189
Answers will vary.

Chapter 10
Exercise 33, page 194

1. simple ballads sung to guitar music
3. An offbeat film about illegal trash dumping
5. a contemporary folk singer and songwriter; *Soul Journey* and *Time (The Revelator)*

Exercise 34, page 200
1. <u>to tell the truth,</u> infinitive (subjective complement)
3. <u>To ignore . . . order,</u> infinitive (subject)
5. <u>to buy up . . . stocks,</u> infinitive (appositive)
7. <u>Raising . . . profile,</u> gerund (subject)
9. <u>your proofreading . . . me,</u> gerund

Exercise 35, page 203
1. The neighbors never suspected <u>that we had a pet boa constrictor in our house.</u> (nom cl, d.o.)
3. <u>Mark's complaining about his grades</u> is getting tiresome. (gerund ph, subj)
5. His problem is <u>getting accepted</u> (gerund ph, sub comp)
7. The knowledge <u>that spring break is almost here</u> makes me happy. (nom cl, appositive)
9. It's almost impossible <u>to predict what will be on the final exam.</u> (inf ph, app to it, a delayed subj) (nom clause, d.o. of inf. ph)

Chapter 11
Exercise 36, page 210
Here are some examples:
1. My sister, who is one of the most conservative people I know, surprised everyone at the family reunion when she showed up in a 1920s-style dress trimmed with beads and feathers, her normally blonde hair dyed red.
3. At the far end of the diner's chrome and plastic counter sat a trucker, an old man with long grey hair, his leathery face a pattern of creases and scars, his fringed jacket worn nearly through at the elbows.

Exercise 37, page 222
Answers will vary.

Chapter 12
Exercise 38, page 235
1. The <u>statement</u> . . . <u>was</u> . . .
3. Apparently the <u>use</u> of robots . . . <u>has</u> . . .
5. Correct

Exercise 39, page 239
1. grief, grieve, grievous, grievously
3. ability, enable, able, ably
5. quickness, quicken, quick, quickly
7. type, typify, typical, typically
9. critic (criticism/critique), criticize (critique), critical, critically
11. appreciation, appreciate, appreciable, appreciably
13. acceptance (acceptability), accept, acceptable, acceptably
15. stealth, steal, stealthy, stealthily

Exercise 40, page 242
Answers will vary. Here are some possibilities.
1. meticulous
3. brusque
5. futile
7. exhausted
9. enthusiastic

Exercise 41, page 244

    1. <u>in</u> a relatively short period of time (noun phrase)

    3. <u>to</u> what the guide told us about the trail leading into the canyon (nominal clause) *and* <u>about</u> the trail leading into the canyon (noun phrase) *and* <u>into</u> the canyon (noun phrase)

Exercise 42, page 253

    1. Claire has always been interested in children and, when she graduates, plans to work with them. Both she and I are majoring in early childhood education.

    3. When . . . , I had no idea Beth was sick . . . . Our grandmother took one look at her called the doctor, and drove her to the hospital. That decision turned out to be a good one: Beth's cramps turned out to be appendicitis.

Exercise 43, page 256

    1. I recall with great pleasure the good times that we had at our annual family reunions when I was young. With our cousins and younger aunts and uncles, we played volleyball and softball until dark. Those games were a lot of fun.

    3. It seemed to my cousin Terry and me that the grownups were different people at those family reunions. Such memories of family reunions may be true for people everywhere.

Chapter 13

Exercise 44, page 266

Here are some examples:

    1. The cost of repairs to the nation's public transportation facilities—roads, bridges, and railroads—is an expenditure that cannot be delayed much longer if the system is to survive.

    3. Normally living in the coastal waters of Japan, the paper nautilus octopus, a rare marine animal, was found recently in the squid nets off Santa Catalina in California.

Exercise 45, page 269

Management is still taught in most business schools as a bundle of techniques, such as budgeting and personnel relations. To be sure, management, like any other work, has its own tools and its own techniques. But just as the essence of medicine is not urinalysis (important though that is) the essence of management is not techniques and procedures. The essence of management is to make knowledge productive. Management, in other words, is a social function. And in its practice management is truly a liberal art. [Note: If you put a comma after *practice* in the last sentence, you have improved on the original! A comma would make the sentence easier to read.]

    The old communities—family, village, parish, and so on—have all but disappeared in the knowledge society. Their place has largely been taken by the new unit of social integration, the organization. Where community was fate, organization is voluntary membership. Where community claimed the entire person, organization is a means to a person's ends, a tool. For 200 years a hot debate has been raging, especially in the West: are communities "organic" or are they simply extensions of the people of which they are made? Nobody would claim that the new organization is "organic." It is clearly an artifact, a creation of man, a social technology.

Index